GROWING GOD'S FA

MW00332662

Growing God's Family

*The Global Orphan Care Movement and
the Limits of Evangelical Activism*

Samuel L. Perry

NEW YORK UNIVERSITY PRESS

New York

NEW YORK UNIVERSITY PRESS
New York
www.nyupress.org

References to Internet websites (URLs) were accurate at the time of writing. Neither the author nor New York University Press is responsible for URLs that may have expired or changed since the manuscript was prepared.

ISBN: 978-1-4798-0038-4 (hardback)
ISBN: 978-1-4798-0305-7 (paperback)

For Library of Congress Cataloging-in-Publication data, please contact the
Library of Congress.

New York University Press books are printed on acid-free paper, and their binding materials are chosen for strength and durability. We strive to use environmentally responsible suppliers and materials to the greatest extent possible in publishing our books.

Manufactured in the United States of America

10 9 8 7 6 5 4 3 2 1

Also available as an ebook

To Mom and Dad, for everything

CONTENTS

PREFACE AND ACKNOWLEDGMENTS

This book is about evangelicals and their social engagement. Specifically, it elucidates the ways in which certain aspects of the evangelical subculture—core ideological commitments, patterns of thought, institutionalized strategies of action—can serve to stimulate activism to address social problems while simultaneously undercutting their practical effectiveness. To accomplish this task, the book focuses on an ongoing effort among evangelicals to serve vulnerable children ("orphans" in a nuanced, theological sense) primarily through adoption and foster care. Although I have written this book to be accessible to a non-academic audience, it is principally a work of sociology. This means (or at least it *should* mean) that I have approached the topic of evangelicals and their activism as a social scientist, not as an advocate or opponent. Readers who are hoping for a scathing exposé on evangelicals and adoption will be disappointed, as will those who are hoping for some social scientific validation of evangelical efforts.

This is certainly not to suggest that I have no skin in the game. Academics often study topics that are of personal relevance to them. I have found this to be especially true for scholars of adoption issues. Some casual digging will reveal that many, if not most, contemporary experts on adoption seem to have adoption somewhere in their personal history.[1] My story is no different. While I do not consider myself an expert on adoption or foster care, my fascination with evangelicals engaging in these activities can be traced back my own life experiences, starting in the early 1980s. When I was four years old, my parents, both white evangelical Protestants, were interested in having more children, but my mother, having already birthed two boys, had no interest in being pregnant again. They were open to transracial adoption and, in 1984, adopted an African American infant girl whom they named Elizabeth. Two years later, my parents adopted another African American infant girl as a companion for Elizabeth—my sister Katherine. Although my parents were well educated and had the best of intentions, they were pioneers in many regards with hardly any support from social workers or the adoptive community, and with almost no resources from which to gain strategies for parenting transracially adopted children. They encountered a number of struggles helping my sisters navigate issues of loss, belonging, and racial identity. The unique racial dynamics and culturally non-traditional experiences of my family instilled in me something of a protosociological sense that was particularly attuned to issues of American culture, religion, family diversity, and racial prejudice.

Along my circuitous path toward becoming a professional sociologist, I also picked up a graduate degree from a flagship evangelical school, Dallas Theological Seminary (DTS). Although my subsequent intellectual development has taken me fairly far afield politically from most of my fellow students and professors at DTS, I remember my seminary days with great fondness. That educational opportunity fostered within me a fascination with the evangelical subculture and its relationship to contemporary American controversies surrounding issues of race, economic policy, and family structure.

As a researcher, I feel it is important to acknowledge these formative experiences up front to discern how they potentially color my conclusions. On the one hand, in approaching the evangelical adoption and orphan care movement as (1) white and middle class, (2) from an adoptive family, and (3) with an evangelical background, I am in many ways talking about "my people." As a result, I have had to interrogate my own feelings continually throughout the project to ensure that I was neither (1) letting common evangelical schemas (that is, ways of thinking), values, and terminology go uninvestigated simply because I am familiar with them nor (2) immediately imputing the best of intentions to movement leaders and families simply because I naturally want to give them the benefit of the doubt (as I would with my own parents and evangelical friends).

On the other hand, I did not want my sincere desire to think critically about the various dynamics of the orphan care movement to bias my interpretation the other way. I found the cynical and ungenerous rendering of evangelicals in Kathryn Joyce's *The Child Catchers* and her related articles personally offensive, primarily because I feel that professional researchers (whether journalists or scholars) have a responsibility to the public and the people they study to be as unbiased and objective as possible.[2] Reading Joyce's work, I found it clear that she has picked a side, and evangelicals are not on it. My own approach has been influenced by the moral psychologist Jonathan Haidt, who argues that researchers interested in morally contentious issues need to first step back and resist their own tendency to moralize, choose sides, and demonize their opponent.[3] To be sure, there are times and contexts in which one should be morally for or against something, but I believe that my job as a sociologist is to be an honest researcher first and foremost.

Although my own life experiences required me to be candid and vigilant about potential biases, I also found these experiences to be incredibly beneficial to my research for a variety of reasons. First, my evangelical seminary training and personal experience with adoption gave me an intimate awareness of the cultural toolkit and jargon of the evangelical subculture and an attentiveness to the multiple challenges confronting families involved in adoption or foster care.

Second, evangelical leaders and families were more open to speaking with me as someone who had personal connections with the group. Knowing that I came from an adoptive family and that I graduated from DTS was often all evangelical leaders and families needed to hear before they agreed to take part in my study and even encouraged others to participate. This insider knowledge of both evangelicals and adoption was critical. Evangelicals are often (justifiably) suspicious of sociologists and journalists, fearing that they will be intentionally caricatured, at best, as culturally backward do-gooders and, at worst, as bigoted religious fanatics.[4] Ultimately, it is possible that my "street cred" within the evangelical and adoptive communities gave me access to leaders to whom few other researchers would have had access.

And last, having grown up in a transracially adoptive family with our own struggles around issues of racial identity, belonging, and rebellion, I was quickly able to empathize with the adoptive and foster families who spoke to me about their trying, and often quite painful, experiences. During our extended conversations about challenges with adopted or foster children, families often asked me how my family dealt with those issues and what we might have done differently looking back. Briefly touching on my own family's challenges (only when directly asked) seemed to make families more comfortable disclosing struggles that were difficult to discuss.

On the subject of the families who shared their stories with me, I now happily give thanks. Above all the people who deserve credit for making this book possible, my sincerest gratitude goes to the many individuals and families who were so kind as to share with me their insights as well as their prayers, joys, and heartbreaks. This includes leaders and grassroots families, both inside and outside of evangelicalism. I conducted formal interviews from February 2013 to March 2014, but a number of these men and women are still in conversation with me as I write these words. Although I have chosen not to identify the grassroots families I interviewed by name, I am so grateful for their willingness to speak with me and even to invite their friends to share their stories with me as well. My debt is too great to repay in words.

Because the leaders and experts who spoke with me have made themselves publicly visible, I feel it is appropriate to thank them by name (alphabetically): David Anderson, Curtis Artis, Phillip Aspegren, Mark Barret, Daniel Bennett, Jon Bergeron, Larry Bergeron, Bill Blacquire, Johnny Carr, Lisa Castetter, Gerald Clark, Dan Cruver, Amy Curtis, Tom Davis, Mike Douris, C. H. Dyer, Diane Lynn Elliot, Sharon Ford, Paula Freeman, Frank Garrott, Sarah J. Gesiriech, Beth Guckenberger, Dwain Gullion, Kerry Hasenbalg, Scott Hasenbalg, David Hennessey, Chuck Johnson, Craig Juntunen, Bruce and Denise Kendrick, Aaron Klein, Jason Kovacs, Daniel LaBry, Andy Lehman, Tabitha Lovell, Tom Lukasik, Brian Luwis, Ruslan Malyuta, Jedd Medefind, Tony Merida, Michael and Amy Monroe, Russell Moore, Rick Morton, John M. Neese, Herbie Newell, Kerry Olson, Katie Overstreet, Paul and Robin Pennington, Ellen E. Porter, Karyn Purvis, Kelly Rosati, Scott and Kathy Rosenow, Maridel Sandberg, Doug Sauder, David Smolin, Matthew Storer, Kathleen Strottman, Elizabeth Styffe, Bruce Thomas, Jodi Jackson Tucker, Carolyn and Kiel Twietmeyer, Scott Vair, Michael Wear, Rebecca Weichhand, Jason Weber, Elizabeth Wiebe, and Lynn Young. These women and men were incredibly generous with their time. In the end, ten books would not be enough to recount the insights they provided, which extend far beyond the workings of the orphan care movement.

Among these leaders, three in particular deserve special thanks: Michael Monroe, Dr. Karyn Purvis, and Jedd Medefind. Michael took a special interest in my research early on and spoke very candidly with me about what he felt were oversights or shortcomings in the orphan care movement. Although he is a passionate advocate for adoptive families and children, he and his wife Amy understand the complex challenges associated with adoption and foster care more than most. I always appreciated Michael's humility, humor, and honesty. Like Michael, his colleague Dr. Karyn Purvis was quite outspoken about her concerns for wounded children within the orphan care movement. She dedicated her scholarship, teaching, and counseling practice to helping these children and their parents. She lost her battle with cancer in April 2016. I will remember her charm, soft-spoken manner, intelligence, and fierce compassion. Jedd Medefind, as the president of the Christian Alliance for Orphans (CAFO), was incredibly generous, often providing email introductions to other key leaders or information and documents from CAFO that I would not have had access to otherwise. I also corresponded with Jedd over email more than with any other leader in the movement. The Christian Alliance for Orphans is lucky to have such a genuine and thoughtful leader.

Although I have done my best to be convincing, I doubt that the families or leaders with whom I have spoken with will agree with everything I have written here. Nevertheless, it has been my sincere goal throughout this project to honor both their gracious participation and my task as a sociologist by being equal parts generous and fair. I earnestly hope they see that effort in these pages.

Several of my academic mentors deserve grateful acknowledgment, above all Omar McRoberts, Kristen Schilt, Gina Samuels, and Robert Wuthnow. Their encouragement and feedback were invaluable at each step in the research process, from the initial inception of this project on through data collection, analysis, and writing. Not only have they shaped my thinking about scholarship in religion, culture, gender, and adoption, but they have also been tireless advocates for me in my career, and I am indebted.

Tremendous thanks go to the various centers and associations that allowed this research to be fully funded. Specifically, I wish to thank the Religious Research Association; the Society for the Scientific Study of Religion; the Center for the Study of Gender and Sexuality; the Center for the Study of Race, Politics, and Culture; the Martin Marty Center for the Advanced Study of Religion; and the Social Sciences Division at the University of Chicago. The Center for the Study of Gender and

Sexuality and the Center for the Study of Race, Politics, and Culture both provided financial support, office space, the occasional snack, and computer equipment from 2013 to 2015 while I progressed through the data collection, analysis, and writing; wrote articles; and applied for jobs. Having an office is a rare privilege for a graduate student, and this was invaluable for me.

My colleagues in the Sociology and Religious Studies Departments at the University of Oklahoma also deserve thanks. They have been especially collegial and supportive as I have worked to get my research off the ground and out the door. Circumstances worked out for me to have a reduced teaching load in my second semester on campus, which provided ample time for me to finish transforming an unbearably dry and technical first draft into something halfway readable (I hope). Here's to years of future partnership.

Thanks also go to Jennifer Hammer and her team at New York University Press. Jennifer initiated a conversation with me about this project some years back while I was still in grad school. She has now patiently seen it through to completion. Shayne Lee at the University of Houston once told me that Jennifer is "the best in the biz." She has lived up to her reputation completely.

Finally, I am forever indebted to my family. My Dad and Mom have been a bottomless well of encouragement for me my whole life. I am so grateful for their support. I dedicate this book to them. My in-laws, Dave and Debbie Jobe and Melinda Jobe-Polvado, have also served in critical roles as sounding boards, cheerleaders, bed and breakfasts, and friends. Last, to my loving wife and children, I will speak directly. Jill, you have been so patient with me as we traveled this journey through graduate school and now into professional academics. You have sacrificed so much so I could do what I love. Saying thank you does not begin to cover it, but I want to work to make sure you know your support and sacrifice is appreciated. As I have said before, I would leave academia tomorrow if you asked me to. But I *am* glad you have not asked me to. Not yet, at least. To my daughter, Ryan, and my sons, Beau and Whit, thank you for filling my life with motivation and joy. Your Daddy loves you very much, always.

Introduction

American evangelicalism needs a good dose of
demythologizing.
—Christian Smith, *American Evangelicalism* (1998:193)

The headlines started appearing around 2007, and by 2013 they had
reached a fever pitch. Dozens of online magazines and news websites
were publishing exposé-type articles throwing light on what had become
the latest American evangelical craze—adopting children, and not just
one or two children, but as many children as possible.[1] One author
explained that "some families adopt as many as five or six new children," declaring themselves "serial adopters" and wearing bracelets that
say "orphan addict."[2] Another author described an "evangelical adoption
boom," in which "Bible-adhering Christians essentially collect children"
and in which the corrupt, global adoption industry reaped billions from
"coercion, racism and wannabe-do-gooders' salvation complexes."[3]
Headlines for these articles included provocative phrases like "The
Evangelical Orphan Boom," "Orphan Fever," the "Evangelical Adoption
Obsession," an "Evangelical Adoption Crusade," "Serial Adopters,"
"Evangelicals Exploiting the Orphan Market," "Preying on the Desperate," "Evangelicals and the Fake-Orphan Racket," and "How the
Christian Right Perverts Adoption." They thus seemed to be describing
something both powerful and alarming, even potentially dangerous.[4]

Most of these articles were either written by or using information and
arguments from Kathryn Joyce, a free-lance journalist specializing in issues of religion, family, and gender.[5] *The Child Catchers: Rescue, Trafficking, and the New Gospel of Adoption* (Joyce 2013b) was the culmination
of several years of attending evangelical conferences, interviewing key
leaders, and reading literature by evangelicals on the topics of Christians and adoption. In the estimation of Joyce and other journalists or
anti-adoption activists, the growing coordinated effort among American

evangelicals to promote compulsive adoption was not motivated by a genuine love for children. Rather, evangelicals were adopting primarily to proselytize the children of poor birth mothers, domestically or abroad, and to promote the pro-life agenda, creating an (at times, coercive)[6] alternative to abortion for women with unplanned pregnancies.

These journalistic descriptions of the evangelical movement to promote Christian adoption, fostering, and orphan care do indeed capture *some* of the stated goals of its leaders (albeit ungenerously and superficially).[7] However, there are at least three important, but questionable, assumptions in their accounts. Each assumption builds on the previous ones. The first is that American evangelicals have *actually* been successful at accomplishing their objectives. That is, in describing an evangelical "adoption boom" or "orphan boom," Joyce and others are assuming that American evangelicals have been successful at mobilizing evangelical families to adopt or foster more than they have in the past—or more than anyone else, for that matter. The second assumption is that the proselytizing, pro-life, patriarchal ideology of the American evangelical subculture is ultimately driving these efforts, making them successful. Finally, building on the first two assumptions, and readily apparent from the tone of the headlines, a major assumption of these treatments is that American evangelical efforts at social engagement should be feared by non-evangelical Americans. The not-so-implicit message is that American evangelicals are both so ideologically committed and effective at social engagement, and their ideology is so at-odds with American democratic values, that America and the world must take warning when evangelicals get involved in particular social issues like the care of vulnerable children.

These assumptions about evangelical social engagement are not new, nor are they limited to evangelical efforts to promote adoption or fostering. In his book *Christian America? What Evangelicals Really Want*, sociologist Christian Smith explains that "today, many journalists, scholars, public leaders, and ordinary Americans are curious and concerned—sometimes frightened—about who evangelicals are and what they want."[8] Toward the end of his book, Smith concludes,

In the American media, in the popular imagination, and often in academic scholarship, American evangelicals are routinely cast as either angels or demons. The angel myth is fostered by many religio-political conservative activists who posture American evangelicals as the country's last bastion of righteousness in a decaying society, a mass constituency of morally upright and outraged citizens prepared to "take back America" for Christ. . . . Likewise, many liberal-leftist activists imagine American evangelicals as demons. They cast evangelicalism as an ominous resurgence of religious oppression, a movement of radical, intolerant, and coercive zealots determined to undermine basic American freedoms in the name of narrow religious supremacy. . . . In the so-called "culture wars" drama—played out mostly by small parties of activist cultural and political elites of both persuasions—American evangelicals are too often projected "larger than life" as angels or demons.[9]

Here Smith argues that journalists, American popular culture, and even academics caricature evangelicals in terms that exaggerate their social influence and ideological commitment and provoke unjustified concern among some Americans regarding their activistic efforts. These thoughts resonate in Andrew Greeley and Michael Hout's book *The Truth about Conservative Christians: What They Think and What They Believe*. On the first page of their book, they explain that

insiders and outsiders alike misperceive, misrepresent, and stereotype this large and diverse segment of American culture. To insiders . . . Conservative Christians defend the core values of both America and Christianity against the onslaughts of a secular and vulgar culture that will, if unchecked, undo both nation and religion. . . . [To outsiders] Conservative Christians are a dangerous juggernaut bent on undoing liberty, equality, and the fraternity of nations. Power-mad hypocrites, they mask hate with love, a judgmental streak with pieties, exclusion with appeals to inclusion, and monoculture in the name of diversity. Neither the insider nor outsider portrait does justice to the variety, complexity, and subtlety of Conservative Christianity.[10]

Throughout both books, these authors demonstrate how dominant characterizations of American evangelicals and their social engagement, while in vogue, are misleading. While I am in agreement, the accounts of these scholars have been based on public opinion data and generalizations about evangelical social engagement without actually focusing on a *specific* empirical case. Their studies are thus unable to elucidate questions like: How do American evangelicals engage particular social issues, not just in theory, but in practice? In what ways do their unique ideological commitments shape their immediate and long-term objectives and methodological approaches? And what are the tangible consequences of their efforts?

This book presents an empirical examination of one such evangelical attempt at social engagement: the evangelical orphan care movement. Using this case study, I extend its logic to evangelical social engagement more broadly in order to provide a sociological analysis of evangelical activist efforts. Throughout the book, I draw on a variety of data sources collected over several years of research on the orphan care movement, including in-depth interviews with over 220 movement elites and grassroots participants involved at some capacity in adoption, foster care, and global orphan care; content analyses of movement literature; ethnographic material collected from three years of participant observation at movement events; and various quantitative data sources including national surveys, government data on adoption and fostering, and a database of orphan care movement organizations.

The overarching argument of this book is straightforward: Evangelical social engagement, because of certain characteristics inherent within the American evangelical subculture, is fundamentally *self-limiting*. While evangelicals are compelled by their subcultural commitments to collectively engage social problems in tangible ways, these same commitments lock them into an approach to social engagement that does not work on a practical level and, in fact, undermines natural advantages evangelicals have at their disposal. Consequently, their attempts at social engagement will ultimately fall short of accomplishing long-term, substantive change in the areas they seek to address.

This argument plays out in several ways with respect to the orphan care movement. First, contrary to the assumptions of journalists like Joyce and even the claims of evangelical activists themselves, I show that there is no concrete evidence to suggest that evangelicals have successfully mobilized American Christians to adopt or foster more children than they have in the past, despite over a decade of effort. To be sure, *some* evangelicals are adopting and fostering children, as they always have, but certainly nowhere near the point where other Americans would have cause for concern, even if proselytizing and pro-life values were driving evangelicals' efforts (which is only partly true at best). Second, I demonstrate that certain aspects of the American evangelical ideology and subculture, far from turning evangelicals into a juggernaut of social change, in many ways actually *hinder* evangelical efforts at social engagement just as much as they facilitate them. And last, based on the first two arguments, I conclude that evangelical attempts at social engagement—specifically, their efforts to address social problems like vulnerable children, but also issues of poverty, racial inequality, homelessness, sex trafficking, the environment, and so on—pose little threat to a secular American democracy, primarily because American evangelical attempts at social engagement are fundamentally self-limiting, being less about solving social problems and more about obedience, religious renewal, and group-boundary maintenance.

But first, I must explain some foundational ideas and concepts that I use throughout the book. In the next two sections, I briefly discuss what we know about the links between culture, social movement participation, and American evangelicalism.

Culture and Social Movement Participation

Sociologists have long been interested in understanding collective action, and since the Civil Rights Movement, research has often focused on a particular type of collective action referred to as a "social movement": a campaign or series of coordinated efforts among groups to bring about social or political goals.[11] Fundamental to the study of social movements is the question of *why* grassroots actors, who are often not directly affected by the problem(s) that the group seeks to address, volunteer their time, resources, and in some cases their own safety and lives to participate in movement activities. Closely related to this question is the question of *how* movement leaders effectively attract, motivate, and deploy grassroots actors to brave the risks and costs of activism to accomplish movement objectives. This is the question of how social movement mobilization happens.

In earlier research on social movements, sociologists often interpreted movement participation as a consequence of emotional reactions to deprivation or structural strain.[12] The basic idea was that if the perceived injustice or grievance was strong enough, a collectivity of outraged actors would respond, akin to a mob. Later work on movement participation drew on organizational and rational actor models of human behavior. Political process and resource mobilization theories argued that central to the task of recruiting and mobilizing participants was the political climate and structure that would facilitate such mobilization,[13] as well as the ability of movements to harness enough social or material resources to coordinate and deploy participants effectively.[14] From the 1980s onward, research on social movements was influenced by what scholars have called the "cultural turn" in the social sciences,[15] particularly in sociology. Movement researchers began to ask about the role of culture (in the forms of norms, symbols, identities, moral understandings, and repertoires of action) in shaping social movement participation.[16]

Two dominant concepts in the literature on culture and collective action have been that of collective action frames and, more recently, cultural schemas. "Collective action frames" are understood as negotiated, interpretive schemata (like maps for interpreting our world) that can motivate and guide collective action. When movement leaders engage in "framing" to mobilize a group of people, they try to attach symbolic meanings to a social problem that will provoke a response from a particular audience. The content of this framing activity is the collective action frame.

Christian ministers do this sort of framing activity every week. Suppose, for example, the pastor of a large, predominantly white, middle-class, conservative Protestant church wants to mobilize his church members to serve the poor downtown. More than just providing handouts, this pastor wants church members to repent of their own affluence, change their patterns of consumption, give sacrificially to those in need, and even rally to address systemic causes of inequality. To accomplish this goal, he will most likely engage in framing. That is to say, he will employ a variety of media (a series of sermons, books, articles, video clips, blog posts, adult education curricula) that connect the immediate problem (poor people and injustice in our city) with the biblical call for Christians to proactively address poverty (a collective action frame), and he will tell the church that this truth applies directly to them and requires radical action. If this framing activity hits home (or finds "resonance") with the church members, they will act, and the pastor will have been successful.[17] As we will see later, most evangelical attempts at social engagement are based on this underlying theory of how mobilization works—ideas or beliefs move people to action, and therefore, if you change their ideas, you will change their actions.

By contrast, research on culture and social action has increasingly drawn on the concept of "cultural schemas" to refer to durable, cognitive structures (i.e., ways of organizing thinking) that "provide meanings, motivations, and recipes" for social action.[18] Though similar to collective action frames, cultural schemas differ in that they derive largely from social structure rather than interpersonal interaction and describe something more cognitive and thus more generative of social action than frames.[19] In fact, schemas can describe thought processes that are pre-reflexive or unconscious.[20] To put it another way, cultural schemas organize our thoughts, motivate our actions, and tell us how to act in a given situation. But they are buried deep and do not originate from what we are experiencing as we interact with other people. Rather, they come from how we were raised and under what conditions. Moreover, these ways of thinking can be buried so deep that we struggle to articulate them; they just *feel* right.

So how does this work when it comes to mobilizing people to address a social problem? Let us go back to the pastor who wants to mobilize his church members to serve the poor. It might be nice to think that average American churchgoers could be mobilized to radical, life-altering social action just by hearing a rousing sermon or reading a book that resonates with what they have always been told about Christians addressing poverty. Certainly, people are often influenced by emotionalism or whatever is popular, but those sorts of individual changes tend to be superficial and short-lived. Experienced pastors know this.

Rather, research behind cultural schemas suggests that people are not easily persuaded to drastically change their lives. First off, people are more self-interested than we like to acknowledge. Research shows that activism—even very altruistic and self-sacrificing activism—often stems largely from a combination of (1) concerns about the approval of one's peers or loved ones and (2) previous life circumstances.[21] But more to the point, people raised in white, American, middle-class, conservative

Protestant households have been raised with certain sets of cultural schemas, or ways of thinking, in this case about what poor people *really* need and how to help them. These cultural schemas—because they are buried deep down, often at the level of intuition and reflex—shape church members' behavior far more than anything said from the pulpit or what they read in a Christian book. Any pastor who seeks to influence his people to drastically change in ways that are contrary to their cultural schemas about poverty, morality, individualism, and social action—even if he could make an airtight biblical case for it—will find it far easier said than done. It is possible, but it requires ways of convincing that are more involved than most framing activities like preaching sermons or showing videos. Throughout this book, I draw heavily on this idea of cultural schemas to help us understand orphan care activism but, also, evangelicals more broadly.

The American Evangelical Subculture and Social Engagement

Before proceeding, some important clarification is needed regarding the group I am describing. First, while I will not always clarify that I mean *American* evangelicals, I wish to state here that I am focusing on American evangelicalism specifically and not evangelicalism in an abstract, decontextualized sense, as if such a thing even existed. American evangelicals are a particular group that has been indelibly shaped by their American-ness, and this is the group about whom I am writing.

Second, the term "evangelical" can be defined in different ways, and these differences have important implications for understanding the size, influence, and opinions of American evangelicals.[22] While some studies define evangelicals by their denominational affiliations,[23] the orphan care movement transcends many of the traditional denominational boundaries.[24] Other studies define evangelicals by whether they self-identify as "evangelical."[25] This can also be somewhat problematic in that lay Christians may not know what that term means or resent the idea of labeling themselves anything besides "Christian," "Christ follower," "believer," or "disciple." For the purposes of this book, I follow previous scholarship that defines American evangelicals as Christians (generally Protestants) who hold firmly to the idea of spiritual salvation through a personal, faith relationship with Jesus Christ (leading to an individualized "born-again" experience and identity), who believe in the supreme authority and reliability of the Bible, and who stress the need for all Christians to share the gospel with others.[26] All of the leaders and grassroots participants I interviewed for this study would fit this description. The vast majority would identify as "evangelical" as well.

Moreover, it should also be kept in mind that when I refer to "American evangelicals" I am using the language of statistical tendency. I certainly do not mean to imply that all sixty million or more American evangelicals (or even all of those within the orphan care movement) think the same way on the issues I discuss in this book.[27] Indeed, sociologists have recently called for greater recognition of diversity within evangelicalism itself, and I wholeheartedly agree.[28] Yet there are enough consistencies across evangelicals to employ what sociologist Max Weber describes as an "ideal type." By this, he means an abstract, hypothetical construct containing elements commonly found in a social group or situation (i.e., "the Protestant work ethic"). When I use the term "American evangelicals" this should be understood as a Weberian ideal type, an idealized category highlighting the characteristics most commonly found among the group.

In thinking about the role of culture in shaping social engagement, American evangelicals have long served as an interesting test case. Although American evangelicalism is in many ways rightly understood as a *religious* movement in that it is concerned with religious reform and renewal and is somewhat inwardly focused, evangelicals are also committed to changing their environment with the gospel.[29] Distinct from their fundamentalist forbears in the early twentieth century, contemporary American evangelicals feel compelled to engage society while remaining true to their theological convictions—what Christian Smith calls an "engaged orthodoxy." The ways unique aspects of the evangelical subculture shape their perspectives on collective action and social change have been the subject of a good deal of study.[30] Research on that topic has identified several dominant cultural schemas that orient, motivate, and dictate strategies for their social action.[31] I take these up in greater detail in later chapters, but I introduce them here.

The central schema orienting evangelical social engagement is what I call "pietistic idealism." This concept is adopted from insights provided by sociologist James Davison Hunter. Hunter argues that evangelicals are influenced by a form of philosophical idealism merged with Christian pietism. By this he means that, for evangelicals, right ideas or right beliefs are foundational. They are just as important as having the right actions, if not more so. More than this, however, individuals must have the right ideas or beliefs about God, and these right ideas are the source of morally righteous social engagement. Conversely, social engagement (even when it is altruistic or self-sacrificing) that is not done explicitly with God in mind is morally suspect, if not idolatrous. The *why* matters most. Serving the poor may be a good action, but if I am doing it because it makes me look generous or it makes me feel like God owes me, then it is a sinful action. Moreover, as we will see later, actions done for the poor as a cause for their own sake, but not for God's sake, still miss the point. Helping the vulnerable cannot be done for self-serving reasons or even for the sake of a cause; it *must* be done for the sake of pleasing God.

In truth, pietistic idealism is often more of an ideal or standard than a practical reality. American evangelicals do lots of mundane activities throughout the day that are not done explicitly for God's sake. Yet pietistic idealism is collectively held up as the guiding principle of social action (especially actions that are in any way sacralized, like adoption or orphan care), so much so that evangelical movements and organizations often structure pietistic idealism into their organizational principles and practices.

While the *why* of social engagement is crucial for evangelicals, the *how* is also critical. A corollary to pietistic idealism is the evangelical schema of individualism or its flipside, anti-structuralism. Right ideas about God matter at the individual level, and thus American evangelicals tend to embrace a perspective on social engagement that sees individual heart transformation at the center of social change. Conversely, evangelicals are often suspicious or even opposed to perspectives that see social structure as the primary target of social engagement. Such an approach is tantamount to absolving individuals of their responsibility to be obedient. Or worse, it smacks of "social gospel" activism that prioritizes practical service over preaching the message of salvation. Relatedly, evangelicals largely hold to what some researchers call "relationalism." This is the idea that personal relationships are the mechanism through which heart transformation takes place. From this schema flows the primary technique evangelicals employ to bring about social change, which Christian Smith calls the "personal influence strategy"—one person affecting another person with the truth of God's word. This is the idea of social change one heart at a time.[32]

Last, while not necessarily a schema per se, numerous scholars of American Christianity like Mark Noll argue that evangelicals exhibit a strong tendency toward populism. By this they mean that evangelicals are often suspicious of secular ideas and academics, while also being highly influenced by the media and easily swayed by fads, sentimentality, and shallow theological reasoning.[33] This inclination toward populism may play itself out in social engagement as evangelicals are often quickly drawn into rash action by emotional appeals.[34]

Despite the considerable attention given to evangelical perspectives on social engagement, relatively little empirical attention has been given to actual, specific efforts at engaging their society.[35] Still less attention has been given to the efficacy of these campaigns and the ways certain aspects of the evangelical subculture may facilitate and/or hinder their efforts—though some researchers consider this from a theoretical standpoint.[36] In his analysis of interviews and national survey data, for example, Christian Smith theorized that the evangelical subculture, while promoting and catalyzing social engagement, might also limit its own effectiveness. He writes:

> We wish to draw attention here to at least one significant way in which American evangelicalism appears to be relatively inaffective: in actually accomplishing distinctively Christian social change. Although evangelicalism does sustain a thriving religious tradition for itself, we will suggest that it does not fare so well when it comes to achieving its goal of transforming the world for Christ. Moreover, this circumstance is not quite as simple as evangelicalism succeeding in some ways but faltering in others. In actuality, the irony of this situation is thick, for the conditions underlying evangelicalism's strength and ineffectiveness are often linked: many of the subcultural distinctives which foster evangelicalism's vitality as a religious movement, we believe, are the very same factors which can foster ineffectiveness as an agent of social change. The sources of both its strengths and weakness are often the same.[37]

Smith identifies three potential (self-induced) hindrances to evangelical effectiveness at fostering social change. First, evangelicals face a tremendous public relations problem in that many Americans do not fully understand what evangelicals really believe or prioritize, and those who do understand evangelicals often do not like them very much. In fact, Smith argues that it is in fact the things that evangelicals consider strengths or assets about themselves (personal conviction, confident evangelism, moral rectitude, fervent devotion) that bother non-evangelical Americans.[38] Second, evangelicals do not recognize that the personal influence strategy is ultimately limited in its ability to address social problems that are structural in nature, like many forms of racial inequality.[39] Last, Smith points to the inherent contradiction evangelicals wrestle with in their commitment to what he calls "voluntaristic absolutism." On the one hand, evangelicals believe that obedience to God must be voluntary and uncoerced. But on the other hand, evangelicals often advocate for laws that privilege a Christian perspective, like requiring that prayer and creationism are taught in public schools. Evangelicals are consequently unable to articulate a consistent public policy in light of this contradiction.

But perhaps Smith is wrong. Perhaps evangelical social engagement is ineffective, not because Christians are *too* evangelical, but because they are not evangelical *enough*. This is a common refrain among evangelicals, as James Davison Hunter explains. Evangelicals believe they could change society if ordinary, grassroots Christians would simply be better Christians: if they would repent and believe the gospel enough, submit to the authority of scripture, take a stand for Christ, engage the culture, and stop buying into secular ideologies and methods.[40] Considering this argument, Smith counters:

> The strategic difficulties that constrain evangelical attempts at social influence demonstrate precisely the powerful authority that evangelical cultural codes still do hold over ordinary evangelicals. The problem is not that evangelicalism is [being secularized]. Quite the contrary. Evangelical cultural structures . . . retain tremendous authority among the faithful. The problem, rather, is that the subcultural codes which evangelicals employ with great conviction are themselves strategically inadequate for the task for social transformation. It is precisely because the strategically

deficient evangelical tradition exercises so much authority among its ad-
herents, then, that evangelicals encounter much of the strategic ineffectiveness described above.[41]

While this book builds on Smith's argument, one significant limitation of Smith's research, and that of others focusing on the topic of evangelical beliefs about social engagement, is that the constraints described
are all at the theoretical level. Smith is unable to point to concrete,
empirical examples of how evangelical attempts at social engagement
have failed for the reasons he suggests. Rather, he infers that they will
be failing strategies based on his sociological assumptions. Smith is also
unable to highlight the actual mechanisms that would limit evangelical
effectiveness at social engagement. In other words, he leaves us without
a clear picture demonstrating the specific social processes that connect
evangelical cultural schemas about social change with actual outcomes.

In this book, I attempt to overcome these limitations by focusing on a
large, well-developed, and ongoing movement among American evangelicals to engage their society—the orphan care movement. In the following
section, I provide some background on evangelicals, adoption, and orphan care and then lay out the history and development of the contemporary orphan care movement.

Evangelicals, Orphan Care, and Adoption

Though Roman Catholics, and particularly nuns and priests, have more
often been associated with the care of orphans in the American popular
consciousness, evangelical Protestants have participated in significant
campaigns to promote adoption and orphan care in the United States
since before the nation's founding.[42] One of the fathers of the First Great
Awakening, George Whitefield, founded the Bethesda Orphanage in
1740 in Savannah, Georgia. Staff at the orphanage provided for the children's physical care, taught them the Bible, and prayed for their eventual
conversion. According to Whitfield's biographer, Thomas Kidd, the
Bethesda Orphanage highlighted two facets of Whitfield's ministry, and
both provide a window into evangelical social engagement. The first is
that evangelicals have long believed that ministering to physical needs
is important, but in light of the reality of eternal judgment, spiritual

needs are preeminent and can never be neglected. The second is that the strategies evangelicals use to address social problems (like vulnerable children) are always shaped by immediate cultural context, sometimes in egregious ways. The Bethesda Orphanage, for example, was the key reason Whitfield advocated for the introduction of chattel slavery to Georgia, the intention being that slave labor would fund the operation of the orphanage.[43] Other evangelical efforts at orphan care have also been guided by this commitment to addressing spiritual needs *first*, as well as reflecting broader cultural commitments in their methods.

While there are other examples of Christian orphanages being founded, the first major campaign to promote forms of orphan adoption spanned from the mid-1800s to the early-1900s. The enterprise involved transporting immigrant children westward on trains (later to be called "orphan trains") to be adopted by rural families around the country. Around the mid-nineteenth century, large cities along the East Coast, and particularly New York City, became home to increasing numbers of European immigrants. With this increase in immigration came thousands of orphans whose families were either dead or too impoverished to care for them. Some have estimated that there were nearly thirty thousand orphans of Irish descent in New York City alone.[44] Lacking opportunities for education or employment, these orphans often became involved in vagrancy and criminal activity. Viewing the problem of orphan delinquency as primarily a lack of Christian education, an innovative evangelical pastor, Charles Loring Brace, believed that a solution to the problem would be to place orphans into homes of hardworking Christian parents throughout the country whose guidance could help the young people mature into upstanding, moral adults. Starting from Eastern cities like New York, trains would carry "orphans" out west to various rural towns where they would be displayed to families who would take responsibility for them (and possibly adopt them) and typically use them as farm hands in exchange for room and board.[45] From 1853 to 1929, orphan trains placed between two hundred thousand and two hundred fifty thousand children into homes in Western states, Canada, and Mexico. Of these placements, ninety thousand were formal adoptions.[46]

This early example of evangelical activism on behalf of white-ethnic orphans was contemporaneous with a similar movement, that of boarding schools for Native American children (some orphans, others forcibly removed from their homes). Also established by evangelical Christian missionaries, Native American boarding schools were intended to "civilize," "assimilate," or "Americanize" the children, teaching them white (Protestant) Christian values and morals, while expurgating the children of their tribal heritage. Within these boarding schools, children were forced to cut their hair, had their native names changed to Euro-American names, and were forbidden to speak in their native language or engage in tribal cultural/religious practices. Unlike the orphan train movement, however, the Native American boarding schools continued well into the twentieth century and were the precursor to a large number of adoptions of Native Americans by whites after World War II and up until the Indian Child Welfare Act of 1978 modified the practice of child custody removal from Native American families.[47]

One other noteworthy campaign among American evangelicals to promote adoption and orphan care was that of Korean adoptions taking place primarily from the 1950s into the late 1980s. In the early 1950s, a middle-aged couple named Harry and Bertha Holt, who already had six biological children of their own, saw a documentary about orphanages in Korea that were filled with the mixed-race progeny of Korean women and American GIs following the Korean War. Because of their mixed-race heritage, these children were stigmatized and abandoned to orphanages, in which they lived in ostensible squalor. The Holts were so moved by this video that Harry traveled to Korea to adopt eight Korean orphans. The Holts subsequently became pioneers in international adoption and arranged hundreds of Korean adoptions for American couples, often ignoring certain standards and practices recommended by social workers and accepting couples who had been rejected by other agencies. The Holts did, however, request that adoptive families be "saved."[48] Pressured for years by authorities in the child welfare system, the Holts eventually began to follow standard professional practices for placing children and even eventually became an official adoption agency, Holt International Children's Services, which still exists today but is no longer explicitly evangelical, as Harry and Bertha had been.

The Contemporary Evangelical Orphan Care Movement

While adoption and orphan care are certainly not unfamiliar to evangelical Protestants, the contemporary adoption and orphan care movement should not necessarily be thought of as a continuation of earlier efforts. While many evangelicals who were previously involved in adoption, fostering, and orphan care in previous decades are now currently affiliated with the movement, the actual coordination and force behind the current campaign began around the turn of the twenty-first century.

Around 2000, an evangelical salesman in Texas named Paul Pennington became convinced that the Christian church had neglected its responsibility to look after orphans.[49] Paul and his wife, Robin, had adopted children in the 1980s because of infertility issues, and Paul felt that Christian adoption was God's primary solution to the problem of vulnerable children worldwide. Paul was also committed to the idea that the local Christian church, as opposed to parachurch organizations or the government, was God's tool for addressing the needs of orphans through Christian adoption. In 2001, Paul founded a ministry in his church called Hope for Orphans, which would educate church members on the Christian's responsibility to look after orphans and promote adoption as the primary means of fulfilling this responsibility.

The year 2003 would witness crucial collaborations that would precipitate the contemporary orphan care movement. That year, Paul Pennington sought out mentorship from established Christian ministry leaders. He contacted Dennis Rainey, who was also an adoptive father and the president of Family Life, which is the family ministry of Campus Crusade for Christ International (abbreviated in 2011 to Cru). Dennis was so moved by Paul's vision and the mission of Hope for Orphans that he asked if Hope for Orphans could become a ministry of Family Life. Paul agreed, and now with the greater resources and influence of Family Life, Hope for Orphans began hosting information sessions around the country promoting Christian adoption called "If You Were Mine" seminars. These would later be held in evangelical megachurches, home to influential celebrity pastors including John Piper (Minneapolis, Minnesota), Charles Swindoll (Frisco, Texas), and Rick Warren (Saddleback, California). Also in 2003, the contemporary Christian recording artist Steven Curtis Chapman and his wife Mary Beth, who were also adoptive parents, established an evangelical nonprofit called "Shaohannah's Hope" (named for their adopted Chinese daughter Shaohannah Hope and later shortened to Show Hope) that would provide grants for Christian couples seeking to adopt children. And later in 2003, Hope for Orphans, Shaohannah's Hope, and James Dobson's Focus on the Family agreed to collaborate in hosting a series of regional conferences called the "Cry of the Orphan," which also promoted Christian adoption.

As this emerging campaign coalesced and gathered momentum and influential evangelical leaders—such as Dennis Rainey, Steven Curtis Chapman, Rick Warren, and James Dobson—and organizations—such as Campus Crusade for Christ and Focus on the Family—began participating, they decided to coordinate their efforts and meet for what they called an "Orphans Summit" in 2004 in Little Rock, Arkansas. This represented the birth of the Christian Alliance for Orphans (hereafter CAFO). The first CAFO Summit was a meeting of thirty-eight key leaders, including the founders and executives of Hope for Orphans, Shaohannah's Hope, and Focus on the Family, as well as evangelical megachurch pastors such as Rick Warren and the presidents and CEOs of large Christian adoption agencies such as Bethany Christian Services and America World Adoption. Paul Pennington, now recognized by many as the "father of the orphan care movement,"[50] was appointed the first president of CAFO and later served as a board member until 2009, when CAFO hired its current president, Jedd Medefind, former special assistant to President George W. Bush and director of the White House Office of Faith-Based and Community Initiatives.

As of 2016, CAFO Summits have attracted over twenty-five hundred attendees, and CAFO as an organization has included over 195 member organizations, over 545 member congregations, and well over 500 individual members. The Christian Alliance for Orphans now represents the central organizing hub for the contemporary evangelical orphan care movement, and thus, to speak about the movement is now essentially to speak about CAFO and its organizations, members, and activities.

Figures I.1 and I.2 illustrate the rapid and consistent growth of CAFO since its founding around 2003–2004. Figure I.1 illustrates the rise in the number of attendees at annual CAFO Summits. As attendance has steadily increased into the thousands, they are now hosted by evangelical megachurches that can accommodate the large crowds. Recent summits

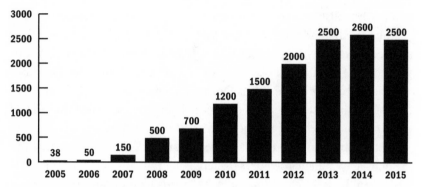

Figure I.1. Approximate number of attendees at CAFO's annual Orphans Summits, 2005–2015. Source: Correspondence with CAFO president Jedd Medefind.

have been held at Rick Warren's megachurch in Southern California, Saddleback Community Church; Willow Creek Community Church near Chicago; and Brentwood Baptist Church in Nashville, Tennessee (twice). The 2015 summit at Brentwood Baptist had over twenty-five hundred in attendance.

The function of summit conferences for CAFO seems to have evolved over the years, corresponding to the growth and visibility of the orphan care movement. The earlier summits were small and primarily served as a networking and discussion group for high-level leaders of various evangelical nonprofits. The primary concern was to promote Christian adoption from overseas or foster care, but other concerns included activities such as AIDS relief, mentoring, and serving in orphanages. Now, along with organizational leaders, summits increasingly attract evangelical grassroots families and individuals as well as family care practitioners who can earn continuing-education credits for attending. As the attendance has grown and diversified, summits have evolved to serve a variety of functions, including casting vision and direction for the movement, facilitating valuable workshops for lay leaders and practitioners, increasing momentum and visibility for the movement within broader evangelicalism, networking, and providing opportunities for orphan care nonprofits to advertise their services.

Despite their high level of visibility, however, annual summits do not represent the central organizational function of CAFO. At its core, CAFO seeks to promote and facilitate the orphan care movement,

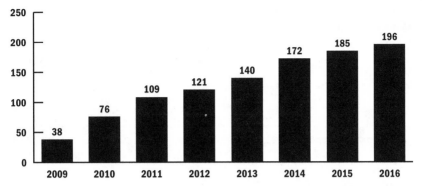

Figure I.2. Number of CAFO member organizations, 2009–2016. Source: Correspondence with CAFO president Jedd Medefind and the author's database of CAFO member organizations.

primarily, by coordinating efforts and getting evangelical nonprofits and congregations to partner with one another in advocacy and service on behalf of orphans. To this end, evangelical nonprofits can be listed on the CAFO website if they agree to CAFO's membership requirements. These include paying dues, filling out an application, submitting tax records to the Evangelical Council for Financial Accountability, and agreeing to CAFO's statement of beliefs and membership standards. Figure I.2 illustrates the growth of CAFO member organizations, from 38 in 2009 to 196 in mid-2016. While the growth of CAFO member organizations over time has been consistent, the growth has not been strictly cumulative, nor will CAFO membership ever encompass the entire universe of evangelical nonprofits that facilitate adoption or other orphan care activities. From year to year, some organizations drop out of CAFO membership for various reasons, while others sign up. Nevertheless, the obvious numerical growth of both CAFO Summits and organizational membership demonstrate that the visibility and scope of the orphan care movement has been on a steady upward trend.

What are these CAFO member organizations like? First, they are on the whole relatively young organizations. Figure I.3 organizes the number of CAFO member organizations by how many were founded in a particular year. While a notable minority of these organizations were founded between 1879 and 1989, over 80 percent were founded after 1990, about 63 percent were founded after 2000, and 46 percent were founded after

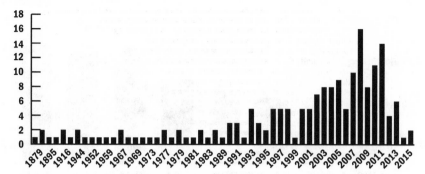

Figure I.3. Number of CAFO member organizations by year of founding, 1879–2015.
Source: Author's database of CAFO member organizations.

2005. In other words, the majority of member organizations affiliated with the main hub of the evangelical orphan care movement were founded *after* the movement started taking shape in the early 2000s. This does not necessarily mean that evangelical nonprofits focusing on orphan care have been founded with greater frequency in recent years than in past years. Unfortunately, there is no record of organizations that were founded but died off. Nor is there any record of orphan care nonprofits that did not become members of CAFO. These trends, rather, only illustrate that the majority of organizations constituting CAFO's membership base are relatively young.

As of early 2015, CAFO organized its member organizations into four ministry focuses: adoption, foster care, global orphan care, and advocacy. The categories were not mutually exclusive, and thus CAFO organizations could fall into any or all of these categories. Over three-fourths of the organizations (77 percent) placed themselves in the category of global orphan care. And over half (53 percent) categorized themselves as engaging in advocacy on behalf of vulnerable children. By comparison, a little over one-third (34 percent) were involved in placing children in adoptive homes, and less than a quarter (23 percent) were involved in foster care. The fact that most of the organizations described their ministry as "global orphan care" and "advocacy" suggests that CAFO member organizations have been primarily concerned with mobilizing Christians to orphan care in a general sense rather than being directly involved in child placement in adoptive or fostering families.

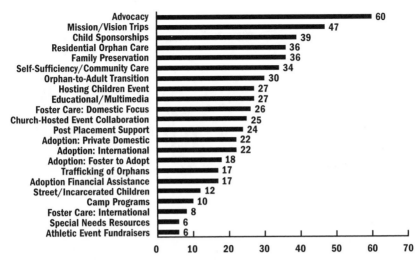

Figure I.4. Ministry focuses of CAFO member organizations, 2016. Source: Christian Alliance for Orphans (2016–2017); and the author's database of CAFO member organizations.

Later in 2015, CAFO divided up ministry focuses into a larger variety of categories, published in a document called "Next Steps."[51] Figure I.4 illustrates the percentage of organizations by all of the categories included in "Next Steps," which again, are not mutually exclusive. About 60 percent of organizations place themselves in the category of advocacy, while collectively one-third (33 percent) do work in adoption placement (private domestic, foster care, or international) and about 30 percent work in foster care placement (domestic or international). Importantly, CAFO has increasingly sought to highlight how its organizations promote orphan care activities beyond adopting and fostering, including child sponsorships (39 percent), family preservation (36 percent), post-placement support (25 percent), and more.

Where are these organizations? It is important to consider the locations of these evangelical nonprofits because this helps us understand the extent to which these activities may be localized to a particular part of the country with a large concentration of evangelicals, such as the Southern or Southeast United States, or "Bible Belt." To the extent that all of these CAFO organizations are located in evangelical hotspots, it would suggest that the visibility and influence of the orphan care

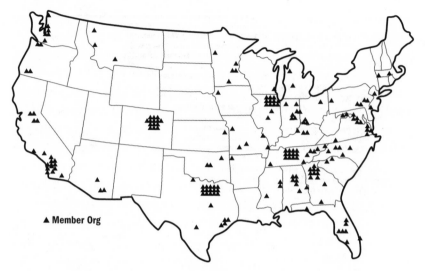

Figure I.5. Map of CAFO member organizations, 2016.

movement would not extend to regions with lower concentrations of evangelicals.

Figure I.5 illustrates the geographic distribution of all CAFO member organizations by plotting their locations out on a map of the United States. While several member organizations have branches all over the United States (e.g., Bethany Christian Services, Lifeline Children's Services), I have only plotted the location of each organization's headquarters. From the map it is apparent that these organizations are scattered all over the nation. Although there are some located in cities known to be evangelical strongholds like Colorado Springs, Nashville, or the Dallas–Fort Worth area, they are also found in Southern California, Chicago, Washington, D.C., the Pacific Northwest, and elsewhere. This distribution would suggest that the orphan care movement's influence and promotional activity are not limited to the Bible Belt.

As of mid-2016, CAFO also included 547 member congregations, which it lists on its website.[52] These congregations serve as resources for other congregations in their regions that hope to establish some sort of ministry to serve adoptive families or vulnerable children. Each congregation is also required to adhere to CAFO membership standards. Although CAFO does not list the specific cities for all these congregations, they do indicate the state. Figure I.6 lists the number of CAFO member congregations by state to illustrate where they are most predominant. This map excludes member congregations in Hawaii (2) and Alaska (1). Similar to the distribution of member organizations, CAFO's 547 member congregations are also all over the nation. The states shaded darker gray represent the top ten states with the most CAFO member congregations. These states contain more than 58 percent of such congregations. Outside of Texas, Tennessee, and North Carolina, these states are not primarily in the Bible Belt; they include California, Colorado, Florida, and states in the Upper Midwest. When we take into consideration the top twenty states with CAFO member congregations (representing about 84 percent of such congregations), we see that these states are also in the Northeast and Pacific Northwest as well. These congregations are also fairly diverse in their denominational affiliations. While a large number are (Southern) Baptist or non-denominational, other denominations are represented including Presbyterian, Lutheran, Methodist, Evangelical Free, Vineyard, and others. Thus figures I.5 and I.6 show that the evangelical adoption and orphan care movement is very much a national movement in its scope.

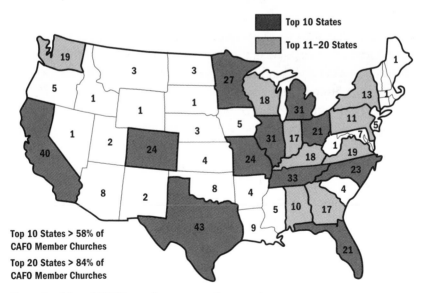

Figure I.6. Map of CAFO member congregations, 2016.

Beyond promoting these member organizations and congregations as resources for Christians already interested in adoption, fostering, and orphan care, CAFO also works to increase Christians' awareness of God's call to look after orphans. The organization's primary strategy for accomplishing this goal is the Orphan Sunday campaign. Established in 2009 by a Christian pastor in Africa, Orphan Sunday is now a major promotional effort in which CAFO seeks to get as many Christian congregations around the world to set aside the first Sunday in November (moved to the second Sunday, starting in 2015) to recognize the church's responsibility to care for orphans and to get Christians thinking about adopting and fostering. Congregations can participate at a variety of levels, and CAFO provides a list of resources to facilitate participation. These include resource manuals, event ideas, advertising materials, inspirational videos, Orphan Sunday merchandise, and specific partner organizations depending on each church's capacities and needs. The Christian Alliance for Orphans estimates that more and more congregations around the world are celebrating Orphan Sundays every year. It keeps a record of the number of countries in which at least one church has reported hosting an Orphan Sunday, which has increased from one in 2009 to at least sixty-four in 2014.[53]

At the national level, CAFO estimates that in November 2014 over two thousand congregations in the United States hosted an Orphan Sunday event. Unfortunately, because congregations do not have to register with CAFO to host an Orphan Sunday, there is no way to verify this number. However, CAFO does publish a record of the names and locations of its 201 Orphan Sunday regional coordinators (as of mid-2016) as well as its seventy-six international coordinators.[54] Regional coordinators are volunteers in a particular area of the country who serve as resources for congregations who want to host an Orphan Sunday. Regional coordinators help these congregations think through how to promote and host the event and where to find materials.

Figure I.7 plots out the locations of all 201 regional coordinators on a map of the United States, excluding those in Hawaii (2) and Alaska (1). Again, we see that the regional coordinators are scattered all over the nation. While some states clearly have more regional coordinators than others (e.g., California, Michigan, Kentucky, Tennessee), these volunteers

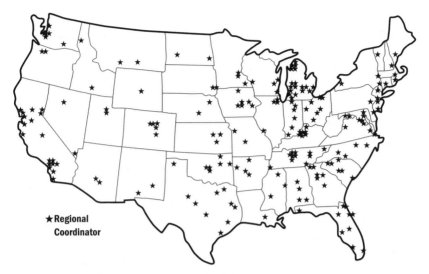

Figure I.7. Map of Orphan Sunday regional coordinators, 2016.

are not limited to the Bible Belt or evangelical hotspots; they are essentially in every state.

Taken together, these various data points suggest that the adoption and orphan care movement—viewed through its central organizing hub in CAFO—is growing both numerically and in its geographical presence. But to what practical end? The foremost practical objective of the orphan care movement has been to promote and facilitate the care of vulnerable children, primarily through adoption and fostering by Christian families. But as we will see, the effectiveness of the movement, as assessed on the basis of whether it has demonstrably accomplished that practical objective, is questionable.

The Preeminence of Adoption and Foster Care within the Orphan Care Movement

While the majority of CAFO organizations have categorized themselves as being involved in "global orphan care" or "advocacy," the most visible and valued form of orphan care in the movement remains adoption and, to a lesser degree, foster care. This has been the case since the movement's inception in the mind of Paul Pennington to the present day, though we will see how this emphasis has become less visible since mid-2015. The movement's primary emphasis on adoption and fostering can be inferred from the prominence of these activities in the promotional materials and campaigns of CAFO and their constituent organizations and board members, as well as CAFO's explicitly stated goals and the advocacy activities of the movement's most influential proponents. Adoption—and to a far lesser extent, fostering—have also received the greatest amount of media attention, both critical and positive. To be sure, caveats are often made by movement leaders, both in popular orphan care books and in my own interviews with them, acknowledging that God does not call every Christian to adopt or foster.[55] Even so, it is impossible to ignore that a central practical objective of the movement is to see adoption and fostering increase within Christian communities to the point where both become normalized and commonplace among evangelical families.

As the central coalition uniting the movement, CAFO serves as the primary mouthpiece for the movement's stated goals and proposed methods. Thus, statements regarding the philosophy and practical outworkings of orphan care—whether published by CAFO, spoken from upfront at summit conferences, or made by CAFO's leaders—provide insight into what activities are most valued and emphasized by the movement.

At the 2012 CAFO Summit hosted at Saddleback Community Church, Pastor Rick Warren, one of the founding leaders of the movement, summarized his understanding of orphan care by stating, "When we say orphan care, it's adoption first, second, and last."[56] Many of the movement leaders cringed at the hyperbole in Warren's words. And the fact that Kathryn Joyce was able to seize upon this declaration to characterize the movement as consumed by an "adoption obsession" likely caused many to distance themselves from such a strong statement. Nevertheless, a survey of CAFO's promotional materials and even self-descriptions reveals that activities surrounding adoption and fostering represent the primary application for Christians and churches answering God's call to serve orphans.

For example, from 2013 to 2015, CAFO posted its mission statement as the first image visitors would see on their homepage (https://cafo.org). The statement read: "To *inspire,* *equip,* and *connect* Christians to make the Gospel visible through ADOPTION, FOSTER CARE & GLOBAL

ORPHAN INITIATIVES rooted in the local church" (italics and capitalization theirs). Two details are worth noting in this statement. First, the overarching goal of CAFO is not a particular form of orphan care but, rather, "to make the Gospel visible." It must be kept in mind throughout that because evangelicals' are committed to pietistic idealism (the belief that righteous social actions must spring from right motives, namely, to obey and glorify God), activism or even orphans themselves cannot be the ultimate end of their efforts. That would be idolatrous. Rather, the *ultimate* goal (at least formally) must be to demonstrably magnify God and communicate the gospel somehow. Keeping this in mind, the second detail to note is that there is a clear emphasis on adoption and foster care as the key methods through which CAFO seeks to "make the Gospel visible." The term "global orphan initiatives" is ambiguous and can encompass a variety of activities including child sponsorship, family preservation, famine relief, medical missions, institutional care, and so on. Notably, it could also include adoption and fostering. But the fact that adoption and foster care are mentioned explicitly, at the beginning, and separate from other global orphan initiatives indicates a clear emphasis on these particular activities.

The articulation of "adoption, foster care, and global orphan initiatives" as the principal activities CAFO seeks to catalyze within Christian churches is repeated throughout CAFO's promotional materials. Elsewhere on CAFO's website, for example, the "About" section includes a few paragraphs that describe CAFO's constituency and overarching goal followed by its more specific goals and methods. As of mid-2016, this section read, "The size and scope of CAFO's work has grown significantly over the years, but the core mission remains the same. CAFO members join in coordinated initiatives that grow effective adoption, foster care and global orphan care rooted in the local church."[57]

This emphasis on adoption and foster care extends to specific initiatives of CAFO, including the summits and Orphan Sunday. For example, when visitors click on the link for CAFO Summits, immediately below an image of beautiful, smiling children are three words in bold: "**Adoption. Foster. Global.**" Further down the page, the website includes an informational blurb: "The CAFO Summit has become the national hub for what Christianity Today called, 'the burgeoning Christian orphan care movement.' Last year's conference drew 2,500 foster and adoptive parents, orphan advocates, pastors and leaders from 30 countries. Together, we explore effective foster care, adoption, family preservation and global orphan ministry."[58] Elsewhere on the website, when readers inquire about Orphan Sunday they are provided with a series of answers to frequently asked questions, including: "What is Orphan Sunday? On Orphan Sunday, Christians around the globe celebrate the love of the God who 'defends the cause of the fatherless' and calls us to do the same. Ultimately Orphan Sunday makes God's true character and the Gospel itself visible as God's people explore and respond to His heart for the orphan in adoption, foster care, and global orphan ministry."[59]

This theme is also repeated in CAFO's correspondence with members. Since January 2016, CAFO has sent out weekly email updates from its blog "The Orphan's Matchbox."[60] At the top of each email, beneath the name of the organization reads, "Adoption. Foster Care. Global Orphan Care." Again, while adoption and foster care would logically be subsumed under "global orphan ministry" or "global orphan care," both adoption and foster care are virtually always mentioned first and set apart as distinct in CAFO materials. This gives off the strong impression that the primary emphasis is on adoption and foster care, while "global orphan care" is essentially shorthand for "everything else." Certainly, CAFO elsewhere encourages individual Christians and churches to engage in orphan care activism beyond and outside of adopting or fostering. Even so, the examples cited above clearly illustrate how prominent the activities of adoption and foster care are within the mission of CAFO and, by extension, the orphan care movement more broadly.

Beyond the explicit statements by CAFO emphasizing adoption or fostering among Christians or the constituency of CAFO's leadership, the adoption and fostering activities of grassroots Christian families and congregations have been virtually the sole focus of media attention regarding the orphan care movement. Moreover, my experiences within grassroots evangelical orphan ministries and congregations suggests that CAFO is far more intentional about at least mentioning some variety of orphan care activities, while grassroots organizations almost exclusively focus on adoption and foster care. Between 2013 and 2016, I attended three Orphan Sunday events at three congregations in three states (Illinois, Georgia, and Oklahoma) as well as other orphan-related functions in various congregations. Without exception, the primary focus of these events was to encourage adoption or, alternatively, foster care. Those in the congregation who could not adopt or foster were encouraged to support families who are involved in either. Virtually no mention was made of other types of activities like child sponsorship, family preservation, or mentoring. Based on my observations, it seems that the emphasis within the broader Christian community on adoption and foster care is even more explicit than that of CAFO, which tends to be more nuanced.

Overview of the Book

This book has been written to inform our understanding of ways culture both facilitates and constrains American evangelical efforts at social engagement. It shows that certain aspects of the American evangelical subculture—particularly the schema of pietistic idealism and its connection with individualism/anti-structuralism and the evangelical tendency toward populism—while precipitating flurries of social engagement among evangelicals, ensure that these attempts at social engagement will ultimately be self-limiting, leading evangelicals to undercut their own efforts in practical ways.

Chapter 1 discusses the failure of the movement to successfully mobilize Christians to adopt or foster more. It draws on available data on adoption and foster care participation as well as recent surveys of Americans to demonstrate that, despite the considerable efforts of the movement, there is no evidence to suggest that Christian families are adopting or fostering more than they have in the past or more than anyone else. Both at the national and state level, adoption and fostering have not increased over the last fifteen years among non-relatives, even in states where CAFO would seemingly have the most potential to mobilize Christian families to adopt or foster. And other evidence suggests that American Christians or evangelicals, as recently as 2013, are not significantly more likely than other Americans to adopt or foster children. The remaining chapters seek to understand some of the empirical reasons why the movement has been unsuccessful at accomplishing its mobilization goals.

Chapter 2 lays the groundwork for understanding evangelicals and social engagement by unpacking how evangelicals think about mobilization. Specifically, it draws on data from movement "mobilization literature" (books written to promote orphan care among Christians) and interviews with movement leaders to demonstrate the mobilization strategies of the orphan care movement. I show how these strategies are almost entirely built on the institutionalized evangelical assumption that cultural change (meaning change in values, beliefs, or worldviews) necessarily (in a moral sense) precedes both individual and collective action and that this cultural change happens through transformative interpersonal conversations and teaching. It also highlights the evangelical skepticism about social change being accomplished through social structure in the form of government intervention or establishing "ministries" to serve orphans, as opposed to influencing individuals with the gospel to take personal action.

Building on the previous chapter, chapter 3 draws on data primarily from interviews with movement leaders to explore how the evangelical cultural schema of pietistic idealism as well as that of the "biblical" (that is, married heterosexual) family model influences movement leaders to draw moral boundaries around the movement cause and activism in ways that severely hinder their mobilization efforts. It demonstrates that, because evangelical leaders are so committed to the evangelical perspective that God-honoring orphan-activism must be preceded by "right motives" (i.e., obedience to divine calling, God's glory, expressing the gospel) and carried out by the "right people" (heterosexual, married, Christian families), their mobilization target to recruit to the task of adopting and fostering is severely limited, excluding Christians who adopt *merely* for family growth, Christian singles, and LGBT (lesbian, gay, bisexual, trans-gendered) individuals and couples, all of whom might make strategic partners in the cause of moving vulnerable children from institutions or otherwise sub-optimal or even harmful environments.

Chapter 4 argues that the orphan care movement has been unsuccessful at generating *new* motives to mobilize Christians to adopt or foster more than they have in the past. Rather, they have been successful at circulating what I call "evangelical vocabularies of motive" that evangelicals now use to justify their adoption pursuits to the evangelical community.

Through in-depth interviews with families involved in adoption and fostering, I demonstrate how many grassroots evangelical families, and even many movement leaders themselves, were initially drawn to adopting or fostering, *not* because of their belief in the importance of orphan care to Christians, but because of a combination of infertility and interpersonal connections with others who had adopted. It is only *after* these families became involved in adoption or fostering that they began to internalize dominant evangelical vocabularies of motive to give an account for why they adopted or fostered. I propose that these evangelical accounts of adoption mislead both movement leaders and outside observers into believing the movement has been more successful than it really is.

Chapter 5 examines the ways certain aspects of the evangelical subculture intersect to hinder the sustainability and effectiveness of evangelical attempts at social engagement. It draws on interviews with both movement leaders and grassroots families to show how the evangelical cultural schemas of individualism/anti-structuralism and pietistic idealism, along with the evangelical tendency toward populism, create a situation in which evangelicals are challenged and exhorted to commit to sacrificial forms of activism through shallow theological rhetoric and pietistic pursuits of obedience at the expense of evaluation and research. Moreover, it shows how the individualism and pietistic idealism of evangelical congregations makes them unwilling to accommodate families to provide the support that they need when they have adopted or fostered children with significant health and/or behavioral challenges. This results in families feeling unsupported and in trouble and ultimately hinders the sustainability of the movement.

Chapter 6 considers how pietistic idealism shapes the evolution of the orphan care movement in tension with other internal and external pressures. First, I show that CAFO and the movement itself have already evolved considerably since the movement's inception in the early 2000s. This evolution has followed a common pattern of religious groups and movements—they have grown in numbers, diversified, professionalized, and gradually become more accommodating to secular society and the state. While these changes have moved the movement toward greater strategic effectiveness in several regards, I argue that this is *in spite of* pietistic idealism, not because of it. I draw on interviews with movement leaders to show that pietistic idealism is fundamentally conservative in that it values preservation over innovation and progress. Thus, while movement leaders would affirm that tactical adjustments are necessary and good for improving strategic effectiveness, effectiveness is not the ultimate goal; obedience is. Those most committed to pietistic idealism will always be more concerned with keeping the movement focused on the main thing—glorifying God and communicating the gospel, even if it means neglecting strategic effectiveness. Evangelical efforts influenced by pietistic idealism will thus be fundamentally self-limiting.

The concluding chapter revisits and clarifies the contributions of the book and establishes comparisons between evangelical orphan care activism and contemporary efforts among evangelicals at addressing race relations and human trafficking. It also provides several recommendation for the orphan care movement moving forward.

1

What Evangelical Orphan Boom?

Now, therefore, thus says the LORD of hosts: Consider your
ways. You have sown much, and harvested little.
—Haggai 2:5–6 (English Standard Version)

Adoption is not the *ultimate* goal of the orphan care movement. Neither is fostering, or serving orphans at all, for that matter. It would be a
mistake to gloss over this point, because to view the goal of the orphan
care movement as, say, "to adopt [or foster] as many kids as possible," as
some have,[1] would be to fundamentally misunderstand the movement
and evangelicals themselves. To be sure, evangelical leaders and organizations should share some of the blame for observers misunderstanding
the goal of the orphan care movement. When titles for the most influential books in the movement include phrases like "The Priority of
Adoption for Christian Families and Churches,"[2] or "Reclaiming Adoption,"[3] or "Awakening to Gospel-Centered Adoption and Orphan Care"[4]
or when leading organizations and conferences are called "Together for
Adoption," one could hardly be blamed for assuming that adoption is
the whole point.

But if you ask movement leaders, adoption and foster care are not the
ultimate goal of the orphan care movement; they are the fruit. For evangelicals, adoption and foster care are what *should* happen when Christians understand their own spiritual adoption in Christ and God's love
for vulnerable children. This is why evangelical books promoting adoption, foster care, or global orphan care so often begin with theology and
only later talk about the practical application.[5] I will elaborate further on
this point in later chapters. But for now, suffice it to say that, for evangelical leaders in the movement, the ultimate goal of orphan care is the
glory and grace of God reflected in the Church's loving care and spiritual redemption of vulnerable children. The goal is "to make the Gospel
visible" as CAFO says. Rather than viewing adoption and fostering as

the ultimate end, it would be more accurate to say that, for most of the movement's existence, and certainly from its inception, adoption and foster care have been the most visible and valued orphan care activities and thus the clearest evidence that the movement is having an impact, for those inside and outside the movement.

But the importance of adoption and foster care must not be minimized, either. As I demonstrated in the introduction, mobilizing and equipping Christians to engage in adoption and foster care have been the principal projects of the movement up to 2016. It is these activities, adoption and foster care, that movement leaders wish to become synonymous with evangelical identity both among evangelicals themselves and the surrounding culture. For example, in his September 2015 blog post, Focus on the Family president Jim Daly wrote,

> Reports show there are approximately 100,000 children in foster care in the United States who don't have a mom and dad because the courts have deemed them unfit and have terminated their parental rights. But think about this: There are about 300,000 churches in the U.S. If just one church out of three had a family who was willing to adopt a child, the number of kids on the foster adoption rolls would be zero. Wouldn't that be a great New York Times headline? "Christian Church Wipes Out Foster Care Adoption Lists!"[6]

Statements like this comparing the number of available children to be adopted with the number of Christian churches in the U.S. are commonly found in movement books, articles, and websites.[7] Given this clear emphasis within the movement, if adoption and foster care are *not* happening in greater numbers and particularly among Christian families, movement leaders would have to question whether they were truly making an impact, whether anything has changed as a result of their efforts, and whether their approach to social engagement has been somehow ineffective.

But no one apparently believes the movement has been ineffective. In fact, while evangelicals themselves, and certainly their recent efforts at promoting orphan care, may be extremely polarizing, virtually all news outlets, critics, movement leaders, and sympathetic defenders are unified in the assumption that evangelical Christian families have recently been adopting (and to a some degree fostering) children in greater numbers than other Americans, that this trend is growing, and that movement efforts are the catalyst.[8] Critics of the orphan care movement, claiming that "evangelical adoptions [have] picked up in earnest [since] the middle of the last decade,"[9] have alerted Americans to a menacing evangelical "adoption boom," arguing that evangelical families have become consumed with "orphan fever" and an "adoption obsession," leading them to recklessly pursue adoptions with little regard for birth mothers, national laws, or whether their pursuits unwittingly promote child trafficking.[10]

So, too, among those advocating adoption and foster care among evangelicals, authors argue that participation in these activities among evangelical Christians is growing and in numbers disproportionate to other Americans.[11] In their 2015 book *In Defense of the Fatherless: Redeeming International Adoption and Orphan Care*, Sara Brinton and Amanda Bennett make explicit claims about the growth of the movement and of Christian adoption in particular, often citing numbers with no reference to empirical support. For example, they write, "Over the last ten years, God's people have awoken to God's heart for the fatherless. There is a growing movement within the Evangelical Christian church to care for orphans. . . . *Thousands of Christian families are adopting* not because of infertility but in response to God's call."[12] And elsewhere, they state: "*A growing number* of Christian families are adopting. . . . The Christian adoption and orphan care movement has been described as a 'revolution that will sweep the world.'"[13]

In support of these claims about rising evangelical adoption and fostering, anecdotes are often told (and repeated) about Christian groups mobilizing to adopt children from foster care or a particular orphanage or village overseas.[14] Most authors, however, fail to cite any broader statistical evidence to verify that evangelical Christians on the whole have been adopting or fostering more than other Americans or even more than they have in the past. A contrast to this came in 2013 when Barna Group, the Christian-based polling firm, conducted two national surveys on the topics of adoption and foster care. In a recent book published by Barna Group, and co-written by elite leaders in the orphan care movement,[15] Barna cites statistical findings from these data as evidence that "Christians are more than twice as likely [as Americans in general] to adopt a child."[16] Barna also claims that "practicing Christians" are "significantly more likely" to consider adoption, more likely to plan to adopt in the next five years, and more likely to foster children or consider fostering. These are remarkable claims, considering both that previous research on the characteristics of adoptive families has seldom found much of a connection between religious identity and adoption and fostering[17] and that overall adoption rates in the United States have actually *declined* within the past decade, with numbers of intercountry adoptions at their lowest since 1981 and declining by over 75 percent since 2004.[18]

To be sure, movement leaders and promotional materials make clear there are a variety of ways to serve vulnerable children beyond adoption and fostering (e.g., child sponsorship, family reunification, mentoring), and CAFO especially has gone to greater lengths to emphasize that point within the last few years. Yet, within the orphan care movement, adoption and foster care have virtually always been the primary application given when believers are corporately challenged to obey God's call to serve orphans. Consequently, adoption and foster care have remained at the forefront of movement activity and are the primary evidence of God's work through the movement. Stemming from their importance, a central goal of the movement up to the present has been to see adoption and fostering increase within Christian communities to the point where both become normalized and commonplace among evangelical families, creating a "culture of adoption" or "culture of orphan care," as numerous evangelical leaders and institutions have called it.[19]

Given this objective, the assumption held by movement critics and advocates that American evangelical families have been adopting or fostering more recently than they have in the past is tremendously important. To the degree that it is true, it would be evidence that the orphan care movement, and its distinctively evangelical approach to social engagement, have been successful in an eminently practical way.

This chapter looks at a variety of data sources to assess whether evangelicals have *actually* been adopting or fostering more than they have in the past or more than other Americans on average. It is by far the most technical chapter in the book, but readers should bear with me; it establishes a major premise on which the remaining chapters will build, namely, that *there is no available evidence that adoption or fostering by evangelical families has increased at the national or state-level since*

2000. In fact, *there is no reliable evidence that evangelicals in particular, or Christians in general, are more likely to adopt or foster children than other Americans.* While news outlets and movement materials abound with gripping stories of evangelical families adopting or fostering, these occurrences are not happening often enough to be reflected in any observable trends. In light of the best available evidence, then, it seems that the orphan care movement's most prominent *practical* objective of mobilizing more Christian families to care for vulnerable children through adoption and fostering has not been accomplished.

Adoption and Fostering Trends in the United States

Although adoption has always taken place in the United States at some capacity, and forms of foster care have been present since the late 1800s,[20] beyond child welfare and family therapy researchers and practitioners, social scientists have paid relatively little attention to adoption or foster care compared to other family relationships.[21] To researchers interested in understanding patterns of engagement in adoption or fostering, a considerable barrier has been the lack of reliable and comprehensive national data. Regarding adoption numbers, the data limitations are largely an unfortunate result of the majority of domestic adoptions being unregulated and transacted through individuals (e.g., family, friends, or "adoption consultants") or private agencies. National-level data based on large, representative samples of Americans have been relatively scarce.[22] As a result, the majority of research on adoption has relied on small, non-random samples of adoptive parents and, far less often, birth mothers or adoptees.[23]

When we look at the most reliable and recent national data on adoptions taken from various sources, an obvious trend is that adoptions have *not* on the whole increased in the United States since 2000; rather, they are in decline. I start by presenting the most aggregate trends and then break down the trends in various ways by the available data. Figure 1.1 presents the percentage and estimated numbers of women and men who have adopted from three previous waves of the National Survey of Family Growth (NSFG) for the years 2002, 2006–2010, and 2011–2013 (see National Center for Health Statistics 2015b). The clear trend is that both the percentage and absolute numbers (extrapolated from the

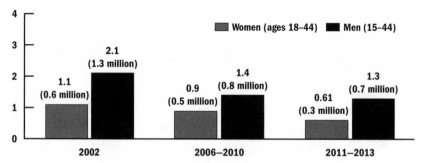

Figure 1.1. Percentage (and estimated number) of women and men who have adopted, 2002–2013. Source: National Survey of Family Growth, 2002, 2006–2010, and 2011–2013 (National Center for Health Statistics 2015b).

percentage) of women and men who have adopted have consistently declined since 2002. Indeed, according to the NSFG data, the percentage of men and women who have ever adopted in 2011–2013 was nearly half that of 2002.[24]

For another perspective, figure 1.2 presents the total number of adoptions in the United States (left axis) along with the rate of adoptions per 100,000 adults (right axis) from 2001 to 2012, compiled by the U.S. Children's Bureau.[25] By both metrics, adoptions have been in steady decline since 2005. While the number of adoptions went up from just over 140,000 in 2001 to about 146,000 in 2005, that number declined steadily to 119,514 in 2012. Similarly, rates of adoption per 100,000 adults in the United States have slowly dropped from 65 in 2005 to 49 in 2012.

Other data sources also confirm the general decline in adoptions. For example, the 2000 and 2010 U.S. Censuses include data for the total number of adopted children. Comparing the numbers for 2000 and 2010, what we observe is an aging of the population of adopted children. That is, there are higher numbers of younger adopted children in homes in 2000 and higher numbers of older adopted children in homes in 2010. This aging population of adopted children suggests that Americans have not been adopting younger children as much as they had in the past. While it is possible that the aging population of adopted children is due to more frequent adoptions of older children (as prospective adoptive parents who are unable to adopt younger children start to look

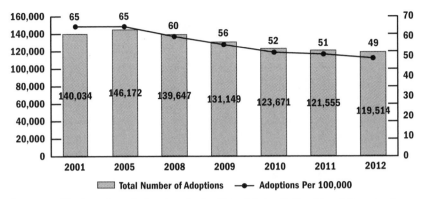

Figure 1.2. Total number of adoptions in the United States (*left axis*) and the rate of adoption per 100,000 adults (*right axis*), 2001–2012. Source: Child Welfare Information Gateway (2016).

into older-child adoptions), this has in fact not been the case among foster children. From 2000 to 2014, the percentage of children adopted from foster care at ages 1–5 increased, while the percentages of foster children adopted at ages 6–15 declined.[26]

These overall declines in adoption are likely due in some part to the slowing of adoptions from overseas (called "intercountry" or "international" adoption) and the recent rise in assisted reproductive technologies (ART), such as in vitro fertilization. Regardless of the reason for these observed trends, however, there is no evidence to suggest an increase in adoptions in recent years; in fact, it's the opposite. Adoptions are declining on the whole.

Yet while adoptions on the whole seem to have been in decline over the last decade or so, perhaps there are other forms of adoption that have been increasing. Figure 1.3 presents trends in adoption from overseas, foster care, and "other" sources from 2000 to 2015. The "other" adoptions category includes private agency, tribal, facilitated, independent, and stepparent adoptions. Although there was a slight increase in the number of such adoptions from 2001 to 2005, the number has declined steadily to 2012.[27] While these "other" adoption numbers in figure 1.3 are somewhat incomplete, other data sources corroborate the declining trend. For example, data from the National Foster Care Adoption Attitudes Survey showed that private adoptions declined 9 percent between 2007 and 2012, and data on private adoptions from previous decades indicates

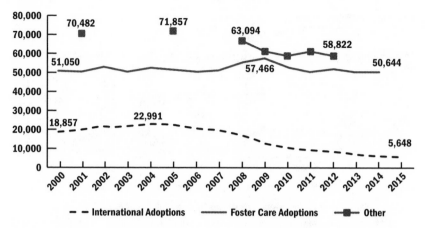

Figure 1.3. Number of international, foster care, and "other" adoptions, 2000–2015. Source: International adoption numbers are reported by the U.S. Department of State. Foster care adoption numbers are taken from the Adoption and Foster Care Analysis and Reporting System (AFCARS) reports (Children's Bureau 1998–2015). "Other" adoptions were calculated from various sources by the U.S. Children's Bureau (Child Welfare Information Gateway 2016).

that the overall trend shows a decline in such adoptions.[28] Moreover, the trends in figures 1.1 and 1.2 above would suggest that adoptions from private agencies or third parties are not high enough to counteract the declining overall trends in adoption.

But another way to test this would be to consider the trends in women voluntarily relinquishing their children for adoption in the United States. If this has been happening more often in recent decades, then perhaps adoption through private agencies or third parties is growing. Data from the NSFG from 1973 to 2011–2013 show that the percentage of children women relinquish for adoption has declined or remained steady in each wave. In addition, both pregnancy and birth rates have been declining in the United States for decades across all ages of women.[29] This means there are not more children being voluntarily relinquished for adoption, and thus it is unlikely that independent or third-party adoptions are growing.

The number of foster care adoptions seen in figure 1.3 have been quite consistent since 2000, from about 51,000 in 2000 to a peak of about 57,000 in 2009 and back down to under 51,000 in 2014 (with an over-all average around 52,000). The number of intercountry adoptions has been in steep decline since its all-time peak in 2004, at almost 23,000 children, down to a thirty-five-year low of 5,648 children in 2015. The decline of intercountry adoption has not necessarily been due to a lack of demand; rather, it is due primarily to a number of prominent "sending" countries such as China, Guatemala, and Russia cutting back or outright shutting down their intercountry adoption programs.

But perhaps these countries slowing or shutting down their intercountry adoption programs are actually due in part to the onslaught of orphan-crazed American evangelicals, thus indirectly confirming how doggedly evangelicals have been seeking to adopt. This has been the contention of movement critics, in lieu of hard evidence for an actual increase in evangelical adoptions. For example, after recounting several stories of alleged child trafficking and government corruption associated with Christian adoptions, Kathryn Joyce claims that "evangelicals—whether driven by zeal or naïveté—have had a disproportionate impact on the international adoption system." Elsewhere she states, "However well intended, this [evangelical adoption] enthusiasm has exacerbated what has become a boom-and-bust market for children that leaps from country to country."[30]

But a closer look at the trends in American adoption from various regions in figure 1.4 suggests that the orphan care movement has had

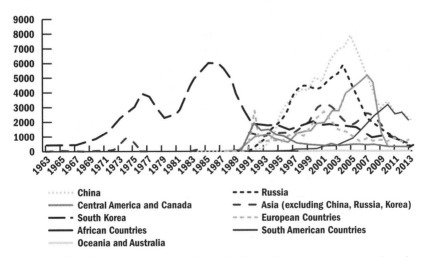

Figure 1.4. Trends in intercountry adoption to the United States, 1963–2013: number of adoptions from different sending regions over time. Source: Data for 1994–2015 from U.S. Bureau of Consular Affairs, Department of State, websites (https://travel.state.gov).

little to do with the boom-bust international adoption economy. Each line represents the numbers of children adopted in the United States from each country or continent between 1963 and 2013. Most obviously, the increases in adoption from each region, except for African countries, began well before the orphan care movement solidified. Moreover, even the *declines* in intercountry adoption from major sending regions such as South Korea (since 1986), Russia (since 2004), China (since 2005), the rest of Asia (since 2001), and Guatemala (since 2007) also started before the orphan care movement had gained significant momentum. Even adoption from African countries (since 2010) began declining just as CAFO started to promote Orphan Sundays, gain organizational members, or attract significant numbers of attendees at summit conferences and before most of the popular evangelical books promoting Christian adoption had been published. It is highly unlikely, then, that the boom-bust pattern in intercountry adoption over the last fifteen years had much to do with the mainstream orphan care movement. The dates simply do not match up. To be sure, Christian adoption seekers from the United States were involved at various points in adoption scandals in Cambodia, Haiti, Guatemala, and elsewhere. Not even leaders in the orphan care movement would deny that.[31] But various instances of corruption in international adoption cannot be laid solely at the feet of Christians, and they were almost certainly not the result of the orphan care movement, as critics suggest.

Yet it is still possible that these national trends showing an overall decline in adoption mask a growing movement among devout Christians or evangelicals to pursue adoption. Perhaps adoptions only among the non-Christian or non-evangelical U.S. population have been in decline while conservative Christians have actually been adopting in greater numbers. Although I cannot test this theory with data from intercountry or private domestic adoptions, data from reports published in the Adoption and Foster Care Analysis and Reporting System (AFCARS) allow me to indirectly test this theory for foster care adoptions.[32]

Figure 1.5 presents the numbers of foster care adoptions from 2000 to 2014 broken down by the relationship that the adoptive parent(s) had with the child prior to adoption—relative, non-relative, or step-parent. These adoptions also include those by relatives or non-relatives who were foster parents at the time of adoption. If a growing wave of

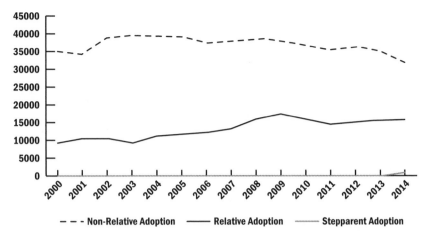

Figure 1.5. Number of foster care adoptions by relationship of adoptive parents to children prior to adoption, 2000–2014. Source: AFCARS reports (Children's Bureau 1998–2015).

American evangelical families have been pursuing adoption from the foster care system, we would expect to see some increase in *non-relative* adoptions somewhere in the last ten or so years. Although the aggregate numbers of foster care adoptions appear to be fairly stable (see fig. 1.3 above), the trends in figure 1.5 suggest that there has been a consistent increase only in kinship adoptions from foster care (i.e. adoptions by relatives), almost doubling from just over 9,400 in 2000 to over 17,300 in 2009 and back down to around 15,600 in 2014. In contrast, adoption by non-relatives has declined steadily almost every year from just under 40,000 in 2003, to under 32,000 in 2014. Stepparent adoptions from foster care (lying at the very bottom of the chart) have remained steady at around 100 every year nationally, except for a recent jump to almost 1000 in 2014.

The AFCARS data also allow me to indirectly assess whether evangelical families are adopting more from foster care by looking at the family structure of adoptive parents. Figure 1.6 presents the number of adoptions from foster care between 1998 and 2014 by whether the adoptive parents were a married couple, an unmarried couple, a single female, or a single male. As will be made clear in future chapters, the evangelical orphan care movement is primarily concerned with mobilizing married, heterosexual Christian families to adopt vulnerable children, as opposed to singles. If American evangelical families are increasingly seeking to adopt children in response to the mobilizing efforts of the orphan care movement, we would expect to see some sort of increase in married couples adopting, as opposed to unmarried couples or singles starting around 2003–2004 when the movement initially started organizing. But there is no sign of such a trend.

The number of adoptions with married couples has stayed around 35,000 each year since the early 2000s. In fact, since around 2008, the number of adoptions with married couples has declined consistently, from about 37,100 in 2008 to just over 33,200 in 2014. Single female adoptions represent the next largest number of adoptions, and these have not shown an increase, either. The only discernible increase in either married couple or single female adoptions came after 1998, which was the result of the federal Adoption and Safe Families Act in 1997, in which states were required to more quickly terminate parental rights and place foster children in permanent adoptive homes. Interestingly, the largest increase may be seen among unmarried couples and single males. While only 455 unmarried couples adopted from foster care in 1998, this number nearly quadrupled to 1,759 by 2014. Similarly, only 699 single males adopted in 1998, growing to 1,574 in 2014. These trends likely represent the increase in placements with same-sex couples who until recently would almost always be adopting as unmarried couples or singles.[33] Overall, the trends in figure 1.6 give no indication that married couples (which would include American evangelical families interested in adoption) are any more likely to adopt from foster care in 2014 than they were over a decade earlier.

I should like to pause here for a moment to stress that these foster care–adoption numbers are in the *thousands*, not millions. The sheer number of evangelical Protestant adults in the United States (somewhere around sixty million)[34] would suggest that, if there were any sort of widespread interest in adopting among this population, as described by either movement leaders or critics, we would at least see some semblance of a blip in adoption trends either among non-relative adoptions or married couple adoptions, and most likely among both. In contrast, these trends provide no evidence of any sort of movement among American evangelical families to seek out foster children to adopt. In

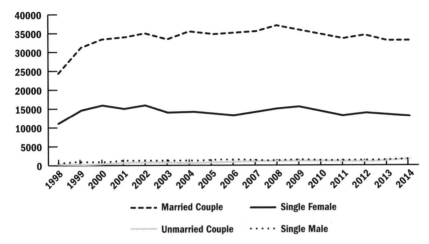

Figure 1.6. Number of foster care adoptions by family structure of adoptive parents, 1998–2014. Source: AFCARS reports (Children's Bureau 1998–2015).

fact, trends would suggest the opposite—since around 2000, foster children are actually being placed more with kin and less frequently with non-relatives.

But perhaps American Christians have increasingly been serving as foster parents without necessarily adopting, which the orphan care movement would also encourage.[35] We would then expect to see some sort of increase in foster children being placed in foster homes with non-relatives. Again, numbers from the AFCARS reports suggest that this has not been the case. Figure 1.7 presents the percentages of children in the foster care system from 2000 to 2014, broken down by their most recent placement. Placements in pre-adoptive homes, non-relative foster homes, and institutions have been stable throughout, while placement in foster homes with relatives has slightly increased to a high of 29 percent in 2014. Only placements in group homes has declined. To clarify, these trends *do not* indicate that American Christians are uninvolved in foster care. Many, no doubt, are. They do show, however, that there has not been a discernable increase in non-relative foster parenting over the last decade or so, which suggests that American evangelical couples are not fostering at higher rates than they had been in the past.

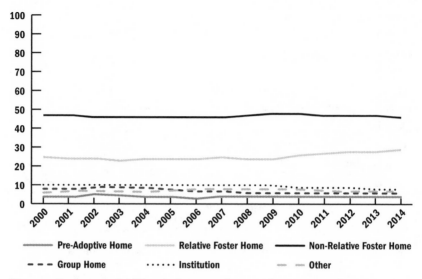

Figure 1.7. Percentage of children in foster care by type of most recent placement, 2000–2014. Source: AFCARS reports (Children's Bureau 1998–2015).

But what happens when we disaggregate these national numbers? Unfortunately, the AFCARS data cannot be disaggregated to the county level, but we can see trends for individual states. Figure 1.8 presents the absolute numbers of children adopted from foster care from 2000 to 2013, excluding adoptions by relatives and stepparents. So these numbers represent just non-relative adoptions, or the kind that evangelicals would be participating in. Numbers are provided for the states where the orphan care movement was most strongly represented. These are the states with the most CAFO member organizations, congregations, and Orphan Sunday coordinators (see figs. I.5, I.6, and I.7 in the introduction). In other words, these are the states where the movement would seemingly have the greatest potential to mobilize families to adopt from foster care. It is apparent that in every state except one (Texas) numbers of adoptions have either gone down or stayed the same. Moreover, the reason foster care adoptions in Texas have gone up is likely because, as most other states have either leveled off or brought fewer children into foster care since 2000, Texas has gradually brought more children into the foster care system.

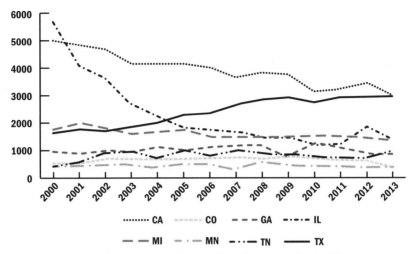

Figure 1.8. Number of non-relative adoptions from foster care for CAFO states, 2000–2013. Source: Kids Count Data Center (Annie E. Casey Foundation, n.d.)/ AFCARS reports (Children's Bureau 1998–2015).

Figure 1.9 presents the percentage of children exiting foster care by non-relative adoption from 2000 to 2013 for CAFO states. Here we see that the percentage of children exiting foster care by adoption in any CAFO state, including Texas, has not gone up. Thus the increasing absolute numbers for Texas are more a reflection of the large and growing supply of children in foster care and corresponding efforts being made by Texas to get the children out. But again, across all states where CAFO has the strongest influence, there is no evidence to suggest an increase in children exiting foster care by non-relative adoption, despite the fact that children are available and waiting to be adopted.

We can observe similar trends for foster care placement. Figure 1.10 presents the percentage of children in foster care placed in non-relative foster homes for strong CAFO states from 2000 to 2013. Although there are slight increases in the percentage of foster children being placed in non-relative homes for California, Tennessee, and Georgia, these changes are small, and most of the other states remain the same or are even declining in the percentage of foster children being placed with non-relatives.

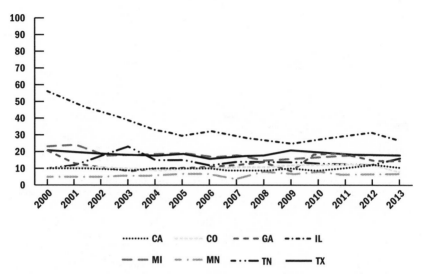

Figure 1.9. Percentage of children exiting foster care by non-relative adoption for CAFO states, 2000–2013. Source: Kids Count Data Center (Annie E. Casey Foundation, n.d.)/AFCARS reports (Children's Bureau 1998–2015).

While data from the U.S. Children's Bureau confirm that intercountry and "other" adoptions have also not increased in strong CAFO states since 2005,[36] I am unable to disaggregate those adoption patterns any further. Thus I cannot replicate the analyses in figures 1.5–1.10 for intercountry and private domestic or third-party adoptions.

It may be that the overall declines in intercountry adoption hide a rising tide of evangelical families eager to adopt. Most evangelical writers believe this to be the case. For example, in a 2016 *Christianity Today* article describing the declines in intercountry adoption, the journalist Sarah Eekhoff Zylstra claimed, "Foreign adoptions have been in short supply while demand has surged among American evangelicals, prompted by Russell Moore and other leaders."[37] But if that were the case, one might expect to see this surplus desire for adoptable children spill over into foster care adoptions, where children are vulnerable, ready, and waiting. Yet we have not seen anything resembling an increase in foster care adoptions due to the unmet demand from the slowing down of intercountry adoption. Rather, foster care adoptions remain stable (see fig. 1.3).

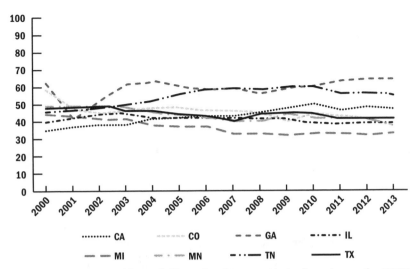

Figure 1.10. Percentage of foster children placed in non-relative foster homes for CAFO states, 2000–2013. Source: Kids Count Data Center (Annie E. Casey Foundation, n.d.)/ AFCARS reports (Children's Bureau 1998–2015).

Another alternative is that evangelical families with a so-called adoption obsession have been flocking to private or third-party domestic adoptions, where we simply do not have the available data to discern their impact. While this is unlikely to be the case, considering overall declines in private adoptions found in other studies[38] and the trends observed in figures 1.1, 1.2, and 1.3, hypothetically, such a trend would be interesting for other reasons if it were true. The push of the evangelical orphan care movement has been to serve children who are the "most vulnerable," "orphans" in the fullest sense of the word.[39] By a variety of indicators, the children waiting in orphanages overseas or in foster care domestically may be characterized as "vulnerable." They have a higher likelihood of experiencing in utero trauma owing to their mothers' poverty, and after they are born, they are more likely to endure poor nutrition, instability, and susceptibility to early childhood abuse and neglect. By comparison, children adopted through private agencies or third parties in the United States would be, by these indicators, far less vulnerable. Indeed, well-to-do infertile couples (both Christians and non-Christians alike) are often waiting in line to adopt such children from the womb, ready to expend thousands of dollars and traverse several states if necessary.

If evangelical couples were turning en masse to private domestic adoptions rather than pursuing foster care adoptions, for example, this would suggest that evangelical adoptive couples are less interested in rescuing the wounded and vulnerable and more interested in old-fashioned family growth. That is not necessarily a bad reason to adopt, but neither is it distinctively evangelical. Moreover, such a pattern *could* be negative to the extent that it implicates evangelical couples in American-style adoption consumerism, in which hundreds of eager and often childless couples shop for "designer babies" with the "right" combination of age (infant), ethnicity (white), and human potential (healthy, not traumatized, not HIV positive, not chemically dependent).[40] If this were the case, it is possible that the orphan care movement would be failing at its goals in other fundamental ways.

These national and state-level foster care trends also drive home another important point. Because the decline in international adoption has primarily been the result of sending countries slowing or shutting down their adoption programs, one could make the argument that the lack of growth in adoption among Americans in general is due, not to lack of interest, but to structural factors completely outside of the control of the orphan care movement. The issue, then, would not be the failing mobilization strategies and subsequent inability of the movement to motivate Christian families to pursue adoption but the political structures undermining their potentially effective mobilization efforts.

But there are no such structural barriers to inhibit Americans' participation in foster parenting or adopting from foster care. There is certainly no lack of available children, since tens of thousands of children remain available for adoption every year at the national level, with over a thousand in most states. Moreover, adopting from foster care is not prohibitively expensive, as it can be with international (or private domestic) adoption, and, in fact, the government provides resources to enable adoption of foster children. Non-adopting foster parents are also paid a modest stipend by the state per foster child with all foster children's health needs covered by the state, which in some ways incentivizes one to become a foster parent.[41] The fact that foster care placements and adoption among non-relatives have not grown since 2000, even in states where the orphan care movement is well represented, suggests that it is most likely *not structural barriers* barring eager hordes of prospective foster and adoptive parents with "orphan fever" from bringing vulnerable children into their homes. Rather, this fact suggests that Americans' *interest* in fostering and adoption has shown no significant sign of increase during the span of the orphan care movement. To the extent that this lack of interest in non-relative adopting and fostering extends to American evangelicals as well, the orphan care movement must question the efficacy of its efforts.

Still Searching for the "Colorado Miracle"

One anecdote that is often cited to demonstrate the practical effectiveness of the orphan care movement in mobilizing evangelical churches and families to adopt and foster is what I call the "Colorado Miracle." The numbers vary somewhat by the source, but the story has been recounted in a variety of different news sources, books, and interviews I conducted. Around 2010, Focus on the Family held a "Wait No More" conference in partnership with various churches and evangelical nonprofits, including Project 1.27, an agency that facilitates foster care adoptions. Speakers at the event challenged attendees to sign up to be foster parents or even to adopt waiting children from the foster care system.

Kelly Rosati is director of the Wait No More initiative, and in 2011 her husband and she co-authored a book by the same name about their adoption experiences.[42] During my interview with Kelly, I asked her about the famed collaboration between Wait No More and the state of Colorado. Recounting the story, she explained, "I remember saying to Sharon [Dr. Sharon Ford, manager of permanency services for the Colorado Department of Human Services and longtime board member for CAFO]—I always tell the story—what would success look like? If we had five hundred people attend the event and one hundred families start the foster care adoption process, would that be success? She said that would be success times three. And we ended up having 1,365 people, or 1,300 people it was, and 265 families started the process [of foster care adoption]."

What was the result of these families initiating the foster adoption process? One 2010 news article ran an astonishing headline, "Adoption Initiative Halves Numbers of Kids Needing Families." In that article,

Electa Draper of the *Denver Post* reported that, in November 2008, Colorado had almost eight hundred children available for adoption, meaning that their parents had lost their parental rights for various reasons. By early 2010, that number had declined to 365 children who were eligible for adoption from foster care.[43] For that number, Draper cited Sharon Ford. Although the religious commitments or motives of the adoptive families could not be verified, the tone of the headline and article strongly implied that the results were due to local churches and Christian families taking action on behalf of foster children. In her 2010 article in the *Wall Street Journal*, Naomi Schaefer Riley reported more general numbers but explicitly credited the mobilization of evangelicals behind the adoptions in Colorado. Referring to the Wait No More initiative, Riley explains, "In Colorado alone, Focus [on the Family] has moved about 500 of the 800 kids in foster care into permanent homes over the course of less than two years." In a 2012 *Relevant* magazine article entitled "Fostering Hope: How the Church Is Changing the Face of Foster Care and Adoption in the U.S.," Tyler Charles repeats the story, claiming: "In Colorado, where Focus on the Family is based, 800 children were in foster care and awaiting adoption in 2008. By 2010, that number had been reduced to 365."[44]

More recently, in his contribution to *Becoming Home*, part of the Barna Group FRAMES series, the president of CAFO, Jedd Medefind, points to the Colorado initiative as an exemplar of what the orphan care movement can accomplish. He explains, "One sees [the Christian community's commitment to foster care] vibrantly in Colorado, where many churches have made kids in the foster system a central focus. Over the past four years, the number of children waiting to be adopted in Colorado has been cut from 677 to less than 300. Dr. Sharon Ford, who oversees foster care adoptions for the state said, 'There is no question who is doing it. It's the church families adopting these precious children that no one else would take in the past.' "[45]

For those working in the child welfare system, these numbers would be truly astounding and would serve as powerful evidence that the orphan care movement was accomplishing much of the change it set out to achieve, at least in this part of Colorado. Unfortunately, these numbers are contradicted by available foster and adoption data for the state of Colorado. As I have shown in figures 1.8, 1.9., and 1.10, according to available AFCARS data going back to 2000, Colorado has not seen any sort of increase in the overall numbers of children being adopted from foster care by non-relatives (fig. 1.8), the percentage of children exiting foster care by non-relative adoptions (fig. 1.9), or the percentage of foster children being placed in foster homes with non-relatives (fig. 1.10).

Moreover, even the numbers of children waiting to be adopted in these reports are impossible to square with the AFCARS data.[46] Figure 1.11 presents the raw numbers of children waiting to be adopted in Colorado along with the numbers of children entering foster care from 2000 to 2014. Two important points are worth noting. The first is that at no time from 2000 to 2011 did the number of children waiting to be adopted in Colorado dip below 1,000. Any claims about the numbers of children waiting to be adopted dropping to between 300 to 400 are wildly inconsistent with government records. The second point is that, while the number of children waiting to be adopted declined steadily between 2008 and 2013—perhaps at first glance suggesting that Christian adoption might have been clearing the rolls of children in foster care—this also corresponds to a decline in children *entering* foster care in Colorado. This would help explain why the total number of foster care adoptions in Colorado *declined* by about 30 percent from 1,067 in

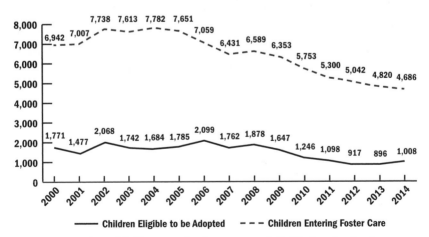

Figure 1.11. Number of children entering foster care and eligible for adoption in Colorado, 2000–2014. Source: Kids Count Data Center (Annie E. Casey Foundation, n.d.)/AFCARS reports (Children's Bureau 1998–2015).

2009 to 769 in 2014.[47] None of this is to suggest that Christians are not adopting children from foster care in Colorado. Anecdotal evidence alone would suggest many have been. But the declining number of children in Colorado foster care waiting for adoption cannot be attributed to a swell of Christian adoptions (or any adoptions); rather, the fact is that fewer children were entering foster care in the first place.

In the end, the inspiring "Colorado Miracle"—in which Focus on the Family and its partner organizations and churches were reported to have quickly mobilized Christian families to adopt hundreds of children out of foster care—is not substantiated by available data.

State-level trends focusing on non-relative adoptions do not include measures of religion. Thus they cannot definitively demonstrate that Christians or evangelicals are not adopting or fostering more than others or increasing in their pursuit of fostering or adopting. Taking a more focused look, in a section below I use recent national survey data collected by Barna Group to examine whether American evangelicals are more likely to pursue adoption or fostering or even to express interest in doing so. But first, I briefly survey what we know about the traditional motivators of Americans to adopt or foster and the potential role played by religion.

What We Know about Religion in Adoption and Fostering
Who Adopts and Why?

Although a wide variety of factors influence Americans' decisions to adopt, the primary reasons to adopt have been, and still remain, either infertility (where pregnancy is an incapability for one or both partners) or sub-fecundity (where conception is possible, but healthy birth is somehow impaired).[48] Because fertility/fecundity declines with age, and as women now more frequently delay childbearing to pursue education and careers, adoption is unsurprisingly most often pursued by women or couples who are older, married later, more educated, more economically successful, and have received some sort of ART treatments prior to considering adoption.[49] Women or men who have been a foster parent, have an already-existing relationship to the child, and/or have had a general exposure to adoptive relationships are also both more willing and more likely to adopt.[50]

Research on the relationship between religion and adoption seeking has been somewhat mixed. Some studies, for example, find no connection between religious commitment (measured in various ways) and adoption-related activities.[51] Other studies find that women who are more religious are more likely to consider adoption, but not necessarily more likely to take steps to adopt.[52] And still other studies find that devoutly religious persons are more likely to both pursue adoption and actually adopt.[53] Interestingly, while religious commitment is often positively linked with Americans' adopting, there is little evidence that Americans adopt because of their religious identity, affiliation, or tradition. For example, numerous studies on the topic have found little to no difference between Protestants, Catholics, other religious groups, or people with no religion in their likelihood to adopt children, or even in their attitudes toward the practice.[54]

Why is this the case? It seems that Americans tend to adopt, first and foremost, because they desire children and are otherwise unable to have them physically and, second, for generally humanitarian or altruistic reasons that might be linked to religious commitment but not necessarily a specific religious identity or tradition.[55] Beyond humanitarian concerns, religious commitment is often connected to "pronatalism," a cultural belief that strongly encourages families to bear many children. When confronted with fertility or fecundity issues, religiously motivated pronatalism can be a strong inducement to consider adoption.[56] Additionally, highly religious persons tend to be more skeptical of ART treatments for ethical reasons and would likely consider adoption a more acceptable alternative when facing fertility or fecundity obstacles.[57] Last, it should be kept in mind that researchers have been finding an association between religious commitment and adoption for decades, well before the orphan care movement emerged. It is possible then that religious commitment, for the reasons described above, may have long been related to adoption behavior and is not necessarily attached to the relatively recent efforts to mobilize American evangelicals to the practice of adoption.

Who Fosters and Why?

As seen in the foster placement and adoption trends I have described, foster parents often include (1) family members of the child who volunteer or are asked to take in the child either on a temporary basis or potentially to adopt the child, (2) non-kin foster parents who have no interest in adopting the child (but sometimes do adopt if a strong relationship develops), or (3) non-kin foster parents who are fostering in the hopes of adopting the child. The formal priority in the child welfare system is family reunification. Where reunification is not possible, the next priority is that the child should be placed with kin. And if that is not an option, children will be placed with either a familiar and willing non-kin foster parent or with a non-kin adoptive family. Because these different streams of potential foster parents can be quite dissimilar in their social characteristics, it is difficult to describe a "typical" foster parent.[58]

Studies of foster parenting most often cite altruistic and care-giving motivations as the primary reason most non-relative foster parents initially sign up. Additionally, along with a desire to help vulnerable children, foster parents tend to be motivated by infertility, by missing their own children, by a desire to have companions for their children already at home, and for some, by the financial incentives.[59] Little explicit attention has been given to the role of religion as a motivator for fostering. Several studies have found no difference among non-adoptive and adoptive foster parents in their being motivated by religious reasons to foster.[60] Other studies have found that, while fulfilling religious duty is commonly expressed as a motive to be a foster parent, other motives—such as serving the child or providing a home—are much stronger factors. Unfortunately, explicitly religious motives to engage in foster parenting may be buried in statements about wanting to rescue children or provide families.[61]

While there are certainly limits to the available research on why Americans adopt or foster children, a consistent trend is that religious commitment is often (though not always) a contributor to why persons pursue adoption or fostering along with other factors. The reasons given for this connection tend to be religion's association with altruism, pronatalism, and suspicion of ART treatments. Despite this connection to religious commitment, however, studies have not found adoption or fostering to be linked with a particular subcultural identity like "evangelical" or even specific to a particular body of religious beliefs. The exception to this trend was findings from the 2013 Barna FRAMES study publicized in the book *Becoming Home: Adoption, Foster Care, and Mentoring—Living Out God's Heart for Orphans.*[62] In the following section, I take a closer look at the Barna data and consider claims made in the book.

The Barna FRAMES Data and Findings

Placed against the backdrop of previous research on religion, adoption, and foster care, Barna Group's recent findings on the propensity of Christians to adopt or foster more than others are somewhat surprising. In *Becoming Home*, Barna Group writes, "Who is adopting? While adopting and fostering remain rare, practicing Christians are more than twice as likely as the general population to adopt and significantly more likely to consider adoption or fostering."[63] Elsewhere, the Barna Group explains: "Today, practicing Christians are the most likely to adopt—5% have done so, compared to 2% of all Americans. They are also more likely, though only slightly, to be foster parents (3% compared to 2% of all Americans)."[64] Barna Group also displays statistics in graph form indicating that "practicing Christians" are more likely to say they will adopt in the next 5 years compared to all Americans.[65]

First, I need to point out that the way Barna Group defines certain terms can obscure what the FRAMES data actually say. The term "practicing Christian" is not defined in the book, and Barna Group sometimes changes the definition depending on the study. For example, in most studies, Barna Group has defined "practicing Christians" as persons who self-identify as "Christian" (Protestant or Catholic), attend worship service at least once a month, *and* say that their religious faith is very important to them.[66] Yet it is often unclear who is included as "Christian." For instance, while Barna Group occasionally distinguishes "practicing Christians" from Mormons, in other surveys it appears that Mormons who identify as "Christians" are included. And in a 2016 report, Barna Group started to include weekly prayer as a qualification for "practicing Christians."[67] I tested out these various combinations to reproduce the findings Barna Group reports in *Becoming Home*, and it appears that they used the more conventional measure—that is, persons who self-identify as Christian (including any Mormons who chose that identification), attend worship service at least once a month, and say that their religious faith is very important to them.

But beyond the fact that the term "practicing Christian" is arbitrary and goes without justification anywhere in the book, it cannot tell us much about which Christians are doing the adopting or fostering. Specifically, Barna's research methodology might very well be masking that it is devout *Catholics* (those who attended worship service last month and strongly agree that their faith is important) who are the ones doing the adopting and fostering, rather than evangelical *Protestants* toward whom the book seems targeted. Another conceptual problem is that Barna simply asks respondents if they have "ever adopted" or "ever fostered." This would also include those who have adopted stepchildren as well as those who have adopted members of their own family (kinship adoption). Barna Group claims to demonstrate that practicing Christians are more likely to engage in adoption or fostering, but there is no way to tease out whether these are religiously motivated or even altruistic endeavors, given the nature of the questions.

There are other practical concerns about the data. The FRAMES surveys consist of one telephone survey and one online survey.[68] In *Becoming Home*, Barna cites percentages primarily from the phone survey, and it uses the online survey for certain questions unique to that component. The claim that 5 percent of practicing Christians have adopted compared to 2 percent of *all Americans* is already questionable given that it compares practicing Christians to the *entire* sample, which also includes practicing Christians. Statistically, this is an inappropriate comparison (more on this in a moment).

But the phone survey data raise other red flags. First, the questions about adoption and fostering were only asked of respondents who are under fifty years old (which eliminates nearly half of the entire sample). Barna does not justify this, but it is possible that it did this to catch Christian families who would be close to child-rearing age and possibly to show a greater contrast between Christian and non-Christian families in their likelihood to adopt or foster. Second, the number of people who adopted or fostered in the entire analytical sample is extremely small (adopted: 13 out of 577, or 2.3 percent; fostered: 11 out of 577, or 1.9 percent). While these numbers are fairly close to the percentage of Americans who are adoptive or foster parents,[69] because the sample size is so small, the reliability of claims that Christians are more likely to adopt or foster compared to others is suspect. Third, and perhaps most serious, when one compares "Christians" (including Protestants and Catholics and whoever else is identified that way) in general to everyone else in the sample, we see that all thirteen of those who have ever adopted are Christians. There are zero non-Christians in the sample who have ever adopted children. Thus it becomes clear why Barna had to compare "practicing Christians" to "all Americans" and include practicing Christians in that comparison: because Barna would have had to argue that non-Christians do not adopt children at all—a claim so outrageous it would have cast serious (and appropriate) doubt on the group's data.

One last point needs to be made about Barna's finding that practicing Christians say they are more likely to adopt or foster a child in the next five years. While this may well tell us something about the valued place of adoption and fostering in American Christian culture, there is a problem in taking these claims at face value. Surveys show that most Americans view adoption and fostering as loving, altruistic acts.[70] Most evangelicals would likely wish to represent themselves in this light and thus might naturally feel internal pressure (what social scientists call "social desirability bias") to answer in the affirmative to such questions, especially when doing so costs them nothing. Moreover, as I demonstrate in later chapters, because the evangelical orphan care movement has gained national attention among evangelicals through Orphan Sundays, mobilization literature, evangelical celebrity endorsements, and so on, there would likely be considerable social desirability biases leading evangelicals to exaggerate their interest in adopting and fostering or their likelihood to do either in the next five years.

Are Evangelicals Really More Likely to Adopt or Foster than Other Americans?

Despite the problems with the Barna FRAMES surveys and what I think are unfounded conclusions, it is interesting to analyze these data to see what they in fact demonstrate: When I analyze the data to compare the percentages of evangelicals who have adopted or fostered to others, I find that there are no statistically significant differences.

Using Barna's category "practicing Christian" is not helpful, first, because it combines Protestant and Catholic Christians (and thus not necessarily evangelical Christians), and second, because it compares those

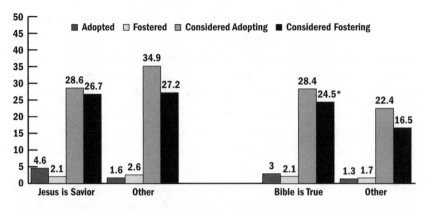

*Statistically significant difference from "Other"

Figure 1.12. Percentage of Respondents by Relationship to Adoption and Fostering and Evangelical Beliefs. Source: Barna 2013 FRAMES survey, phone component (Barna Group 2013).

Protestants and Catholics who attend church monthly *and* say that their faith is important to them with other Americans who may have selected only two out of the three criteria and thus may consider themselves committed Christians but not "practicing," as defined by Barna. More standard measures of evangelical Christianity are (1) a personal conversion experience and relationship with Jesus Christ, and (2) affirming the ultimate authority and truthfulness of the Bible.[71] These measures would provide greater indications of evangelicalism than Barna's "practicing Christian" measure.

Figure 1.12 presents the percentages of respondents who have (1) adopted, (2) seriously considered adopting, (3) fostered, or (4) seriously considered fostering by whether they believe they are going to heaven when they die because they have confessed their sins and trusted in Jesus as their personal Savior or "strongly agree" that the Bible is completely true in all that it teaches. The results first indicate that adopting and fostering are extremely infrequent situations even for Americans who claim to have Jesus as their personal Savior or believe that the Bible is totally true. Moreover, there are no statistically significant differences between these believers and other Americans in their adopting or fostering rates.

When I compare the percentages of those who have seriously considered adopting, results show that there are no significant differences between those who have accepted Jesus as their Savior and others, nor are there significant differences between those who believe the Bible is totally true and the rest. In fact, those who have *not* trusted Jesus as their Savior appear to be slightly more likely than those who have trusted Jesus to seriously consider adopting a child, although again, this is not a statistically significant difference. And when comparing those who have trusted Jesus as their Savior versus those who have not, there are no significant differences in the percentage who have considered fostering. The only significant difference in these comparisons is between those who "strongly agree" that the Bible is completely true and those who did not affirm that response in the percentage of those have seriously considered fostering. Those who hold a higher view of the Bible seem slightly more likely to consider fostering a child, which again, may be in some part due to social desirability.

What Evangelical Orphan Boom?

Across the United States, a growing number of evangelical nonprofits, congregations, and leaders have been marshalling energies to mobilize families to "defend the cause of the fatherless," primarily by participating in adoption and foster care.[72] Over the last few years, these mobilization efforts have kicked up a firestorm of media attention from those in favor of the movement, as well as staunch critics. I have shown in this chapter that—despite recent claims from critics about an "evangelical adoption boom," stemming from "orphan fever" among conservative Christians,[73] or claims from evangelical advocates that "a growing number of Christian families are adopting" or that "Christians are more than twice as likely [as Americans in general] to adopt a child"[74]—there is in fact *no reliable evidence* that evangelicals are adopting or fostering more than they have in the past or that they are adopting or fostering in significantly greater numbers than other Americans.

At this point, I expect a large number of readers will still be skeptical about the claims I have made—especially evangelicals. The typical reaction I get when I talk to evangelicals about my findings is something like, "But how could that be possible? What about all those families in my church? And my pastor? And in the news?" This was my initial reaction, too. When I started studying the orphan care movement, my goal was not to show that evangelicals were not adopting or fostering more than they had in the past. Like most others, I thought they were! But my only evidence, like that of all the other families and leaders I have interviewed since, was anecdotal. And unfortunately, even handfuls of anecdotes are unreliable for making strong claims about broader trends. Like many readers, over the last few years I have personally interacted with dozens of evangelical families serving vulnerable children through adopting and fostering, often at tremendous costs to themselves. But available data suggest that this is just not happening in large enough numbers to cause any change in national or state-level trends. Now, it is possible that members of CAFO or some related organization, upon reading this book, will respond with mounds of data showing that, *because* of the movement (or at least coinciding with the movement), evangelicals have indeed been adopting and fostering in increasing numbers. But if such data exist, the movement has been hiding it quite effectively for some time.

Moreover, several of the movement leaders I interviewed were forthcoming about the fact that adoptions have been in decline and the movement's efforts have not been successful. The most direct statement came from Elizabeth Styffe, director of orphan care initiatives at Rick Warren's Saddleback Community Church. In my interview, I asked Elizabeth about her involvement with the orphan care movement. While she has been involved with CAFO since the beginning, she interjected, "I don't believe there is a movement. I think people like to think there is. But you always have to look at results. And if more churches have an orphan care ministry than used to have an orphan care ministry, then you have somewhat of a movement. But you have to look at the fruit. And we have fewer kids getting into homes than ever before. And so I don't think there's a movement yet." Others who have been around the movement from its inception expressed similar concerns. Scott Hasenbalg is former executive director of the agency Show Hope, which funds Christian adoptions. During our interview he confessed to me that their monthly pool of applicants had declined from 120 to 100, and he concluded that this was likely due to fewer people adopting, specifically Christians. Tom

Davis, former CEO of Children's HopeChest and author of *Fields of the Fatherless*,[75] was part of the original CAFO Summit meeting in the early 2000s. He has since backed away from the mainstream orphan care movement, explaining: "I felt like I was going to the same place, talking to the same people, the same kind of interactions, year in and year out, and I was like, Wait a minute, are we accomplishing anything? Are adoptions in the United States going up? No? Well, why are we spending all this money? Why are we still having these conferences with no result?"

But an important question remains. If evangelicals are *not* adopting or fostering more now than in the past, how then do we account for the seemingly endless news reports and even leaders' testimonials suggesting they are? I offer two likely explanations. The first is what social scientists call "confirmation bias." Basically, when a credible source tells us something, and we believe it, it implants a bias in our brain. Without thinking about it, we start to look for evidence that confirms our belief while systematically ignoring all evidence to the contrary. The clearest example of this is racial or ethnic prejudice. When someone we trust like a grandpa or uncle warns us that members of a particular ethnic group are lazy, dishonest, or violent, we naturally start to see evidence of this everywhere and ignore all the individuals who contradict that stereotype. So, too, with evangelicals and adoption. When a credible source like a journalist or Christian leader tells us evangelicals are pursuing orphan care with reckless abandon, and we believe them, then every evangelical adoptive or fostering family we see becomes another confirmation of that "fact." We then unintentionally ignore the tens of millions of evangelicals who have no involvement in adoption or fostering.

The second explanation I will discuss at length in chapter 4. For now, I summarize by saying that, in my interviews with leaders and families, I repeatedly noticed a discrepancy between why evangelicals *say* they are adopting or fostering and what personal circumstances initially got them going in that direction. Remember that most adoptive families, historically and today, adopt because of fertility/fecundity issues. That is also true among evangelicals, and always has been. And while the movement to date has *not* been successful at mobilizing more evangelical families to adopt or foster, it has been *very* successful at teaching evangelical adoptive and fostering families to articulate their activities in very gospel-centered, missional ways. While more evangelicals may not be adopting or fostering because of the gospel, more evangelicals are articulating their motives for adopting or fostering using gospel language, even when it was infertility that initially got them interested. Taking their accounts at face value gives the impression that evangelicals are recently adopting or fostering for *new* reasons (those generated by the movement), rather than for the same reasons they always have been (because they want kids and adoption or fostering is the best or only option). That would explain the lack of numerical impact.

Readers should also keep in mind I do not mean to argue that the orphan care movement has been unsuccessful in *every* regard or that nothing significant has been accomplished by their efforts. Vulnerable children in the United States and abroad *are* being helped at various capacities. While the numbers are not as great as anecdotes would suggest, *some* vulnerable children are indeed being placed in loving Christian families as a result of the movement's efforts. Moreover, as international adoption becomes less of a possibility owing to programs shutting down, evangelicals are promoting other strategies for serving vulnerable children abroad. The Evangelical Council for Financial Accountability publishes annual giving reports, which indicate that donations to general orphan care activities have been increasing since 2007.[76] It is possible that orphan care activities outside of adoption and fostering have genuinely been increasing across the globe. Even domestically, alternative ways to serve orphans beyond adoption have become a growing theme within movement organizations, conferences, and literature.[77] Not least of all, as a result of the movement, American evangelicals, and perhaps even American Christians more broadly, are becoming educated about the needs facing vulnerable children and their birth families globally and in their own communities. A better awareness of the challenges confronting vulnerable populations may, one hopes, lead evangelicals to support policies that are more informed and compassionate down the road. These successes should not be overlooked or discounted. They should be celebrated.

But none of these successes of the movement have ever been considered the foremost practical goal, which has always been to awaken the church to God's heart for the orphan and to mobilize families primarily to adoption and foster care. When so much time, effort, and expense has been spent to accomplish that goal over the last ten years, with so little discernable impact, the only reasonable question to ask is: Why? In the remaining chapters, I set out to answer that question. In the end, there is more than a little irony in the answer. Critics of the movement seem convinced that evangelical mobilization efforts are made dangerously successful by elements within the evangelical subculture. In reality, it is the subculture itself that renders evangelical efforts strategically ineffective.

2

Culture Building for Change

What can you do [for orphans] practically? Aim to create a culture of adoption in your church community. Do not settle for merely adding a program to the list of hundred other good things your church is doing. Aim to stir within the ethos of the church the heart of God for the fatherless. Aim to be a church community that has been so gripped by the heart of God for the fatherless and the gospel that you are known for it in your city because of the fruit it bears.
—Jason Kovacs, "Creating a Culture of Adoption in Your Church" (2009:17–18)

Contemporary evangelicalism is an activist religion. Emerging out of dissatisfaction with the defensive separatism of Protestant fundamentalism in the first half of the twentieth century,[1] evangelicals by and large have been, and remain, committed to what Christian Smith calls an "engaged orthodoxy." This is distinct from numerous mainline denominations that have sought to be socially engaged while liberalizing their theological commitments to be more in line with post–Christian American culture. Rather, Smith defines evangelical engaged orthodoxy as a commitment to "maintaining and promoting confidently traditional, orthodox Protestant theology and belief, *while at the same time* becoming confidently and proactively engaged in the intellectual, cultural, social, and political life of the nation."[2] This tension between evangelical commitment to activistic social engagement and theological distinctiveness, Smith contends, is the source of its enduring vitality as a subculture in the pluralistic United States. The commitment to activist faith is so central to evangelical culture and identity that some researchers (myself included) consider it a defining characteristic of evangelicalism.[3] For instance, sociologist and president of Gordon College D. Michael Lindsay, in his research on evangelical elites in the United States, defines an evangelical as one who believes along with other traditional theological commitments that "one should take a transforming, activist approach to faith."[4] And in his critique of the methods and ideological underpinnings of Christian engagement in American social and political life, James Davison Hunter summarizes the evangelical mindset: "To be a Christian is to be obliged to engage the world, pursuing God's restorative purposes over all of life, individual and corporate, public and private. This is the mandate of creation."[5]

But how does one engage the world? Where does one start? Hunter explains that evangelical Christians tend to believe genuine societal change is accomplished, not in the transformation of structures like the economy or legal system, but in transforming "culture." For evangelicals, he explains, "the essence of culture is found in the *hearts and minds of individuals*—in what are typically called 'values.'" Values are moral preferences that guide all of the day-to-day decisions we make. In the minds of evangelicals, then, "culture is made up of the accumulation of values held by the majority of people and the choices made on the basis of those values."[6] Citing teachings from a number of prominent evangelical leaders, including James Dobson, Chuck Colson, and Bill Bright, Hunter demonstrates that evangelicals tend to believe that durable, positive social change happens when Christians are able to promote cultural transformation, that is, when the "values" or "worldviews" in the hearts and minds of individual actors are changed, leading those individuals to make better decisions and, ultimately, make a better society. Conversely, societies are degraded because of the bad decisions of individuals owing to the widespread spiritual and moral corruption in their hearts. Only by changing the hearts of individuals on a large scale can a society be redeemed. Undergirding the activist spirit of evangelicalism is an enduring optimism regarding the ability of single individuals to enact large scale societal change.[7]

Corresponding to this view on social engagement, the dominant method that evangelicals prescribe for transforming culture is what Christian Smith terms the "personal influence strategy," explaining that "American evangelicals are resolutely committed to a social-change strategy which maintains that the only truly effective way to change the world is one-individual-at-a-time through the influence of interpersonal relationships."[8] For most evangelical Christians, the most important changes they are obliged to bring about is, first, in their own lives by bringing their values and practices under the authority of the Bible and, second, in the hearts of their unbelieving neighbors via their spiritual conversion or re-birth through a personal relationship with Jesus Christ. Indeed, the individual salvation experience represents a cosmic example of the personal influence strategy—one's entire value system and world-view being transformed by a personal relationship with Jesus himself, made possible by the personal relationship one had with an obedient Christian who shared the "good news." Consequently, efforts to foster social change that neglect *internal* transformation (bringing individuals' hearts and minds in submission to Jesus Christ and the Bible) are super-ficial and fall short of the comprehensive transformation God desires for the world, which he commands Christians to pursue.[9]

As a corollary to this perspective, evangelical Protestants, though certainly understanding the importance of politics for furthering their goals, tend to view the role of government as limited in its ability to en-gender authentic social change. Collective action that transforms culture (i.e., it changes the hearts and minds of individuals with God's truth, then their actions) is more effectively accomplished through voluntary associations like congregations and parachurch organizations that equip and empower grassroots individuals to take responsibility for influenc-ing others.[10] Correspondingly, evangelicals locate failure to catalyze cul-tural transformation at the individual level, in Christians' unwillingness to embrace the right values and believe the right things about God and his will for their lives, and act accordingly.[11]

Hunter contends that evangelical views about cultural change are shaped by their particular ideological allegiance to two dominant tradi-tions in Western thought: idealism and individualism. "Idealism" is the view that the non-physical ideal is the primary reality, and thus ideas are principally important over matter or action. "Individualism" is the belief that individual actors—rather than social structures such as systemic racism, sexism, or classism—are solely responsible for life outcomes and social change.[12] In evangelical Christian thought, idealism and in-dividualism are linked together by Christian pietism (the view that one's personal relationship with God is paramount), and thus American evan-gelicals hold that the struggle for promoting social change through right behaviors *must* begin with the struggle to help *individuals* to embrace the right *ideas*, and chiefly the right ideas about God. Conversely, right behaviors that are not founded upon the right ideas fall short of what God desires for individuals and society.

Exemplifying this idea, in his ethnographic study of activism in two evangelical megachurches, Omri Elisha describes how socially engaged evangelicals distance themselves from terms such as "activism" or "activist" because these terms convey a commitment to a cause as an end in and of itself. Rather, evangelicals wish to convey that their actions are acts of obedience, with God's glory as their ultimate end, rather than for the sake of the act itself. In other words, their actions *must*, as an issue of moral correctness, spring forth from right ideas.[13] This formal standard for evangelical social engagement I simply refer to as "pietistic idealism."

Following from this research on evangelical approaches to social change and collective action, we would expect the mobilization philosophy and teaching of evangelical movement leaders, and in this case, the orphan care movement leaders, to be characterized by commitments to pietistic idealism and individualism. Specifically, we would expect to see a vision for cultural transformation (as opposed to structural transformation) evidenced in individual action and motivated by the "right" beliefs and ideas about God and his commands for Christian living. We would also expect this broad orientation to be coupled with suspicion of reliance on institutions, programs, or public policies that potentially absolve individual Christians of responsibility to act in obedience to God's commands. This would be accompanied by efforts to ensure that adoption and orphan care activities are being done with the proper, distinctively Christian, ideological commitments in mind. Indeed, this is exactly what I find.

Many of the popular books written by orphan care movement leaders since 2003 were written with the goals of both mobilizing evangelicals to adoption and orphan care and equipping them to mobilize others in their respective congregations. These books thus provide an ideal data source through which to understand how evangelicals approach the task of mobilization. In the remainder of the chapter, I use data primarily from the orphan care movement mobilization literature, supplemented by in-depth interviews with leaders, to clarify the strategies by which the orphan care movement has sought to mobilize Christians to participate in adoption and orphan care more generally. I show how the institutionalized evangelical beliefs and expectations about social action described above limit the mobilization repertoires that movement leaders have at their disposal. More specifically, I show how dominant evangelical schemas of pietistic idealism and individualism require movement leaders to (1) uniformly frame orphan care mobilization in terms of individuals being personally compelled by the "right ideas" to engage in orphan care activities, and (2) avoid dependency on government or ministry programs for vulnerable children in favor of establishing "cultures" in local churches in which all individual members are enjoined and expected to participate in orphan care activities like adoption and fostering. I argue that this institutionalized philosophy of social action promotes a single model of mobilization in which espousing movement ideology *must* precede individual activism. In later chapters, I demonstrate why this approach is strategically ineffective.

Evangelical Adoption and Orphan Care Mobilization Literature

Since the mid-2000s, dozens of evangelical books and articles have been written to promote adoption, fostering, and other forms of orphan care among the American evangelical community. A number of these books are biographical or autobiographical, recounting stories of evangelical women and men who were either orphans themselves and were served by evangelical families or who traveled to foreign countries to adopt orphans or serve them in some capacity.[14] Other books fall into a "how-to" category, written to guide interested Christians through the adoption process or to provide strategies for parenting children with special needs.[15]

Many of the Christian books on orphans and adoption, however, can be classified under the category of "mobilization literature." These books are written with the explicit intent both to persuade evangelicals about the biblical importance of adoption, fostering, and orphan care and to promote these activities within their church community.[16] Moreover, several of these books contain short essays by multiple authors providing perspectives on mobilization from a variety of movement leaders.[17] The subtitles of these books often state the intended mobilization thrust clearly with phrases like "Be the Solution—Change Your World," "Mobilizing the Church for Global Orphanology," "Launching an Orphans

Ministry in Your Church," "Developing a God-Centered Ministry to Orphans," and "Winning the Battle for the Children."

Because these books not only implore evangelicals to engage in orphan care activities but quite often also instruct interested readers on *how to mobilize* orphan care activity in their own churches, their contents can provide key insights into how evangelical leaders, and evangelicals more broadly, think about mobilization strategy. Movement leaders always seek to mobilize participants within a particular cultural milieu, and thus social movement researchers have long understood that leaders must select or construct their message and medium in ways "resonate" with their target audience.[18] The orphan care mobilization literature is written *by* evangelicals *to* other evangelicals *about* mobilizing evangelicals. Thus the content of these works informs our understanding not only of particular or idiosyncratic strategies and ideas used by orphan care movement leaders, but also of American evangelical philosophies and methods of mobilization more broadly. I also interviewed most of the authors whose books I analyze (see the list below), and thus I was able to ask follow-up questions regarding their thoughts on how to mobilize evangelicals to engage in adoption, foster care, and other orphan care activities.

TITLES OF EVANGELICAL ADOPTION AND ORPHAN CARE
    MOBILIZATION BOOKS, 2003–2015

Barna Group. 2013. *Becoming Home: Adoption, Foster Care, and Mentoring—Living Out God's Heart for Orphans.*

Daniel Bennett. 2011. *A Passion for the Fatherless: Developing a God-Centered Ministry to Orphans.*

Lawrence Bergeron. 2012. *Journey to the Fatherless: Preparing for the Journey of Adoption, Orphan Care, Foster Care, and Humanitarian Relief for Vulnerable Children.*

Randy Bohlender and Kelsey Bohlender. 2013. *The Spirit of Adoption: Winning the Battle for the Children.*

Brian Borgman. 2014. *After They Are Yours: The Grace and Grit of Adoption.*

Sara Brinton and Amanda Bennett. 2015. *In Defense of the Fatherless: Redeeming International Adoption and Orphan Care.*

Mardie Caldwell. 2011. *Called to Adoption: A Christian's Guide to Answering the Call.*

Johnny Carr. 2013. *Orphan Justice: How to Care for Orphans beyond Adopting.*

Dan Cruver, ed. 2011. *Reclaiming Adoption: Missional Living through the Rediscovery of Abba Father.*

Philip Darke and Keith McFarland. 2014. *In Pursuit of Orphan Excellence.*

Tom Davis. 2008. *Fields of the Fatherless: Discover the Joy of Compassionate Living.*

Cheryl Ellicott. 2010. *This Means War: Equipping Christian Families for Foster-care or Adoption.*

Diane Lynn Elliot. 2012. *The Global Orphan Crisis: Be the Solution—Change Your World.*

Michelle Gardner. 2013. *Adoption as a Ministry, Adoption as a Blessing.*

Ron Maggard and Ransom Maggard. 2013. *Why Care for Orphans.*

Tony Merida and Rick Morton. 2011. *Orphanology: Awakening to Gospel-Centered Adoption and Orphan Care.*

Russell Moore. 2009. *Adopted for Life: The Priority of Adoption for Christian Families and Churches.*

Russell Moore, ed. 2012. *A Guide to Adoption and Orphan Care.*

Russell Moore. 2015. *Adoption: What Joseph of Nazareth Can Teach Us about This Countercultural Choice.*

Rick Morton. 2014. *KnowOrphans: Mobilizing the Church for Global Orphanology.*

David Platt. 2010. *Radical: Taking Back Your Faith from the American Dream.*

David Platt. 2011. *Radical Together: Unleashing the People of God for the Purpose of God.*

David Platt. 2013. *Follow Me: A Call to Die. A Call to Live.*

David Platt. 2015. *Counter Culture: A Compassionate Call to Counter Culture in a World of Poverty, Same-Sex Marriage, Racism, Sex Slavery, Immigration, Abortion, Persecution, Orphans and Pornography.*

Kelly Rosati and John Rosati. 2011. *Wait No More: One Family's Amazing Adoption Journey.*

Together for Adoption. 2009. *Our Adoption in Christ: What It Means for Us and for Orphans.*

Jason Weber and Paul Pennington. 2006. *Launching an Orphans Ministry in Your Church.*

Kristin Swick Wong. 2005. *Carried Safely Home: The Spiritual Legacy of an Adoptive Family.*

Promoting a "Culture" of Adoption and Orphan Care

A dominant theme in the orphan care mobilization literature is the commitment to addressing the orphan crisis by developing "cultures" within congregations. Authors repeatedly explain that mobilizing believers to engage the problem of vulnerable children requires the development of a "culture of adoption" or "culture of orphan care" within local churches. In her 2013 exposé on the orphan care movement, Kathryn Joyce picked up on the pervasive "culture of adoption" language as well. She writes,

> At the local level churches report a "contagious" spread of "adoption culture" that inspires fellow congregants to adopt, with even smaller congregations witnessing as many as one hundred adoptions in just a few years. Often parents adopt multiple children, and many adoptive families swell to eight or ten kids or more. . . . The viral effect is intentional. Addressing an audience at the Southern Baptist Theological Seminary in 2010, The ABBA Fund's director of ministry development Jason Kovacs, had counseled the crowd that the key to building a church-wide "adoption culture" is to "Get as many people in the church to adopt, and adopt as many kids as you can." He added that they should also "Pray that your pastor will adopt," noting a precedent a pastor can set.[19]

Although, as will be understood from analyzing the writings of the movement authors, Joyce grossly misinterprets Kovacs and other leaders, she is nevertheless correct in implying that the "adoption culture" language is used throughout the movement. The published programs of annual CAFO Summits routinely include seminars on the topics of "Preaching toward a Culture of Adoption and Orphan Care," "Creating a Healthy Culture of Adoption in Churches," "Cultivating a Culture of Adoption in Non-adoptive Cultures," and "Creating a Church Culture Where Foster and Adoptive Families Thrive."[20] And the late Dr. Karyn Purvis, a renowned evangelical child psychologist who counseled Christian foster and adoptive families around the nation through her Empowered to Connect conferences, taught an online instructional video entitled "Creating a Healthy Adoption Culture in Your Church"[21]

This concept of adoption or orphan care culture has also made its way into official denominational statements. In their 2009 resolution "On

Adoption and Orphan Care," the Southern Baptist Convention wrote, "RESOLVED, That we pray what God is doing in creating an adoption culture in so many churches and families can point us to a gospel oneness that is determined not by 'the flesh,' or race, or economics, or cultural sameness, but by the Spirit, unity, and peace in Christ Jesus."[22]

Churches have also embraced the "culture of adoption" concept. Bethlehem Baptist Church in Minneapolis, Minnesota, formerly pastored by John Piper, who is himself an adoptive father and vocal advocate for Christian adoption, states on their website that "adoption is a part of our culture." Celebrating his church's commitment to adoption, Piper exults, "Few things bring me more satisfaction than seeing a culture of adoption flourish at our church, Bethlehem Baptist. It means our people are looking to their heavenly Father for their joy rather than rejecting the stress and cost of children in order to maximize their freedom and comforts."[23] Megachurch pastor, adoptive father, and best-selling Christian author David Platt describes his church in Birmingham, Alabama: "A widespread adoptive culture had infused the church I pastor before I arrived . . . We found that families at Brook Hills adopted four or five children at a time! This adoptive culture has only grown in recent years."[24] And at Ashland Avenue Baptist Church in Richmond, Kentucky, often used as an exemplar among churches participating in orphan care,[25] their website read: "At Ashland, we seek to create and cultivate a culture of adoption, not settle for an adoption ministry. We want adoption to be viewed as central to who we are not just something we do."[26]

Culture vs. Programs or Government

Reflecting the sentiment conveyed on Ashland Avenue Baptist's website above, within the mobilization writings of orphan care movement authors, the idea of adoption or orphan care culture was often contrasted with the creation of more church "programs" or "ministries" that were characterized as removing the responsibility for action from each individual Christian and placing it on the pastor or a few volunteers assigned to orphan ministry.

Russell Moore, president of the Southern Baptist Ethics and Religious Liberty Commission, penned the 2009 book *Adopted for Life: The Priority of Adoption for Christian Families*, which movement leaders and

grassroots adoptive families repeatedly cited as a watershed text articulating the importance of adoption and orphan care for Christians.[27]
Moore, himself an adoptive father of two sons from Russia, was among
the first evangelical leaders to articulate the "culture of adoption" or
"orphan care culture" idea in print. In numerous places throughout his
book, Moore describes a "culture of adoption," emphasizing its importance for fulfilling God's will for his church regarding orphans:

> Adoption is not just about couples who want children—or who want
> more children. Adoption is about an entire culture within our churches,
> a culture that sees adoption as part of our Great Commission mandate
> and as a sign of the gospel itself.[28]

> When we adopt—and when we encourage a culture of adoption in our
> churches and communities—we're picturing something that's true about
> our God. We, like Jesus, see what our Father is doing and do likewise
> (John 5:19). And what our Father is doing, it turns out, is fighting for
> orphans, making them sons and daughters.[29]

> I'm afraid some people will think I'm referring to the church program-
> matically as a set of initiatives. In the case of adoption, some of the need
> is for programs and strategies. But far more important than more "special
> emphases" is a culture of bringing Christ's presence to orphans. This has
> to do with creating a culture of adoption.[30]

Moore's descriptions here portray a "culture of adoption" as a pervasive ethos or worldview within a congregation that views adoption
not merely as an alternate means of having children, but one that is infused with symbolic significance, representing the transcendent reality
of Christian's adoption in the gospel, partnering with God the Father
in his mission to rescue and adopt vulnerable children, and fulfilling
the mandate to bring children to Jesus himself. He contrasts this idea
with establishing church "programs" or "special emphases," which,
though necessary at times, fall short of establishing a strong adoption
culture that motivates action throughout the community of believers.
In a *Christianity Today* op-ed entitled, "Abba Changes Everything: Why
Every Christian Is Called to Rescue Orphans,"[31] Moore clarifies that

cultivating an adoption culture is more than mere activism; it serves a more transcendent purpose, as a visible representation of God's Kingdom. "When we contend for orphans—born and unborn—we are doing more than cultural activism. A culture of adoption, orphan care, and ministry to mothers in distress announces what the kingdom of God looks like and to whom it belongs. We're contending for the faith once for all delivered to the saints (Jude 3)."[32]

Moore's emphasis on developing an adoption culture also came out in my conversation with him. Speaking about the international orphan crisis, Moore talked about the ideal strategy for ensuring that orphaned and vulnerable children were taken care of. Moore stressed that congregations and denominations should avoid investing resources in institutions and orphanages; rather, the solution to the problem of orphans would be found in families—birth families, extended families, and adoptive families. He advises:

> Don't go raising money in your church or your denomination to build more orphanages. That's not what we need. We don't need to institutionalize more children, what we need is to find ways, first of all, to keep families together. And so why are there orphans in Ethiopia and Rwanda and China and other places? Well, in some cases, it's because of extreme poverty, in some cases it's because of war, in some cases it's because of a variety of things. Well, how do we work toward the kind of economic development or the kind of diplomatic solutions that would keep that from happening? And then, how do we work first of all to say, can we place these children, who are orphaned, into extended families? If not extended families, then create the kind of adoption culture within those communities that can welcome these children. And not to simply create more and more orphanages.

Again emphasizing culture over institutions or structures, Moore explains that, for local communities in countries like Ethiopia, Rwanda, and China to consider adopting the orphans in their midst, the Christian community should develop within those countries an adoption culture that welcomes orphaned children, rather than build more orphanages.

Pastor Jason Kovacs, based in Austin, Texas, is co-founder (with Dan Cruver) of the adoption-advocacy ministry Together for Adoption and

current director of ministry development for the ABBA Fund, an organization that manages congregational resources designated to help support Christian adoptions. Kovacs has also frequently written about a
"culture of adoption." Similar to others, he stresses that new "programs"
or "ministries" are ultimately not the goal; rather, he emphasizes the
importance of developing cultures of adoption or orphan care within
congregations as the best strategy for mobilizing Christians to embody
God's love for vulnerable children:

> Many of these churches are asking how they can serve the fatherless most
> effectively? The best advice I can give is to not simply start an orphan
> care/adoption "ministry" but aim to see an orphan care/adoption culture
> established. What do I mean by that? It may be semantics but I see a
> difference that has great implications: Ministry tends be an optional pro-
> gram that a small group of interested individuals can take part in. Culture
> is something that the whole church community takes part in by virtue of
> being part of the church. Ministry does not necessitate the involvement
> or the vision casting of the church leadership. Culture will be sustained
> by the preaching of the gospel and the particular ways it is worked out.
> Ministry is not always clearly connected to the mission of the church.
> Culture is a means to work out the mission of the church.[33]

Kovacs negatively characterizes "ministries" as optional, specific to a
few individuals, and detached from the underlying ideals that ought to
drive adoption and orphan activities, namely, the church's message and
overall mission. This is in contrast to "culture," which pervades the entire congregation as an essential part of membership. He also emphasizes
that culture is sustained by preaching; that is to say, it is reproduced as
church leadership imparts the right ideas and right values to congregants,
emphasizing the centrality of adoption/orphan care to the Christian message. Elsewhere, in Dan Cruver's edited book, *Reclaiming Adoption: Missional Living through the Rediscovery of Abba Father*, Kovacs elaborates on
the importance of developing an orphan care culture, here again contrasting culture with establishing orphan or adoption ministries. "What does
it look like practically for the Church to care for the orphan as part of its
gospel mission? Here is my encouragement for how churches can engage
missionally with respect to horizontal adoption and orphan care. Do not

simply adopt orphan care as one ministry among many in the church. Integrate orphan care into the church's missional culture. Teach, train, and speak about the connection between our mission to the world and adoption. Create a culture that deeply values the fatherless because God does."[34] Thus, again, Kovacs describes adoption/orphan culture as a universal recognition among congregants of God's concern for orphans and the vital link between adoption and the Great Commission.

In my interview with Jason Kovacs, I pressed him to further expound on what it looks like for a congregation to develop a "culture of adoption/ orphan care." He explained,

> Instead of seeing adoption as a ministry that's among many ministries that are optional, like, oh, that's your passion, well, you can get involved in that ministry. The [idea of] culture is, like, every church wants to have a worship culture, a missions culture, a community culture. Every church would say, every person, every believer in our church should be living on mission, should be worshiping, should be in fellowship, should be walking with Jesus, and that's cultural. We value these things and we're about these things, worship, fellowship, the word of God, prayer, and I think adoption needs to be a part of that—so it needs to be woven into the very DNA and ethos of and culture of the church so that no matter who you are and what your passions are, if you're a part of this church family, you can't go for very long without feeling like, okay, if I'm going to be included in this family, I've got to care for the orphan. I've got to care about adoption. A Christian can't say, I'm not so much into missions, that's not my calling. It's like, no, you're made in the image of Jesus, and you're becoming more like Jesus, and Jesus is passionate about missions, is passionate about adoption, so you can't be a Christian and not be passionate about the things he's passionate about. Another way to say this—and I think Charles Spurgeon said it this way, he's like, You're either a missionary, or you're an imposter. So I think you can say you're either passionate about caring for the orphan as a Christian, or you're an imposter. You can't be a Christian and not care about the orphan for very long.

While reiterating several thoughts already discussed, here Kovacs also portrays the culture of adoption/orphan care as something that becomes essential to the membership in the Christian community, just like worship or evangelism. In a congregation that has developed a culture of adoption or orphan care, enthusiasm for adoption and orphan care becomes a part of the "DNA and ethos" of the community; Christians, by virtue of their membership, are expected to be passionate about caring for orphans. Indeed, those who do not share this passion are considered "imposters," that is, not everything a Christian is expected to be, or perhaps not even Christians at all.

Tony Merida and Rick Morton, both adoptive fathers, co-authored another influential book encouraging Christians to promote adoption, fostering, and other activities entitled *Orphanology: Awakening to Gospel-Centered Adoption and Orphan Care*. Similar to Moore and Kovacs, Merida and Morton implore Christians to cultivate a "culture of orphan care" within their congregations. They express that such a culture is essential to accomplishing the task of mobilizing the church to serve orphans: "To see these dreams [of Christians fulfilling God's call to look after orphans] come to life in the local church, we believe the goal is to develop a culture of orphan care," which they believe is represented in "a church where the spirit of God's heart for the fatherless permeates the church with unmistakable power and clarity." [35] In their view, the "culture of orphan care" is an ethos within congregants reflecting God's love for orphans. [36]

In my interview with Tony Merida, I asked him to elaborate on what he envisioned as a "culture of orphan care" in local churches. He explained, "I think the goal in any church is that you don't want orphan care to feel like a maverick ministry that's over running by itself. You know, where you just have a few people zealous about orphans, but if it's going to be something the entire church gets behind, there has to be an aroma of caring for the orphan." Similar to Kovacs, Merida emphasizes here that a culture is a pervasive ethos ("an aroma") of caring for vulnerable children, rather than a separate ministry run by a few interested individuals.

A related theme in the movement mobilization literature is that orphan care and adoption were to be the responsibility of "the Church" or "Christians," rather than the government. Movement authors repeatedly expressed that Christians had abdicated a responsibility that had historically been theirs in caring for vulnerable children to the state and should therefore seek to reclaim that responsibility. In his 2008 book, *Fields of the Fatherless: Discover the Joy of Compassionate Living*, Tom Davis, former president of Children's HopeChest, rejects the excuse that Christians do not need to serve orphans because the welfare system provides for the poor. He writes,

> Without getting into the dynamics of what problems the welfare system has generated, I think it's important to note that it is not a biblical idea. Biblically, the needs of the poor were absorbed into society. After all, the needs of the fatherless aren't only financial, so throwing a check at the problem once a month isn't the answer. Their needs are also social, emotional and spiritual—needs money alone cannot solve. And that's where you and I are supposed to come in. Providing a portion of our fields involves our money, but it also means giving of our time to enter into the lives of the suffering in a way that makes a community and a family available to them.[37]

Davis here contrasts the limited help provided by welfare aid, which he stresses is not a biblical idea, with the comprehensive, holistic investment Christians are to make in the lives of "fatherless" children, which is their biblical responsibility.

Similarly, Merida and Morton assert plainly, "I believe the Scripture teaches that orphan care is the responsibility of the church and not the state."[38] The authors point to the example of Charles Loring Brace—the nineteenth-century evangelical pastor who started the orphan train program—as an example of Christians fulfilling (albeit imperfectly) their biblical responsibility to look after orphans. In contrast, the authors explain, "Today . . . the government is present and active in the lives of thousands upon thousands of abused, neglected, and abandoned children in America. Sadly, in many cases, we, the church of the Lord Jesus Christ, are the ones who are absent. As Christians, have we decided that since these children are provided for on some level by the government, they are not our problem?"[39]

Larry Bergeron, founder of A Child's Hope International and author of the 2012 book, *Journey to the Fatherless: Preparing for the Journey of Adoption, Orphan Care, Foster Care, and Humanitarian Relief for Vulnerable Children*, stresses the issue of Christian responsibility to look after orphans repeatedly. He writes, "Millions of children starve to death around the world. There is hope however, and that hope is in the Church (and not the government) when people follow the Jesus of Servant-hood."[40] Later in the book, he elaborates: "The governments of the world can be involved and perhaps should be involved in resolving the orphan care crisis. Yet the primary role of caring for the orphan belongs to the Church of Jesus Christ and those who proclaim His glory on earth."[41] Elsewhere, Bergeron expounds on this idea and laments that Christians have abdicated their responsibility to take care of orphans:

Many believe . . . that it is the responsibility of the government to care for the orphan. I don't. In the early church, orphan care was a Christian innovation because the Roman government didn't care about human life. Centuries later, we have defaulted to the government what Jesus asked of us, the redeemed orphans of God. He asked us, the sheep called by His name, to care for these children—to look after the orphans![42]

Are government programs the preferred solution? Was it always that way? Not really. . . . We know that the early church was actively involved in caring for abandoned and unwanted children but somewhere along the way in history, we (the Church) relinquished the role which we once embraced. Perhaps the inconvenience of caring for the fatherless, the cost of their care of the opportunity to create "cleaner" ministries convinced us that the government could do a better job. After all, who wants to care for and shelter cockroaches? The problems have progressively worsened in the past few decades—not that I am blaming the world governments for the crisis we see. In fact, these programs have helped tremendously, but no glory has been bestowed upon Christ in the process and no mes-sage of salvation has been presented. Nonetheless, we can either stay the course (government programs) or go back and examine the biblical and historical record again to see how it was done.[43]

Similarly, in her 2012 book *The Global Orphan Crisis: Be the Solution—Change Your World*, Diane Lynn Elliot makes the argument that

in many developed countries, except for a small contingent of private and Christian child welfare organizations, we have largely depended on the government to care for our country's vulnerable children. As helpful as this is in developed societies, systems are often flawed and can cause more complications for children who are already in a vulnerable state. Part of the problem of depending on government systems is that it gives us the false assumption that we are absolved from responsibility. This could not be further from the truth. As human beings, and specifically as Christians, we have a responsibility to be part of the global orphan solution, and governmental policies are no substitute for our wholehearted involvement.[44]

And president of CAFO, Jedd Medefind, in his 2013 book *Becoming Home*, also contrasted the government's important, but ultimately limited, role in caring for vulnerable children to the central role that ought to be played by Christians. He writes:

Yes, I've observed that the government can often create new problems even as it tries to solve old ones. But I've also seen firsthand that government can—and must—play a vital role for vulnerable children. Healthy justice systems protect children from abuse and exploitation. Government can also help marshal physical goods like disaster relief or medicine on an enormous scale. But as vital as these things are, government alone can never meet the deepest needs of a child. As a veteran of Colorado's child welfare system once said to me, "Government makes a terrible parent." The things that matter most—love, nurture, and belonging—can only be provided person to person as individuals and families care for each precious child. James 1:27 says, "Religion that God our Father accepts as pure and faultless is this: to look after orphans and widows in their distress and to keep oneself from being polluted by the world." This is a high charge. And it is something governments cannot do. That's why the church cannot outsource James 1:27 to government or NGOs [nongovernmental organizations]. As Christians, as people God has expressly called to love the orphan, we have an irreplaceable role to fill.[45]

These ideas, repeated by movement leaders and authors, stress that *all* Christians have been specifically and individually called to take care of vulnerable children. Consequently, the issue at stake is both their personal obedience to God and, from the authors' point of view, their ability to carry the job out more effectively and comprehensively than the government can.

In sum, orphan care movement leaders explicitly and repeatedly communicate that "programs," "ministries," and "government" represent somewhat necessary, but ultimately limited, parts of the solution to the problem of vulnerable children. Organization and resources are helpful, but what orphans ultimately need is the holistic—spiritual and physical—care that only individual Christians (in families) can provide. But pragmatism is not the main issue. Of even greater consequence than governments or programs being limited in their effectiveness, movement authors emphasize that Christians have a personal responsibility that they abdicate only in disobedience. Consequently, movement leaders stress that, rather than organizing "ministries" within churches, advocates must develop robust "cultures" within local congregations that will provoke each individual Christian to embrace and obey his or her God-given call to orphan care.

But how does a "culture of adoption/orphan care" influence action? That is, how do the movement leaders envision the connection between developing a culture of adoption/orphan care and whole congregations engaging in orphan care activity on a broader scale?

First Things First: How a Culture of Adoption/Orphan Care Promotes Action

In their discussions of adoption/orphan culture in the mobilization literature, as well as their interviews, it is apparent that movement leaders view mobilization through the schema of pietistic idealism—the belief that right ideas are paramount and necessarily antecedent to right actions and that the most important ideas are those about God and one's relationship with him. Adoption advocate and evangelical megachurch pastor John Piper exemplifies this perspective on Christian action. He exhorts pastors: "Why Christians do what they do is just as important as what they do. Bad motives ruin good acts. . . . Therefore, we must not be content that our people are doing good things. We must labor to see that they do good things from God-exalting motives—lest they find in the end that their sacrifices were for nothing."[46]

In answering what the "right reasons" for Christians to adopt are, Merida and Morton simply state: "The 'right' answer is that we adopt as an outworking of our faith—no more, no less."[47] Indeed, some movement leaders articulated that to pursue orphan care and adoption activism as ends in and of themselves, rather than as acts of worship or faithful obedience, would be morally wrong. In his 2011 book, *A Passion for the Fatherless: Developing a God-Centered Ministry to Orphans*, Pastor Daniel Bennett contrasts the activism of liberal Christian denominations and thinkers with what he considers a biblical approach to social engagement:

> There is a real problem with [liberal Christians'] call to social action. It focuses on social change at the *expense* of the gospel instead of in *conjunction* with the gospel. . . . Worship, not social activism, is the ultimate goal of the church. Justice flows from worship as surely as the melted snow causes the rivers to flow down the mountains in spring. Defining the church primarily as an agent for social change fundamentally alters its purpose. Instead of social good flowing from the ultimate goal of the church that is worship, social good becomes the ultimate goal. . . . In short, ministry to the poor must be theologically grounded.[48]

This quote from Bennett perfectly expresses the evangelical adherence to pietistic idealism; right action must flow from the right ideas, or it is not right action at all. If the right ideas are present, right action will inevitably follow. But social activism, in this case adoption and orphan care, that does not flow out of obedience and worship to God is ultimately wrong action. Bennett calls this "passionless compassion." He argues, "The problem with passionless compassion is that it sees the means—compassion—as an end. It focuses on the good deeds without first focusing on the worship that should motivate the believer to engage in them."[49] And later, Bennett concludes, "True compassion for the needy is always fueled by a passion for God to be worshiped among them—and a passion for God always manifests itself in compassion for others."[50] Thus, orphan care and adoption activism *must* be preceded and motivated by right ideas (obedience, worship to God), or it is not "true compassion," and right ideas will *necessarily* be followed by right action.

Similarly, other movement leaders repeatedly stressed the consequence of embracing the right understandings about God and the link
between adoption/orphans and the gospel as *inevitably* translating into
right action. Russell Moore, for example explains, "Once children are
seen as a blessing, and once adoption doesn't seem strange or exotic, an
adoption culture tends to flourish in gospel-anchored churches. This
is why you rarely see in healthy churches just one or two couples with
children who've been adopted. Once a family or two adopts, there tends
to be a flurry of adoptions."[51] Elaborating more fully on this idea, Jason
Kovacs writes:

> The greatest thing you can do to establish a culture of adoption/orphan
> care in your church is to be gripped by the reality that God has adopted
> us as His children. The church is God's great trans-racial adoptive family.
> As the gospel takes root in our hearts and we recognize that adoption
> is central to the heart and mission of God it also becomes something
> we care about. We will naturally begin to reflect our vertical adoption in
> our horizontal efforts. This is the foundation for creating a culture that
> believes that every Christian is called to care for the fatherless in some
> way.[52]

> An orphan-valuing culture will have a radical impact on the way a church
> conducts its orphan and adoption ministry both inside and outside its
> walls. In this way, orphan care becomes much more than a ministry for
> a select few. The entire congregation takes ownership of it. The children's
> ministry is equipped and mobilized to care for adopted children. The
> small-group ministry is equipped to care for adoptive and foster families.
> The financial ministry has thought through the implications of adoption
> for a family's finances. The church budget reflects the heart of God for
> the fatherless. A passion for adoption grown in the heart and mission of
> God will translate into a thousand different actions. Some church mem-
> bers will adopt. Some will foster. Some will finance adoptions. Some will
> pray and support families. Some will go overseas and give their lives to
> orphans and the gospel.[53]

Kovacs teaches that a congregational culture that values orphans will
transform the entire congregation and influence all of the ministry

structures (e.g., children's ministry, small groups, the church's allocation of resources) as well as individual activities. As Christians are gripped by their own spiritual adoption and God's heart for orphans, this will "translate into a thousand different actions," all involving some aspect of orphan care. It is clear in this account that Kovacs envisions the ideas influencing the structure and practices of activity, not the other way around.

Recounting his arrival at Bethlehem Baptist Church in Minneapolis, Minnesota, Kovacs illustrates how the culture of adoption/orphan care manifests itself in practical activity:

> Although new to [Bethlehem Baptist], I soon began to realize these families were part of a much bigger group and a much bigger vision: to be a people who care passionately for the orphan. Over the years this church had developed a culture of adoption that had resulted in hundreds of children being placed in homes. It didn't matter who you asked in the church, adoptive family or not, they would tell you the same thing: We adopt and care for the orphan because God adopted us in Christ when we were without hope and home.[54]

Again, Kovacs connects embracing God's view of orphans and the transcendent reality of the Christian's adoption into God's family with the adoption and orphan care activities of those families in the congregation. Merida and Morton describe a similar outcome when those in a congregation embrace an orphan care culture. "[A] church with an orphan care culture will have ministries, teams, printed materials, media, common language, Bible studies, and regular discussions on the topic. They will pray about orphan care in public and private, develop fellowship groups to discuss it, and host events to bring awareness about it. They will celebrate with couples that adopt. They will support the orphan ministries with passion. *The church will have an aroma of Christ's love for the fatherless*."[55]

Rick Morton, co-author of the 2011 book *Orphanology*, published a follow-up book in 2014 entitled *KnowOrphans: Mobilizing the Church for Global Orphanology*. Similar to Kovacs, in several places throughout the book, Morton emphasizes the connection between having the right ideas or understanding about God and his passion for vulnerable children and engaging in orphan care activism. Talking about the growth of the orphan care movement itself, Morton explains:

> [Adoption] Stories like mine are becoming commonplace as evangelicals rediscover orphan care. What is happening reminds me a great deal of Israel's recovery of the Law in Nehemiah 8. The city was in shambles as a result of the desertion and inattention of the exile years. The Law of God had been lost to the people. In rebuilding the city, the people rediscovered the Law, but, more importantly, they reconnected to the heart of God. In similar fashion, the church today has recovered a passion for orphan care by return to deep biblical exposition.[56]

Elsewhere, Morton reiterates how properly understanding the Bible (through the proper preaching and teaching of church pastors) will inevitably lead to right actions. Conversely, Morton also points out that the failure of Christians to engage in orphan care almost certainly stems from failing to understand the Bible's teaching about God's character and heart for orphans:

> Wrestling to know God through His Word will inevitably bring us face-to-face with Him. We cannot ever encounter God and walk away unchanged. Ultimately, good theology in the hands of true disciples will always lead to ministry. Discovering the deep connection between His heart for orphans and the gospel in God's word challenges us to mobilize the church to act. Passivity or intellectual assent to the plight of orphans will not satisfy God, and it cannot satisfy us. We must find practical ways to bring our theology into action.[57]

> Another reason that Christians aren't passionate about orphan care is they haven't seen God's heart for the orphan in the Scriptures. They don't know how important orphan care is to displaying God's character to people or telling the gospel to the world. To change that, we have to teach the Bible differently.[58]

Johnny Carr is a former pastor and formerly the national director of church partnerships at Bethany Christian Services, the largest adoption agency in the United States. In his 2013 book *Orphan Justice: How to Care for Orphans beyond Adopting*, Carr encourages evangelicals to consider the variety of ways they may serve orphans outside of adopting them (although that is certainly included as an option). Similar to other movement leaders, Carr believes that orphan care begins with a culture rooted in the hearts of individuals, which he broadly terms a "culture of life." Drawing a contrast between the "culture of abortion" and the "culture of life," Carr explains, "Creating a culture of life encompasses much more than just protesting murder [abortion]. It must fundamentally begin with our hearts."[59] Addressing the disproportionate number of minority children in the foster care system, he argues that deep-seated racial prejudice that is "a part of our culture" inhibits white evangelicals from participating in foster care and adoption.[60] In order to counteract this racist culture, he explains: "Confronting the racist in each one of us starts with a new understanding of the gospel that begins to transform our often-hard hearts . . . As we consider orphan care, this new understanding changes the way we see children and go about helping them."[61] For Carr, the racism that discourages white evangelicals from fostering or adopting minority children is fundamentally a heart issue, and necessary transformation only takes place when Christians understand the gospel anew. Elsewhere, he stresses the importance of changing the culture of racism into a culture of diversity in order to stimulate adoption and orphan care:

> Acts 1:8 offers a tangible model for cultural influence and change—"you will be My witnesses in Jerusalem, Judea and Samaria, and to the ends of the earth." We must ask ourselves how we can confront racism in our "Jerusalem" and begin to live in such a way that we become culture-changers. . . . Supporting and encouraging families to adopt children from other races here in the U.S. is one huge step in welcoming orphans of every tribe, language, people, and nation into your local church body. . . . If we are going to encourage adoption and orphan care without racial boundaries, we have to begin thinking about the cultures we are creating and perpetuating in our churches, our workplaces, and our homes. Racial reconciliation involves far more than just putting people of different skin colors in the same room. It includes cultivating and celebrating a church and family culture of diversity.[62]

For movement leaders, a culture of orphan care and adoption (i.e., an ethos that recognizes the truth about God, the gospel, and our responsibility to orphans) that pervades the entire congregation necessarily *precedes* Christian activities and ministries organized to serve vulnerable children. This view of mobilization is based on pietistic idealism—the belief of evangelicals that right ideas necessarily precede right actions, and the most important ideas are those about God and one's proper relationship with him. Right activity will necessarily and inevitably flow out from this. But how does one foster a culture of adoption or orphan care in one's congregation?

One Heart at a Time: How to Develop a Culture of Adoption/Orphan Care

When articulating how a culture of adoption/orphan care is cultivated within congregations, movement leaders recurrently articulate both a bottom-up (grassroots) and a top-down (leadership) strategy. At the grassroots level, movement leaders recommend something of a "personal influence strategy" in which individuals take action to convince other individuals about the centrality of adoption to the gospel and God's general call to orphan care. At the level of leadership, movement leaders instruct readers to emphasize the importance of affecting the broader congregation through consistently preaching about the connection between adoption/orphan care and the gospel itself and the broader Christian responsibility to engage the world with the gospel message.

Focusing on grassroots influence, Jason Kovacs, explains how cultures can be transformed by individuals acting in faithful obedience to God's call. "If you cannot move the culture of your church from the top down, be encouraged that many churches have had their cultures transformed by one couple or one person stepping out in radical, patient, and persistent faith. Often the example of one ordinary family or individual doing something that the world thinks is extraordinary is enough to tip the scale for a hundred others who are just waiting for something to happen."[63] Also emphasizing the importance of individuals acting in obedience, Johnny Carr argues, "We will change our culture of abortion only as we develop a culture of life—as each one of us develops a sacrificial lifestyle that honors every human life."[64]

Russell Moore emphasizes both the strategy of personal influence and gospel preaching in cultivating a culture of adoption: "In many ways, this [culture of adoption] is carried through more in thousands of conversations in hallways, fellowship dinners around a common table, and gospel preaching than in new initiatives and curricula and plans."[65] And elsewhere, Moore explains, "The primary means of furthering adoption as mission, though, may seemingly have little to do with adoption at all. The most important aspect of creating an adoption culture is preaching the gospel."[66] This statement also clearly reveals Moore's assumption that, when Christians fully understand the gospel (right idea), this will result in adoptions happening within the church (right action).

Merida and Morton also stress the dual importance of personal influence and gospel preaching in cultivating an orphan care culture within congregations, which they again contrast with promoting "programs." They write: "You don't have to have massive programs for developing an orphan care culture; you simply need to teach the Bible and influence individual believers to answer their personal, direct, and challenging questions. And then keep on teaching and emphasizing orphan care throughout the church."[67] Expounding on the idea of personal influence, the authors later explain, "Think about this. The most powerful means of advertising today is still word of mouth. You can change a church by structure partially. And you can also change it by the power of influencers embodying and sharing the dream as well."[68] Focusing explicitly on the importance of preaching to an orphan care culture, Merida and Morton teach that "the congregation should not only hear about adoption and orphan care when a [Bible] passage is solely devoted to it. To cast a biblical vision that sinks into the minds of the people, it needs to be mentioned regularly. Something about adoption and orphan care should appear in sermons regularly, if the church is going to create a culture of orphan care. Every teacher needs to refer regularly to the subject by means of application."[69]

In my interview with Tony Merida, he elaborated on how he sees a culture of orphan care being accomplished practically within a congregation, focusing on teaching, interpersonal conversations, and repeated references to orphan care and adoption every week:

At a high level, [fostering a culture of orphan care] has to do with what's said from the platform, what's promoted on the website, kind of the air war. And then there has to be a ground war, as well, where everything from tables in the lobby to your pictures and your building, to bullet points in your bulletin for ways to care for the orphan. You just can't talk about it once a year, you know, on Orphan Sunday or whatever. I don't think that's the way to do it. I prefer to talk about it as the drip method, you know, where every week there's just a little drip about orphan care in teaching, in conversations throughout the week that people are having. We just showed the movie STUCK on Friday night to our church and had a panel discussion,[70] and we've been plugging that for a while. In terms of teaching, any time there's a topic like love or hospitality or mercy, just to drop in a little application. Caring for orphans is one of the ways to do this, and boom, you just keep on moving along. But there's just a steady stream of it that has to be talked about to create that type of culture.

Pastor Jeremy Haskins, adoptive father and contributing author to Russell Moore's edited volume *A Guide to Adoption and Orphan Care*, echoes the importance of gospel preaching to cultivating an adoption culture: "As the preaching of the gospel cultivates a culture of adoption, we will change the way we view seating charts in church."[71] He repeatedly elaborates on this idea, viewing the preaching of the gospel as the only way to engender the kind of heart-transformation necessary to mobilize the church to serve orphans through adoption:

Our desire is to cultivate a culture driven by the truth of our adoption in Christ. A culture of adoption when cultivated by the constant and consistent preaching of the gospel not only leads to church unity but to a greater fervency to rescue children from around the world who need adopting. . . . An adoption culture begins with the constant reminder that we are all ex-orphans. What changed everything for us? Adoption! . . . The danger of creating an adoption ministry apart from this truth is that it only leads to another line in your church's budget. It will become a ministry relegated only to adoptive families and social workers in your church—people personally affected by the orphan crisis on a daily basis. In an adoption culture, everyone has been transformed by the act of adoption and this naturally leads to a desire to rid the world of orphans, both physically and spiritually.[72]

Here Haskins points to the danger of orphan activism without properly understanding one's adoption in the gospel, that orphan ministry just becomes an activity for those who have a common idiosyncratic interest in vulnerable children, rather than everyone being gripped by God's concern for the spiritual and physical state of orphaned children. Haskins goes on to explain:

> Apart from the gospel, the call for every church member to care for orphans makes no sense. By cultivating an adoption culture, through connecting the dots for people, they realize that no matter who, they all have a responsibility to care for orphans physically and spiritually in some way. In an adoption culture, this reality is constantly pressed upon us.[73]

> An adoption culture is much bigger than one segmented group of people who are simply more passionate than everyone else in the church about helping kids in need. It's the whole church realizing we all are needy kids. We all need a loving Father to rescue us and give us a family. We need his care and discipline that teaches us how to love one another and serve those apart from our family. This need can only be met by the power of the Spirit, through the kind of consistent preaching of the gospel that constantly presses its implications upon the church, the adopted family of God.[74]

Thus, in the orphan care mobilization literature, leaders instruct Christians to develop a culture of adoption/orphan care in their congregation through two means: (1) by having conversations with other Christians to draw their attention to the gospel significance of orphan care and God's love for vulnerable children, and (2) the consistent preaching of the gospel that relates Christians' spiritual adoption to the practical needs of vulnerable children to be adopted, fostered, or served at some capacity. Through both of these means, movement leaders believe, the hearts and minds of individuals are influenced, a culture (meaning something like an ethos or worldview) of adoption or orphan care that understands God's heart for orphans is cultivated, and Christians in the church are properly motivated and mobilized to minister to the needs of orphans through adoption, fostering, or global orphan care.

Limiting Mobilization Repertoires: Pietistic Idealism vs. Pragmatism

Orphan care movement leaders express nearly identical ideological presuppositions about social engagement from which they prescribe common strategies or repertories for mobilizing Christians to address the problem of vulnerable children. Movement leaders consistently teach that Christians should redirect their efforts away from establishing "ministries" or "programs" to serve orphans and must not rely on "government" to meet the needs of vulnerable children. Rather, individual Christians, recognizing their own adoption in Christ and God's mandate to serve orphans, are charged with the responsibility of helping to cultivate a culture of adoption or orphan care in their congregation. That is, through interpersonal conversations and the preaching of the gospel, they are to cultivate a pervasive ethos among believers that recognizes the theological connections between God's adoption of his spiritual children, the Great Commission, and each Christian's responsibility to address the needs of vulnerable children primarily through adoption, but also by including foster parenting and other orphan care activities.

This culture-building strategy reflects the underlying evangelical cultural schemas of pietistic idealism and individualism. Social engagement must be preceded and compelled by right motives, and thus any orphan care activities that are motivated by the cause of orphans for its own sake or any other reason are potentially idolatrous and ultimately wrong. It is "passionless compassion," to use Daniel Bennett's phrase. So, too, social engagement must be carried out by individuals with right motives. Otherwise, believers are guilty of abdicating their individual call to action. Moreover, pietistic idealism demands that individual hearts ultimately need to be transformed, as opposed to social structures (i.e., patterned social arrangements that shape life outcomes such as the educational system or criminal justice system). Any activism, then, that focuses on changing social structures but stops short of individual heart transformation is insufficient and wrongheaded. Thus, movement leaders envision a "culture of orphan care," where individual Christians are motivated by the right ideas about God and his love for children (established through interpersonal conversations and the preaching of the gospel and the Bible), and then adoption, fostering, and other ministry to vulnerable children will inevitably follow.

To be sure, evangelical commitments to pietistic idealism and individualism provide evangelical efforts at social engagement with a number of important strengths. D. Michael Lindsay argues that evangelicalism's lack of a central leadership structure, owing to its democratized, individualist character, encourages creative and enthusiastic entrepreneurial activity.[75] And Christian Smith points out that, in religious activism, such enthusiasm and activity benefits from ready-made structures of leadership and communication within congregations. Thus, it is unsurprising to see evangelical initiatives like the Promise Keepers, or the orphan care movement, or recent efforts at confronting human trafficking spring up quickly in a frenzy of promotional activity. Moreover, Smith also argues that the evangelical commitment to theological distinctiveness provides evangelical efforts at social engagement with a healthy tension that engenders solidarity among believers while defining the group against who/what they are not.[76] This can be seen in statements by movement leaders who contrast their efforts with liberal Christians, whom they perceive to have mistaken the means for the ends and to have lost sight of the ultimate goal in orphan care, namely, God's glory.[77]

Despite these beneficial contributions, however, Christian Smith argues that the individualist commitment of evangelicalism, though invigorating to evangelical faith, limits its social impact.[78] Similarly, James Davison Hunter theorizes that the approach of evangelical Christians, rooted in pietistic idealism and individualism, is a failing strategy for promoting lasting societal change: "Every strategy and tactic for changing the world that is based on this [evangelical] working theory of culture and cultural change will fail—not most of the strategies, but all."[79]

But how specifically do these evangelical cultural schemas limit the practical effectiveness of their social engagement? At its core, the evangelical schema of pietistic idealism and its associated approach to social engagement is at odds with a *pragmatic* approach to social engagement. A pragmatic approach to addressing the problem of vulnerable children would be to start with a practical goal—for example, increasing the number of children from the foster care system who would be placed in stable homes over the next two years—and then think strategically about *all* available means by which to accomplish that goal. Approaches to mobilizing participation would be evaluated with the practical goal in mind. Conversely, a pragmatic approach to addressing a social problem would not, as a matter of principle, be ideologically bound into a certain method of addressing the problem because the primary concern would be to accomplish the goal. Thus different methods could be tested under the rationale of "whatever works." Certainly, these practical options for increasing foster placements in stable homes would be filtered through a broad set of ethical considerations, ideally ones that a maximal number of participants could agree upon. Yet a pragmatic approach would not be concerned with the *motives* (or beliefs or values) of participants, primarily. Rather, it would be more important whether the participants shared the same practical goal and were willing to do whatever it took (within established ethical limits) to accomplish that goal.

Because of their commitment to pietistic idealism, evangelicals tend to be opposed to a pragmatic approach to social engagement, at least formally. The orphan care movement leaders, in their mobilization writings and teachings, either imply or, in some cases, state directly that adoption and orphan care activity that pleases God *must*, as an issue of moral correctness, emerge out of a sincere conviction about God's character and the Christian gospel itself. To engage in adoption or orphan care activism because it is important in and of itself is morally suspect because a Christian's first priority is to have her or his will fully submitted to God's and the Bible. God himself is the primary obligation, and social engagement for an evangelical should flow from that obligation. Thus evangelicals are theologically obliged to frame adoption and orphan care activities, as well as all other forms of social engagement, in terms of obedience and worship, not practical objectives.

Moreover, because evangelicals reject pragmatism as an approach to addressing social issues, they are unable to quickly adjust their tactics based on a rational calculation of "whatever works." Rather, they must engage social problems by using a method that they can arguably say is "biblical"—that is, there is some sort of precedent or model that God has laid out in the Bible. Or at least the method cannot be blatantly *un*biblical. Mobilizing persons to change unjust social structures is often not understood as a biblical approach to social change because evangelicals view salvation and moral rightness as rooted in individual hearts, not in patterns of behavior or policies that can be implemented without proper intentions. Rather, mobilization through personal influence and the preaching of the gospel represents *the* institutionalized method through which evangelical movement leaders *must* seek to mobilize Christians, *regardless of whether it is practically effective*. And unfortunately, as we will see in chapter 4, interpersonal conversations and inspiring sermons are *not* effective techniques for motivating average American Christians to drastically change their lives. Even with regard to the actual strategies of addressing the problem of orphans, placement into a family, and adoption more specifically, provides a central biblical and soteriological metaphor that evangelicals can use to link the gospel with orphan care. Thus, adoption or other family-based strategies are strongly emphasized as the primary strategies for serving vulnerable children.

Even if their methods of mobilization do not practically work (and we have seen that they have not, thus far), evangelicals are bound to them ideologically. Indeed, they must be faithful to their approach even when confronted with a lack of practical results because to deviate from the "biblical" strategy would be to compromise with pragmatic, secular thinking and ultimately miss the point. The point is *not* orphans or cause for its own sake; the point is obedience. And evangelical pietistic idealism demands that mobilization happen in ways that allow evangelicals to personally influence the hearts and minds of others, either through one-on-one interactions in conversation or through preaching and teaching from up front in sermons, at conferences, or through other media. Correspondingly, the idea of creating and promoting structures or programs that may remedy the problem of vulnerable children not only is unattractive to evangelicals but is rejected outright because such an option absolves Christians from being obedient to God and taking personal responsibility for social change. These ideological commitments ultimately limit the mobilization repertoires and solutions that evangelicals will have for addressing any social problem, not just that of vulnerable children—because all mobilization will involve some variation of a personal influence strategy in which ideals must precede action and solutions will involve transforming "culture" in the hearts and minds of individuals, one person at a time.

Last, the evangelical schema of pietistic idealism predictably will limit the strategic effectiveness of mobilization efforts by constraining not only *what* action "counts" as morally legitimate social engagement (action done with God's glory as its ultimate end) but also *who* is able to engage in that activity for it to count. That is, dominant evangelical schemas about what sort of people can please God with their actions (Christians with God-honoring motives) and what sorts of situations are God-prescribed means to address social problems like vulnerable children (heterosexual, married couples) will circumscribe the options evangelicals can promote to address the orphan crisis. In the following chapter, I draw on in-depth interviews with movement elites to explore how they establish moral boundaries around the issue of orphans and disqualify certain groups of people from being able to address the problem in a way that God desires, again placing a practical limitation on their strategic effectiveness.

3

Orphans Need Families! Just Not *Those* Families

Herbie Newell is executive director of Lifeline Children's Services, one of the largest Christian adoption and foster care ministries in the country. A surprisingly young man (thirty-three years old at the time of our interview) to be at the helm of such a large international organization, Herbie graciously agreed to speak with me by video call while he and his family were on sabbatical visiting orphanages in China. When I asked Herbie about the broader goals of Lifeline as an organization, he spoke about what he hoped would be Lifeline's core contribution to the orphan care movement:

> I would hope that our contribution would be to keep the eyes of the Christian adoption movement on the gospel and the glory of God, and that would probably be where we would be most honored, if someone were to give a testimony to say that that was our contribution. As an organization, we're not looking to say we've placed more children than anyone else. We're not looking to say we're bigger than anyone else. We're not looking to try to say we're in that top five. We're really seeking the heart—as we say to our staff—we're not seeking the face of the fatherless, and I think a lot of times as believers, as followers of Christ you can even get into that trap of we're seeking the face of the fatherless, we're motivated by the child that's sick, or motivated by the child that needs to rescued, in a sense—and we tell our staff all the time, we're not motivated by the face of the fatherless, we're motivated by the face of the father to the fatherless. We're motivated by the gospel and by the glory of God, and we want to see ourselves not as rescuers, but we're rescued. We've been rescued by God through his grace, and that's why we do what do. So, I mean, it would be the greatest honor if someone were to say that our role had been to keep the main thing the main thing in the focus on the gospel and the glory of God, and that's what we preach to our staff.

Herbie's explanation embodies the recurring theme among movement leaders that "the gospel and the glory of God" are the ultimate goal of orphan care, that one's motivation should not be the child herself but, rather, one's own rescue in the gospel. For evangelicals in the orphan care movement, focusing on the gospel and glory of God keeps "the main thing the main thing." Just as important for movement leaders and activists, however, is avoiding what Herbie describes as the alternative, namely, focusing on the "face of the fatherless," which he views as a trap that Christians can fall into. Reflecting this sentiment, Daniel Bennett, pastor and author of *A Passion for the Fatherless*, explained in his interview that

> [the orphan care movement's] goal isn't to get people excited about the orphan, ultimately. Our goal is to get people excited about God. We believe that, as a person gets excited about God, begins to want the things that God desires them to do, orphan care ministry's going to be the result. . . . I think that's the role of the church and the orphan care movement is not necessarily to become an adoption agency or to, you know, even hold a bunch of conferences. . . . But I think the local church, our strength is really presenting a biblical vision of life and how to glorify God and compassion flows as a result of that.

For evangelicals, actions of any kind (including actions that serve others) are morally right to the extent that they spring forth from right ideas or beliefs and wrong when they spring from wrong ideas. Thus evangelical social action must not be motivated by *a* cause, but by THE cause. This core commitment orients evangelical social engagement, including the orphan care movement. This is why the Christian Alliance for Orphans frames its mobilization initiatives like Orphan Sunday as "Ultimately [seeking] to make God's true character and the Gospel itself visible" rather than to promote "adoption, foster care, and global orphan ministry" for their own sake.[1] For evangelicals, the former necessarily precedes the latter. As Dan Cruver, in his book *Reclaiming Adoption*, writes:

> Our confusion comes when we look at human adoption and end up focusing on the fact that a child needs parents. God focuses on the fact that

a lost person needs saving. . . . The *ultimate* purpose of human adoption by Christians, therefore, is not to give orphans parents, as important as that is. It is to place them in a Christian home that they might be positioned to receive the gospel, so that within that family, the world might witness a representation of God taking in and genuinely loving the helpless, the hopeless, and the despised.[2]

In his book, *Rumors of Another World*, best-selling evangelical author Philip Yancey sites an old Puritan proverb: "God loveth adverbs." In a chapter by the same name, Yancey explains that this little statement reflects the Puritan belief that "God cares more about the spirit in which we live than the concrete results."[3] That is to say, God cares less about *what* you do than *why* and *how* you do it. As American evangelicals are ideological and theological descendants of the Puritans,[4] this statement also embodies their commitment to pietistic idealism. To repeat John Piper's statement, "Bad motives ruin good acts. . . . Therefore we must not be content that our people are doing good things. We must labor to see that they do good things from God-exalting motives."[5] As outlined in the last chapter, the schema of pietistic idealism holds that social engagement must, as an issue of moral correctness, be subordinated to the right beliefs and values. Ostensibly altruistic actions that are not done for the right reasons (e.g., God's glory, embodying the gospel, furthering the Great Commission) become the wrong actions—pharisaical by definition. In other words, for American evangelicals, social engagement is principally about *obedience*, about one's relationship to God. Therefore to make social engagement about something else besides God (e.g., human rights, the environment, orphans) is the very definition of idolatry. Extending this idea, right actions that are not done by the *right people* with the right beliefs, are also wrong, or at least less preferable to the right people doing the right actions for the right reasons.[6]

Numerous studies have shown how social groups erect cultural and moral boundaries around group membership, social and physical spaces, and identities.[7] Much less is written about how actors within social movements (a type of social group) erect moral boundaries around particular causes and movement-related activities. In this chapter, I draw on interviews with orphan care movement elites to show how evangelical leaders and activists erect moral boundaries around their activities and goals that ultimately limit their own ability to mobilize action toward a particular cause. These boundaries demarcate what actions "count" as an appropriate solution to the problem of vulnerable children and when the very same actions, done by people with the wrong beliefs, values, or life situation, do not "count." Although the orphan care movement promotes a variety of orphan care activities, I will focus primarily on the most visible and valued orphan care activity in adoption. I show how some moral boundaries have become institutionalized in organizational practices, while other boundaries were not expressed as official practice but only emerged in action. Indeed, many of the evangelical leaders I spoke with had never articulated these expectations before I asked about them. Even in these instances, however, there was remarkable consistency across their answers. My findings here demonstrate a pattern of evangelical thought that limits the target of mobilization efforts to a small group while excluding a large number of persons from being able to serve orphans in a way that God would approve of and who might otherwise be considered strategic partners in the cause of orphan care.

I argue that the patterns I observe in the orphan care movement reflect broader trends that take place when evangelicals seek to rally action around a particular social issue. Put simply, evangelicals engaged in social action will self-limit the scope—and in some ways the efficacy—of their efforts because their adherence to pietistic idealism hinders their willingness and ability to partner with non-evangelicals or actors who fall outside of the ideal standard.

Cultural Boundary Work

A fundamental characteristic of social groups is that they *must*, in order to stay a coherent group, establish and defend boundaries around who may be in the group and who is excluded. All groups do this, including families, tribes, ethnic groups, sports teams, fraternities and sororities, civic organizations, nations, religious groups (including broader religious traditions and local faith communities), and even social movement groups. These boundaries are "cultural" to the extent that they are based on symbolic markers that signify whatever core qualities are collectively deemed necessary for group membership. In some cases, these symbolic markers can even take on a quality of being morally obligatory—these

are moral boundaries. While the practice of boundary work is ubiqui-
tous across all social groups, groups vary considerably regarding (1) the
specificity with which the boundaries are codified, (2) the nature and
content of the boundaries, (3) the practices through which boundaries
are policed, and (4) the malleability of those boundaries.

For all groups, there are certain unspoken—but often still quite
clear and rigid—expectations as to what constitutes group membership. These unspoken requisites for membership often remain unspoken because they are simply taken for granted.[8] As groups grow and
evolve, however, the need to establish clear and codified standards for
membership becomes more necessary. A small student-led community-
service group may have little need for establishing formal expectations
for group membership. But as that group grows in numbers, establishes
a leadership hierarchy, develops a budget, makes decisions about what
projects it will take on, and interacts with other student groups, it is
more likely to codify finely detailed boundaries around membership for
the sake of efficiency and organization. Thus the specificity with which
groups establish their standards for membership and participation in
the group is a good indicator of the organizational development of that
group. Nascent or emerging groups leave a good deal unspoken, while
more developed groups maintain detailed expectations.[9]

There is also considerable variation among groups regarding what
attributes qualify a person for group membership or, conversely, disqualify him. For membership in a family, the requirements usually include a biological connection and/or legal recognition. For membership
on a competitive sports team, however, the primary requirement is one's
skill at that particular sport. While ideological allegiance and solidarity
with one's family or sports team are most often desirable, they are not
prerequisites for belonging to a family or team. Family members are
often at odds with others in the family, and professional sports team
members are often quite vocal about their dissatisfaction with the team
in general. To some degree, this may be the case among particular religious groups as well. Someone may call herself an Episcopalian or Jew
and hold few if any beliefs in common with others who subscribe to all
the central tenets of those faith traditions. In these cases, membership
may stem from one being born into such a religious tradition. And that
membership may be maintained simply by a formal recognition from

some religious body and a very nominal identification on the part of the individual. Yet membership in many conservative religious groups, as well as volunteer organizations and social movement organizations, often requires allegiance to group ideologies. This ideological allegiance is demonstrated symbolically through whatever qualifies as faithful practice. Faithful practice may include positive actions (such as signing a doctrinal statement, attending religious services, protesting certain government policies, adopting orphans, or using certain code words like "missional," "biblical," or "gospel-centered") or negative actions (such as abstaining from alcohol, smoking, caffeine, or sexual immorality or shunning relationships with those outside the group). These expectations for faithful practice are often left unspoken.

Faithful practice that demonstrates ideological allegiance to the group represents a marker of moral boundaries; that is, boundaries that differentiate "right" action from "wrong" action and thus reveal one's *true* membership in the group.[10] Sociologist Michelle Lamont and her colleagues have described how moral boundaries, evidenced in certain appropriate patterns of behavior, signify membership within particular social classes within French and American society.[11] Moral boundaries are policed by group members, and violations of those boundaries are punished with group sanctions, including formal rebuke, shunning, expulsion from the group, and even death.[12] These practices of policing boundaries differ across particular groups and are informed by the broader societal culture and the group's own collective history.[13]

Last, group boundaries vary in the degree to which they are relatively rigid or malleable. These differences often depend on the extent to which such boundaries protect the core identity of the group and which boundaries protect more peripheral, situational interests. Certain boundaries, for example, may be relaxed given changes in the broader social context of the group. For example, prior to the 1970s, my own alma mater, Dallas Theological Seminary (DTS) formally excluded Christians of color from admission. Thus, while a central boundary marker for DTS has always been ideological allegiance (students and faculty must affirm a statement of faith), from DTS's founding until the 1970s, another important boundary marker was the broader social meaning attributed to race. White Christians were in the group; non-white Christians were left out of the group (no matter what they believed). However, as the expectations of the broader society changed following the Civil Rights Movement, DTS removed the racial boundary for admission and admitted students of color. Other boundaries, however, such as the expectation that admitted students subscribe to a particular set of religious doctrines, have not been relaxed. Religious institutions like DTS will likely be far more reluctant to relax their doctrinal boundary markers because they represent part of the group's core identity.

Social Movements, Boundary Work, and the Orphan Care Movement

Despite the large amount of research on boundary work in everyday life, scholars have paid less attention to cultural and moral boundaries within social movements or their constituent social movement organizations (SMOs).[14] Existing research has focused primarily on the role of boundaries in forging and maintaining what scholars call "collective identities"[15] or identities that unite participants around some quality they share as a group. For SMOs, or even entire movements, defining the criteria for group membership and partaking in the collective identity has to do with identifying the "good guys" (us) and the "bad guys" (them) for the purposes of solidarity and mobilization. By erecting and maintaining the boundaries of "who we are" and "who is against us," SMOs are able to engender solidarity around who they are as a group and motivate action by associating certain activities with actors' collective identities.[16] For example, pro-choice SMO leaders and activists might seek to mobilize women who would otherwise never have an abortion by appealing to and shoring up their sense of identification with all women and painting the pro-choice movement as an issue for all women to be concerned about.[17]

As with other SMO leaders, orphan care movement leaders certainly do appeal to collective identity as a means of mobilizing evangelicals to engage in particular activities. As Jason Kovacs put it in his interview: "You can't be a Christian and not be passionate about the things [Jesus is] passionate about. . . . I think Charles Spurgeon said it this way, he's like, you're either a missionary, or you're an imposter. So I think you can say you're either passionate about caring for the orphan as a Christian or you're an imposter. You can't be a Christian and not care about the orphan for very long."

Similarly, Kay Warren (wife of evangelical megachurch pastor and key leader in the orphan care movement, Rick Warren) challenged an audience of thousands at their church in Saddleback, California, saying, "If we are doing little to nothing, how dare we, how dare we claim to be followers of Jesus Christ. Followers of Jesus Christ care about widows and orphans and they understand that it is a litmus test. It is not an option." Simply put: "*We* must look after orphans because *we* are Christian and that is what *we* do." Such is the boundary work of collective identity construction: Faithful practice (orphan care) is promoted as the symbolic criteria validating one's membership in the collective identity of being "Christian." In this regard, then, boundary work can be seen as advancing the task of mobilization. Establishing and promoting a particular criterion for membership in Christianity (orphan care activities) puts pressure on those who wish to be considered Christians to get involved.

And yet boundary work also functions in a different sense for evangelicals. Because evangelical social engagement is to be done out of obedience to divine calling (pietistic idealism), these boundaries are infused with *moral* significance. Kay Warren went on to say, "[Serving orphans] has nothing to do with personality, it has nothing to do with spiritual gifts, it has nothing to do with economic status, it has nothing to do with your season of life. It has to do with accepting the responsibility that God will one day hold us accountable." In other words, fulfilling one's Christian identity as one who takes care of orphans is a command to which Christians must be obedient, a universal calling for the faithful regardless of one's station in life. Moreover, for leaders in the orphan care movement, orphan care takes on a transcendent, moral significance because of the transcendent reality it represents. Warren explains further,

> What our Heavenly Father does for us spiritually, He expects us to do physically. You and I were spiritual orphans. We're not just cleared of the guilt of our sin. We belong in God's family. He has taken us and made us part of Himself. . . . When you understand the theology of it, you will not be able to push it away; you will not be able to put it on the backburner. You need to understand that adoption represents the heart of what Jesus Christ has done for us.[18]

For the Christian, as Kay Warren explains, orphan care and adoption reflect what God has done for his people in the gospel and thus is a special responsibility to which God will hold his people accountable. To be sure, these sorts of moral boundaries around action do define who *is* and *is not* a group member. The collective identity *does* serve as a tool to challenge evangelicals to action as leaders seek to "extend" collective action frames to "resonate" with evangelical audiences.[19]

But the sorts of moral boundaries evangelicals put around social engagement (or any type of action) are not done for the purposes of advancing a cause in and of itself, but they are done to advance THE cause. All activities are to be done with God's glory as their end. And thus adoption and orphan care, for evangelicals, are principally about obedience to a divine calling implied in the Christian identity. Illustrating this idea, Jason Weber, director of foster care initiatives for CAFO and co-author with Paul Pennington of *Launching an Orphans Ministry in Your Church*, summarized the proper Christian motivations to adopt children: "I think ultimately we want our motivation to be with anything, not just, this isn't just an adoption issue. This is, as an evangelical Christian I want my motivation ultimately to be obedience to Christ and a desire to honor and glorify God. And that sounds churchy and all that. I understand that. But there's real truth to that. That's real. That's not made up. That's not fake." For evangelical Christians, in Jason's words, motivation for adoption as for anything else in life should be "obedience to Christ and a desire to honor and glorify God."

Jon Bergeron is a licensed family counselor, director of family care with Hope for Orphans, and a listed speaker on CAFO's website. Jon's response to the motivation question was similar to Jason Weber's:

> Well, [motivation is] certainly something that comes directly from my faith. Because I don't believe there's any other system of knowing that gives us that answer about what should I do and why should I do it. And so what my faith tells me is that the ultimate purpose of man is to bring glory to God, to speak the truth about who God is and to show him to the world. And so, if anything in our lives, including foster care and adoption, doesn't fit within that framework then—that in a primary way—then we are off track.

Here Jon affirms Jason Weber's statement that all of life for the Christian is to glorify God. But he goes a step beyond Jason Weber to say that, if anything in a Christian's life, *including adoption or foster care*, is not done with the ultimate purpose of bringing glory to God and showing him to the world, that activity has fallen short of God's desired goal.

An issue then arises, however, regarding how to promote *only* those activities and situations that qualify or "count" as the sort of orphan care activity that God approves of. Orphan care movement leaders in my study were clear that the goal was not necessarily to get as many children as possible into *any* stable home. Rather, the moral and transcendent significance of adoption and orphan care—as acts of obedience reflecting one's Christian identity—requires movement leaders and organizations to consider what situations are acceptable and then demarcate boundaries around them. Clearly illustrating this point, up to mid-2015 the CAFO website listed a set of standards for all "Adoption and Child Placement" organizations that join the alliance as members. Organizations had to agree to several stipulations, including:

2. Affirm commitment to evangelism and discipleship. Each program, outreach and resource—while meeting physical, emotional and spiritual needs in different ways—will point ultimately to the unfailing love of God in ways that make the Gospel plain and grow believers as disciples of Jesus Christ. . . .

10. Place children only in Christian families (based on the Biblical model of family and qualified singles) who sign a statement of faith consistent with the Alliance's Statement of Faith (unless country/government restrictions do not allow for this distinction). Example: US Foster Care where federal funds are included and state does not allow this requirement.

In these points, CAFO member organizations devoted to adoption and child placement are expected to hold evangelism and Christian growth as the end goal of placement, and because this is the goal, member organizations are only to place children in "Christian families (based on the Biblical model of family and qualified singles)." The parenthetical qualification is critical here. Many families might affirm a Christian identity or belief, especially if it means getting access to an adoptable child they desperately want. But the statement specifies that "Christian families" are to be understood according to the "Biblical model of family" (*read*: a heterosexual and married couple) and "qualified" singles. These are clear boundaries that the CAFO leadership establishes and maintains around the sort of adoption and orphan care activities that qualify as being acceptable before God, given that evangelism and discipleship are the end goal of such activities.

Evangelical adoption and child placement agencies like Lifeline Children's Services express similar standards that both explicitly state the religious requirement for families to be allowed to adopt while implicitly reflecting the symbolic criteria that serves as evidence for the faith commitment. As of mid-2016, the qualifications for domestic adoption with Lifeline state: "The applicants must give evidence of Christian commitment. This means that the applicants must each give evidence of having made a personal decision to accept Jesus Christ as his/her personal Savior and to accept Jesus Christ as the Lord of his/her life. The applicants must have a firm commitment to live these beliefs and teach them to their child. Both husband and wife must belong to the same church. Applicants should be pro-life."[20] The explanation here spells out what Christian commitment entails in a theological sense, but it also emphasizes the standard for marriage as being between a "husband and wife." This is also expressed elsewhere in the listed qualifications where it states, "A *husband and wife* should be married at least three years prior to filing an application" (emphasis added). Also interesting in the above statement is that there is a clear expectation regarding the religious commitments of adoptive families that they be pro-life. Moreover, these are not empty symbolic stipulations. Rather, in the online application for domestic adoption, Lifeline asks each candidate, mother and father, specific open-ended questions related to each of the requirements.

Lifeline's expectations, and those articulated above by CAFO, make clear that there are cultural and moral boundaries set around what "counts" as an acceptable (or at least ideal) adoptive family before God. The symbolic markers include affirmation of particular theological beliefs, but also being in a heterosexual marriage, and, in Lifeline's case, a commitment to being pro-life. These moral boundaries around the activities of adoption and orphan care are institutionalized in other organizational standards as well. For example, the ABBA Fund is an organization that provides grants and interest-free loans to Christian adoptive parents. Speaking to the proper motivation to adopt, the ABBA Fund loan application specifies, "Our heart is to help orphans be placed into loving, nurturing Christian family environments where the child will not only experience the love of Jesus Christ but be introduced to the person of Jesus Christ—and prayerfully one day trust in Jesus so that he or she will be adopted into ABBA Father's family through salvation. As we review your application, we are looking for evidence of that same heart. If this is not your heart, we would encourage you to explore other assistance options."[21]

The ABBA Fund explicitly stipulates not only that parents be Christians but also that they should be adopting with a "heart" or motivation to see their adopted children become Christians as well. The ABBA fund goes so far as to say that if this is not the prospective parents' motivation, they would like for those parents to explore other assistance options. In other words, they will not be receiving funding support for their adoption.

But are the only requirements spiritual and motivational? On their webpage, the ABBA Fund responds to a question about whether they will provide adoption loans to singles. They explain, "ABBA Fund's priority is to steward its limited resources toward God's biblical model for a family, which includes both a father and mother. Accordingly, The ABBA Fund makes its adoption assistance resources in the general loan fund available only to married Christian couples."[22] In this instance, the boundary issue is not religious identity or motivation at all but conformity to God's standard for raising children. God has established a "biblical" model for families, and that means only Christian heterosexual couples. It is these families that the ABBA Fund wishes to support, and thus Christian singles—regardless of *why* they want to adopt—are disqualified.

Evangelical Moral Boundary Work: What Counts as Acceptable Adoption Activism?

In my interviews, movement leaders elaborated on the cultural and moral boundaries described above. For each interview, I asked a series of questions regarding the possibility of different groups who might fall outside the "biblical model of family" adopting orphaned children or even partnering with or facilitating adoption for such families. I started this series of questions by echoing back the respondents' own words about the seriousness and scope of the orphan crisis and the understanding that children need loving homes, stability, and support. Starting from the understanding that these leaders viewed the "ideal" adoptive family as two married, Christian, heterosexual parents, I proceeded to ask the leaders about how they would feel about unbelieving parents adopting, single parents adopting, and same-sex parents adopting. I varied the order with which I mentioned these alternative adoption situations in order to ensure that the patterned responses I got were not due to the order of the questions. Leaders' responses were reflective of the ways in which movement spokespersons, thought leaders, executives, and activists establish and maintain the evangelical cultural and moral boundaries around adoption and orphan care activism.

Tension Involving Adoption by Unbelieving Families

Movement leaders were of two minds about the possibility of placing children with unbelieving, secular families. While acknowledging that unbelieving parents were not necessarily unqualified or harmful to the child, these leaders were committed to the idea that the child's eternal future was at stake and must be kept the central focus of discussions around adoption. Mike Douris is president of Orphan Outreach and chairman of the board of directors of CAFO. When I asked him about the prospect of Christian agencies partnering with and placing children with unbelieving families, he explained:

> I think within the Christian movement, as far as unbelievers, part of the Alliance has been to engage the church, and that a significant part of our ministry is that we want to see kids be exposed to the gospel, and we do this in the name of Christ, and so we can't do that if you're not a believer. And that doesn't mean that we feel like families that are not believers can't adopt and provide a good family for kids, they can. But it's not part of the mission of churches and Christian NGOs, necessarily, to place with unbelievers.

Like virtually all evangelical leaders I interviewed, Mike does not wish to convey that non-Christians cannot provide stable families or adopt children. But he affirms that the commitment of the movement is primarily to see children placed in families where they will be exposed to the gospel, ultimately glorifying God with their conversion and worship, and this removes unbelieving families from consideration as possible targets of recruitment or mobilization efforts.

Likewise, in my conversation with Herbie Newell, I asked him about Lifeline's commitment to placing children with Christian families exclusively. Specifically, I asked him to elaborate on why a Christian family would be preferable to an otherwise moral, secular family. He explained:

HN: I don't know where your worldview is or where you stand, if you're a follower of Christ, but as a follower of Christ, I would believe that there are no moral people. I'm not moral. I'm not good. The Bible says that we've all sinned and fallen short of the glory of God, so not one is righteous, no, not one. It says that our good deeds are but like minstrel garments, so I would probably say there aren't any moral people. Christian people aren't moral people, they are people who are weak in a sense, and realize they need a Savior, and realize they need the manifest presence of God through his son Jesus Christ, so our mission is that children will hear the gospel. I think any follower of Christ—and I know that there's been an NPR article recently that kind of negatively—I know the lady's name, it's just not coming to me right now.

SP: Kathryn Joyce?

HN: Yeah, Kathryn Joyce. And I know she's criticized the evangelical movement and orphan care, and, you know, yeah, I guess I fall into her trap to say 100 percent as a believer, I want to bring children into homes where they're going to hear the gospel of Christ, because I believe it's the hope for the world. I believe it's the hope for the nations, and it's truth, and it's manifest truth, and I've seen it. I've been privileged to travel all around the world. I've met believers all around the world, and I've seen and felt the Holy Spirit in my life, I've seen it witness with other people's lives. I believe the truth of God's word, and because I believe the truth of God's word, my heart would be that orphans would be placed in the homes where they could hear God's word and be discipled in God's word.

Herbie's commitment is echoed by other movement leaders and organizations as well. America World Adoption (AWA), a large evangelical adoption agency that focuses on international adoptions primarily, expresses as its vision statement: "America World desires for every adoptable orphan to be placed in a Christian home." Its mission statement is also clear: "To build Christian families according to God's design of adoption."[23] In April 2013, I attended an "Adopted by Design" seminar in Indiana put on by AWA for prospective adoptive parents. A representative of AWA explained at the beginning of the seminar:

> So one of the major things with America World, though—and our biggest goal is to get these orphans—not just to give them a home here in this world, but to give them an eternal home in heaven. If all we do is just get them adopted here and they still live and die in their sins and they don't accept Christ as their Savior, we've helped them a little bit but we've missed the big picture. The big thing is to get them adopted into Christian families who will bring them up as God says, in the nurture and admonition of the Lord, in hopes that they'll get saved—ask Jesus Christ into their hearts and then go to heaven. So my wife and I are concerned—we want to build eternal things, not just an—even a forever family here on this earth but an eternal family in heaven as well, and so one of the prerequisites with America World is that an adoption family—the couple has to be saved. They have to know for sure they're going to heaven.

These explanations reflect the dominant sentiment among movement leaders and activists, and clearly among the CAFO leadership as seen in their membership standards above, that Christian families are the ideal (and thus morally justifiable) families for orphans because they are able to influence the children toward Jesus Christ and raise them as Christians. As the AWA representative shared, to just get them into a home that takes care of their physical needs is insufficient and "miss[es] the big picture" because "they still live and die in their sins and they don't accept Christ as their savior." The priority of placing children with Christian families exclusively reflects orphan care organizations' commitment to the eternal good of the child rather than the immediate, but ephemeral, material good.[24] Brian Luwis, founder and president of AWA, affirmed this sentiment when I asked him about whether recruiting and facilitating adoptions by otherwise moral but secular parents would help solve the orphan problem:

> Well, I guess it's how we look at the earth. If this is our home, if this is it at the end of this life—that it's done, we turn to dust again—I'd say yeah. I'm totally wrong. If this life is everything, then get that kid into any type of family, it doesn't really matter. But, since I don't believe this is the only life we have—that eternity is the greater span of time and that God came and Lord Jesus came to redeem us from this world—that making a statement saying that we place exclusively with Christian families that will basically establish that eternal relationship for the child—give that child the opportunity to meet their creator—it's all in that context. If you have, obviously, for people that don't have faith, that don't believe that there's a creator, that there's a God, there's an eternity, there's a Heaven, there's a Hell—it's ridiculous, obviously. It makes no sense because then it's all about comfort and education, the health and well-being of that child. Take God out of the equation, then yeah, that makes sense. But if God's in the equation, then, yes. God has standards of what is a family. You know, a man and a woman. What is best? It's a healthy relationship with people that are teaching this child about God so they would know their creator and that they would be with God forever.

I need to stress that these leaders and organizations are not against the idea of unbelieving families adopting and raising children per se. They acknowledge that unbelievers can provide stable, healthy adoptive homes as well. But, because adoption and other forms of child placement are not just about getting kids in homes but are of eternal, moral significance, these leaders and organizations cannot justifiably recruit (or even work with) unbelieving couples.

Other influential movement leaders, however, expressed a qualified acceptance toward otherwise moral, unbelieving families adopting children. Leaders generally justified this stance in one of two ways. Some conceded that Christians are not the only acceptable parents and that a non-Christian home would still be preferable to a child being in foster care or an orphanage, or in need of medical attention that an unbelieving couple could provide. Johnny Carr, former director of church partnerships with Bethany Christian Services and author of *Orphan Justice*, acknowledges the practical reality: "I think kids need families, and certainly, when we look at certain parts of the world, if we truly want every child who's living outside of a family to be in a family, then there are going to be certain areas of the world where finding a Christian family to adopt that child is not even going to be a possibility." Paul Pennington, former chairmen of the board of directors for CAFO and founder of Hope for Orphans, expressed a similar sentiment:

> It kind of depends on the context, but . . . I just—my highest value is to know Jesus. But on the other hand, if you've got a starving and dying child and—and we're in the middle of the Sudan and a really nice couple from Alpharetta, Georgia, who has a Christian memory, who are responsible and they're not sex offenders [*laughs*], say you know what, I think we can get that little boy out of here and save his life and take him to Emory University and fix his heart, of course I would be for that, and the reason is because I believe in the sovereignty of God and I've seen God many times bring children through amazing channels. How many people do you know who are believers whose parents weren't? Because in the end, salvation is a work of God, not the manipulation of parents.

Likewise, Tony Merida, pastor and author of *Orphanology*, was compelled by the dire need of orphans to welcome adoption by unbelievers, especially given the possibility of converting them:

> I'm okay with [non-Christian, heterosexual couples adopting]. Again, because I think the orphanage is so bad, in international context, I really would like to see them brought out of that. And because I believe God is sovereign, I think he can work in any mess of a situation, and bring forth good—including the conversion of these [unbelievers]. I just feel like the orphan, in many ways, is such an urgent need. For them to be brought out, fed, nourished, taken to the doctor, just basic stuff, and then I want to worry about the people's souls and their morality, you know what I'm saying? I just, I don't want adoption to be restricted to believers. So, just like I'm not going to say only Christians should have a baby, you know?

As Merida's explanation alludes, other movement leaders seemed to recognize the tension implicit in affirming adoption by non-Christian parents as good solutions for vulnerable children. These leaders justified the contradiction by expressing that working with non-Christian parents to adopt provided Christian orphan care organizations the opportunity to evangelize those parents. Such was the case with Larry Bergeron, founder and executive director of A Child's Hope International and author of *Journey to the Fatherless*.

> SP: You know, the problem out there, lots of orphans need to be taken care of, and you've talked about a solution to that being the Church. And believers mobilizing to take care of those needs, and for the right reasons, and so let's just say some otherwise moral unbelieving couple comes up to you—they're not interested and they're secular humanists, but don't drink, don't smoke. Would the otherwise moral people, they say, we want to adopt and we want all of our friends to get involved in orphan care as well, do you feel like that helps solve the problem?
>
> LB: Sure. What's my job? My job is called to love them. And if they don't know the Lord—I want them to see Christ in me. I won't ever condemn them. I will help them and I will walk with them on the journey, and maybe through walking on the journey with them they'll say, maybe there's something here we're missing, maybe we need to look into. That would be a privilege for me to introduce them to the Savior.

Dan Cruver, author of *Reclaiming Adoption* and co-founder of Together for Adoption, responded similarly to the same question:

> I think that's more of an image-bearer issue and, not preferably but, yeah. I would support [unbelievers adopting], and then you have to get Christians who are thinking in terms of engaging within that context—or that who are missional thinking—develop relationships with these [unbelievers]. We need that. That needs to be happening in every sector of human society, and so if humans who are seeking to live in ways that are consistent with the Bible's understanding of family and love for children, and discipline, and instruction, and raising children who contribute to the

good of society—I'm all for that, and at the same time I'm saying the
responsibility of the Church is to be so missionally minded that we are
living in those same cultural contexts, and so over time—families are going to be families regardless of how those families are formed, and so
Christians need to be relationally involved with those families and living
out a theology of adoption within that context. So yeah, I don't think it's
an issue where you can say, totally for it, totally against, but no. A common grace—they're demonstrating what it means to live in the image of
God, so I commend that. I want to see it happen, and at the same time
we're called to go to everyone who has not named the name of Christ.

For these leaders, though they certainly prioritize adoption by Christian couples, supporting unbelievers in adoption and orphan care would
give Christians the opportunity to walk with them and live out a Christian witness in the hopes of seeing them converted. This perspective
allows movement leaders to "keep the main thing the main thing," as
Herbie Newell said, keeping eternal salvation and God's glory at the
forefront of their efforts, while also allowing for the practical reality that
unbelieving parents would be a better alternative to institutionalization.

Unequivocal Rejection of Same-Sex Adoption

The written standards for membership in CAFO, adoption with Lifeline Children's Services, or receiving financial help from the ABBA
Fund make it clear that the orphan care movement desires not only that
adoptive families be Christians or even Christians who are adopting for
the purposes of raising children as Christ followers. They also required
that these families be married or spelled out "husband and wife," either
implying or stating explicitly that same-sex couples and/or singles
would be excluded from consideration. For many evangelicals, including
leaders in the orphan care movement, the "biblical" (i.e., married-
heterosexual) family model is not only God's ideal but, for many, it is
the *only* morally acceptable context in which adoption could be God
honoring. While same-sex couples were assumed to be non-Christians
by virtue of being homosexual, even Christian singles (usually assumed
to be women) were often disqualified by virtue of their being biblically
incomplete with respect to the qualifications of a family.

Although movement leaders expressed some ambivalence about the prospect of supporting unbelieving families in adoption, their thoughts on secular heterosexual adoptive families were often far more positive when they were contrasted with leaders' unequivocal rejection of same-sex families, whom they assumed to be non-Christian out of hand.[25] These contrasts came out clearly as I posed alternative scenarios. Russell Moore, current president of the Ethics and Religious Liberty Commission of the Southern Baptist Convention, has been one of the leading thinkers and spokespersons for the orphan care movement. When I asked him about the prospect of same-sex families charitably seeking to adopt children, he responded:

RM: I'm not interested in keeping same-sex couples from adopting. I'm interested in calling evangelicals and Roman Catholics and other Christians to adopt. I think that's a difference. I think with same-sex couples, I think that problem is related to the larger question of same-sex marriage itself. As an evangelical Christian, I have a cosmic view of marriage that suggests it signifies something else. It's a picture. It's an icon of a larger reality of an archetype of Christ and the Church. So that the one-flesh union of marriage is impossible in a same-sex configuration. So, I think my gay and lesbian friends are not going to find what they're looking for by simply defining this to be marriage. And I had a conversation just a couple of weeks ago with a lesbian—a woman, who said why would you want to keep me from having what you have. And I said, well, we just disagree whether—it's not that I'm trying to restrict this, it's that I'm saying, you're saying that the state can come in and create it ex nihilo, by simply defining it, and I don't think you can. And the same thing is going to be the case [with adoption]. I think that there is a reason that God has created families with both mother and father who bring different, but complimentary aspects to, not only to marriage, but also to the task of child rearing. And so I think that's going to have detrimental results later on, but having said that, that doesn't mean that I question the motives in any way of gay and lesbian couples who want to have children. I see, at the base of that, there's a sense of a family that can be formed in ways that I just think that don't form that family. Because it's based in something that's beyond—it's not only beyond state actions, beyond nature, some-thing else.

SP: Okay, say it's not a same-sex couple, but it's an otherwise moral secular humanist couple that says, hey, we want to adopt and we've got lots of—you know, maybe a bunch of University of Chicago professors. Do you feel like that helps gets toward the problem, or do you feel like even that still falls short?

RM: Yeah, absolutely, I mean, families are an aspect of God's creational goodness, so I would say the same thing to a secular humanist couple who comes and says, Should we have children? I'm not going to say, Well, show me your baptismal certificate. I'm going to say, yes, you should have children. And a secular humanist couple who says, We want to have children and we want to adopt, you have my blessing in doing that. So, that doesn't mean that I think an evangelical adoption agency ought to empower that or a Roman Catholic adoption agency, we are a specific mission. But, that's something that we can certainly say is a good thing.

While Moore does not conceive of his role as about preventing same-sex couples from adopting, he believes same-sex couples cannot reflect the cosmic reality of the biblical man-woman marriage that represents Christ and his Church. Same-sex couples thus categorically fall outside of the bounds of morally acceptable families for children. Regarding unbelieving, heterosexual families, however, Moore explains that such families would have his blessing in adopting because their unions fall within the boundaries of acceptable families. And while he doesn't nec-essarily think Christian agencies should have to facilitate those adop-tions because of their specific mission, he believes unbelievers pursuing adoption is a "good thing."

Other movement leaders, while certainly expressing a preference for Christian parents, felt that the severity of the child's situation would jus-tify their compromising on the need to have parents who were Christian but not on the need to have them be heterosexual. Kerry Hasenbalg is founder of the Congregational Coalition on Adoption Institute and wife of Scott Hasenbalg, former executive director of Show Hope, a fund-ing agency for evangelical adoptions. During our conversation, I asked Kerry for her thoughts about "non-traditional families" and adoption.

While I did not refer to same-sex couples specifically, she replied, "I mean, hate the sin and love the sinner, right? I think it's confusing for children to grow up with two dads and two moms. And I don't believe that's God's intended order of things. Is that the battle that God's called me to? Not yet."

As a follow-up question, I asked Kerry if it changed the situation for her any if the couple was still a non-Christian couple but was heterosexual, if that would that make her feel more at peace with that possibility of kids being adopted by those kinds of families:

> Yeah. It does. I mean I never really thought—never really said it out loud. But if I'm standing in Africa and I have—let's say it's my cousin. I come from a Jewish family on one side. So I've got my Jewish cousin Josh and his beautiful new bride, and they can't have a baby, and they want a baby, and there's, you know, Timon over there and he's just—I mean it's a mess. What would I choose? I would choose to put him in that home. And you know what? I think that it would be fine—an evangelical would be hard-pressed to say that that child should stay [in the orphanage]. And so what if I've got like George and Paul standing there and going, you know? That would be a harder one for me. But I would probably be able to say to George and Paul, like, you guys are great guys but I am really concerned for this child. . . . So, I don't think I'd let George and Paul adopt.

This explanation most powerfully demonstrates the salience of family structure for evangelicals as a symbolic marker of cultural and moral boundaries. The boundary is not necessarily between Christians and non-Christians in this case. Indeed, Kerry believes that an evangelical would struggle to argue that an orphan should stay in an orphanage rather than be placed with a heterosexual Jewish American couple. But for Kerry the boundary between the morally acceptable man-woman family structure and same-sex family structure is so strong that, with no other options visible, she would rather a hypothetical orphan remain in an orphanage rather than be adopted by a gay couple. As she explains, having two moms or two dads violates "God's intended order of things."

Interestingly, while all movement leaders, citing theological convictions, were unfavorable to the idea of same-sex couples adopting, several leaders felt like it would be more strategic for the orphan care movement to focus on what they understood to be scientific evidence suggesting same-sex parenting was harmful to children and that best practices were to place children into a heterosexual married family. One leader expressed,

> I think that what the Alliance has to do is really talk about the value—I don't know this research data off the top of my head, I'd have to go look into it—but basically, I think our response has to be, What is the most credible research on what's in the best interest of a child, not is it biblically wrong? But we have to go back to what is the emotional, physical, relational health and success of children who have been parented by—which is hard because that's pretty biased stuff, I think—but anyway, children who have been parented by same-sex couples and those by heterosexual couples, and I know there's some data out there that says, Hey, you know, here's why a child is healthier in a traditional family—I mean, I can't quote that, I don't know that, and, frankly, you know, I mean, I haven't validated any of that research, so who knows?

Another leader made a similar argument: "I would also argue that best practices adoption—objective scientific evidence demonstrates that the best outcomes for children are when they have a mom and a dad. I know that's controversial. I know that's not politically correct, but there is a few thousand years of evidence that demonstrates that the best outcomes for kids is when they have a mom and a dad. That's what we believe."

C. H. Dyer, who is president and CEO of an evangelical sponsorship ministry called Bright Hope, also made reference to research evidence in conjunction with his theological convictions to account for why he would be unfavorable toward same-sex adoption. Referencing scientific evidence also allowed Dyer to explain why he would be more favorable to non-Christian parents adopting children by comparison:

> CHD: I think you have to look at the data, and you need to look at what is the best possible help that you can give a child, and my understanding of that research is that a child does best in a family where both a father and a mother are present, and I mean, they do better in school, they do better in health, they do better jobs, I mean, there's just a whole bunch of data that points toward that that is the

best of the best. And to me, in my faith context, that works really well, and that's where I would want to focus. Why would we settle for something less than that? So I want the best for those kids, and where we can, we need to encourage that. I don't want to run away from scripture that would talk about homosexuality—I don't want to run away from what I believe scripture teaches about homosexuality, and so I think that would prevent me from supporting [same-sex adoption]. And so I look at the scriptural basis for my beliefs and my right to believe those things, and I look at the data that shows what's best for children, and I can put those together in a context that will work for Bright Hope and for us. I'll leave it to society to figure out what they want to do, but for my energy and the funds that I raise and for the religious organization—that faith-based organization that I lead—we're going to hold to scripture and hold to best practices, or what's best for kids.

SP: Okay. Do you feel like the situation would be different in your mind if it was an otherwise moral, heterosexual, but non-Christian couple?

CHD: I don't see any data that says non-Christians—or Christians— are better parents than non-Christians, so I don't make—I wouldn't make that distinction.

None of these movement leaders who referred to the "most credible research," "objective scientific evidence," or "a whole bunch of data" demonstrating that heterosexual parenting led to superior outcomes to same-sex parenting ever cited a specific study. Nevertheless, they cite such evidence as being consistent with their faith convictions that the heterosexual married family is God's design and standard and, thus, is the only proper context for children to be placed. They also seem to recognize that, while their theological convictions on this topic would not be popular, referencing research supporting their views provided a more stable platform on which to maintain their stance.[26]

Ambivalence toward Adoption by Single, Christian Parents

Movement leaders often spoke about God's ideal for children being the married man-woman family, and this was often given as the primary reason for rejecting same-sex couples since children need a mom and a dad by their understanding. It was thus important for me to inquire as to how these leaders would think of Christian single parents adopting. Such parents would be Christians and presumably seek to raise their children as Christians, and yet they would fall outside of the bounds of the married man-woman standard.

Some leaders rejected the idea of a single Christian woman adopting. To these leaders (exclusively men), God's ideal family requires both a man and a woman. C. H. Dyer stated simply, "Again, I would just go back to the data shows it's best for a father and a mother. And, you know, if you're going to strive to help kids in the best way, why would you accept anything less?" Consequently, the counsel of these leaders for single women would be to wait until they find a husband to adopt children. Russell Moore explained:

> Probably the most controversial thing, the second most controversial thing that I ever talk about anywhere is whenever I'm asked somewhere— there will usually be a single woman, evangelical woman—I remember at one church, a woman stood up, she said you know, I'm single, not married, I know there are a lot of orphans out there, should I adopt? And I said, not now. I said I think that a child needs a mom and a dad. And so, if God's calling you adopt, I think God's calling you to be married in order to do that. I said, Now, this isn't Thus sayeth the Lord. This is Thus thinketh Moore. Those are very different things, but I think that's important. And there was a woman who came up after who was crying and screaming at me, who said, "I am single, I adopted my daughter, you're saying that my daughter would be better off back in the orphanage." I said, No, I'm not. Any more than if someone had asked me, I'm single, should I have a baby via sperm donation? I would say, No, but that doesn't mean that I'm saying everybody who has ever been born to a single mother would be better off not alive. That's just not the case. But, there's a sense in which there could be an emphasis upon adoption.

For Moore, the ideal situation for children is in the families of Christian heterosexual married parents. All of these aspects (Christian, heterosexual, married) are important, and he is consistent in saying situations outside that ideal—in this case an evangelical woman wishing to adopt—is not to be promoted. Dan Cruver expressed sentiments similar to Moore:

> I'll have single people come to me and go—I want to adopt, I want to adopt, I want to adopt, and these agencies won't let me, and—so one of my questions is, Why do you want to adopt? Well, I want to be a mother, I want to be a father, and I want to give a child a mother or a father, and I say, Well, if that's where your passion is—is it more that you want to be a mother or a father, or more that you want to see a child in the family? And so I press them on that and they'll eventually say, Well, yeah, child in the family. So, have you thought about making it your mission—objective—to help get this child in that family, or is your need to have a child for whatever reason—to fulfill yourself or to give yourself a sense of identity that you've been looking for, you know—it's a really sensitive—really sensitive—topic.

Here Cruver turns the question back on the Christian single seeking to adopt. He questions whether her motives are to get a child in the ideal situation (a Christian two-parent family) or simply to have a child. The latter motivation he characterizes as seeking "to have a child . . . to fulfill yourself or to give yourself a sense of identity that you're looking for." In other words, through his questioning he implies that the single Christian woman is being selfish by wanting a child, rather than doing the selfless thing, which would be to help get the adoptable child into God's ideal family situation.

Other movement leaders, however, were far more accepting of the prospect of Christian singles adopting children, provided they had the support of their church and necessary resources to do so. Katie Overstreet, former program director for adoption and orphan care at Focus on the Family, while stating up front that her preference would be for a married mom and dad to adopt a child, acknowledged, "We know there are great single parents, and especially for those families who can be intentional about saying, No, I don't have a spouse, but I've got great brothers who live close by and so my child's uncles will be a great male influence for them, or, you know, females or whatever may be." Elaborating more on the expectation of support around the single parent, Dwain

Gullion, president of the ABBA Fund and the North Carolina director of Lifeline Children Services, explains:

> I know single [adoptive] moms. We have them in our adoption sup-
> port groups, and they do a wonderful job. And I even know a single dad
> through Living Hope and he was doing an amazing job with the little boy
> he adopted from China. I think if the single definitely [have] an under-
> standing of the gospel, and they're going to share that with the child, and
> they have a support system in place through their church—this might
> be a double standard, I don't know—they have a support group in place
> at their church, and in their immediate family who will support them
> spiritually and through the nurturing and care of that child. I know with
> ABBA Fund we've always stayed away from singles, outside of a church
> partnership. But, if a church funds a specific partnership fund, and they
> want to help a single mom in their church, then we will administer that.
> With Lifeline, there are certain programs that singles can adopt through,
> and it's the same situation. If they have a clear understanding of the gospel
> and have a support group in place . . . depending on the support around
> the single, I'm okay with making an exception.

It was also interesting that, while I never provided a gender of the hypothetical Christian single, movement leaders typically assumed I meant
single woman. In their experience, single Christian men rarely, if ever,
expressed a desire to adopt a child, but lifelong single women commonly
expressed this desire. Herbie Newell was open to placing children with
single Christian women, but was skeptical of placing with single men:

> Typically, wherever it's allowed, we would definitely work with Christian
> single women. We don't currently have any countries that would work
> with Christian single men, and—I think even if we did, I don't know
> how—I think obviously in the design it's always best for a child to have a
> mom and a dad. I think that if you have to do without one—and I don't—
> it's hard to say that, but I can't see—as a single man, I can't see being able
> to give my children the things that my wife gives them that I think are
> completely foundational. So I think a lot of countries realize that, and
> honestly, we have never had a single man apply—but we would work with
> single women.

Thus, while all movement leaders were clear that their preference would be to see adopted children placed with Christian married heterosexual parents, they negotiated the issue of single Christians adopting in different ways, typically either by holding to the biblical man-woman standard and discouraging singles from adopting or by reluctantly accepting the practicality of single (almost always understood as female) Christians adopting, given that such singles are devout Christians and have enough Christian support around them.

Limiting the Mobilization Targets

How does the moral boundary work described above limit the orphan care movement's effectiveness at mobilization? In figure 3.1, we can see how leaders and organizations in the orphan care movement functionally limit their own mobilization targets. I make no claims that this diagram is drawn to any sort of mathematical scale. Rather, the diagram—including the size and positioning of spheres—is intended as an illustration of how these boundaries are marked off. There are those who qualify as having the "biblical" or "right" family structure (married, heterosexuals) and those who are living according to the "right" reasons (Christians living in obedience, seeking God's glory in all things). And the small area where they intersect is the mobilization

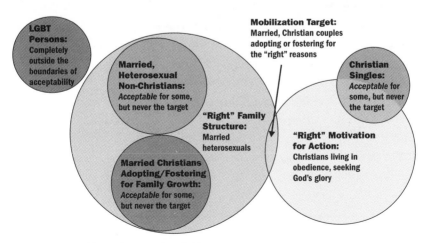

Figure 3.1. Moral boundaries and mobilization targets

target—the population whom CAFO leaders and organizations are seeking to mobilize toward engaging in adoption and foster care. But the moral boundaries require the movement to avoid recruiting those who fall outside of those boundaries of morally appropriate adoption and orphan care activism.

Put another way, CAFO and its constituent organizations, by their own written standards and interview accounts, are not interested in recruiting married Christian couples who are adopting solely for the purposes of family growth, married heterosexual non-Christians, Christian singles, or LGBT persons to adoption and foster care. Certainly, CAFO organizations and leaders would consider some of these groups to provide *acceptable* adoptive situations, that is, they are not necessarily harmful for children. But they are *never* the target of mobilization efforts because they fall outside of the boundaries of God's ideal for children— Christian, married, heterosexual parents adopting primarily with missional intentions.

Boundary Work and the Dilemma of Pietistic Idealism

Pietistic idealism is a double-edged sword. It is in many ways a source of strength for evangelicals engaged in addressing social concerns like the care of vulnerable children. The boundary work associated with pietistic idealism unites evangelicals around a collective identity. Among the most committed, the belief that adoption and orphan care are central to the Christian's identity stimulates flurries of service and sacrifice on behalf of vulnerable populations. Many Christian couples have indeed been motivated to adopt, foster, and serve orphans in order to "make God's true character and the Gospel itself visible," as CAFO says.[27] Even the fact that moral boundary work excludes certain groups from recruitment or participation can be viewed as a functional strength in that it further solidifies who American evangelicals are as a religious subculture—those who are committed to glorifying God in all of life and hold uncompromisingly to a biblical standard for what makes a family.[28] This practice prevents the movement itself from becoming indistinguishable from a worldly social movement for any number of causes—or watered-down "social gospel" or "passionless compassion," as Daniel Bennett calls it.

But pietistic idealism, and the boundary work that it requires, has a strategic drawback. The orphan crisis is enormous in scope, as movement leaders often point out. About one hundred thousand children are waiting for adoption in U.S. foster care, and there are millions of adoptable "double orphans" (those who have lost both parents) overseas, particularly those with special needs whom other Americans are reluctant to adopt. The boundary work of the orphan care movement has functionally limited the size of its mobilization target to a small population of married Christian couples who are not only committed to living missionally but also have the resources to drastically alter their lives through adoption and fostering. In believing that this small group of families can put a dent in the orphan crisis, movement leaders grossly overestimate the number of American Christian couples who are sufficiently committed and equipped for such a calling.

Conversely, the moral boundaries through which leaders and organizations limit the mobilization targets exclude a large number of potentially sympathetic allies and parties interested in adopting or fostering. In doing so, the movement forfeits a tremendous amount of human and political resources that would help address the social problem of vulnerable children domestically and overseas. This includes Christian and non-Christian couples with fertility issues, Christian and non-Christian singles desiring children, and LGBT individuals and couples. In other words, these moral boundaries exclude many of the individuals and couples who would be most interested, well resourced, and easily mobilized to adopting and fostering. This helps us understand why there has not been any measurable impact on adoption and foster care numbers, despite all of the movement activities and efforts over the last ten years.

To clarify, the fact that movement leaders hold that certain *ultimate* priorities must maintain primacy over orphans themselves should *never* be taken to mean that these evangelical leaders and activists are uncommitted to serving vulnerable children in practical ways. For many of these leaders, providing food, medicine, shelter, and—most important— families for orphans is their entire life's work! Indeed, this tension between pietistic idealism and their passion for helping vulnerable children often caused an obvious dissonance in their thoughts. On the one hand, they saw only certain orphan care activities and family situations as morally acceptable before God, and yet orphans are often in quite dire situations needing immediate help that might not be readily available from mission-minded Christian parents. In those situations, some movement leaders stuck to their ideals, while others were more willing to concede exceptions, though they were *never* enthusiastic about these alternatives.

At the risk of being tedious, I wish to reinforce the understanding that movement leaders and organizations insist that adoption and orphan care should emerge out of a motive to reflect the gospel and glorify God by caring for children and leading them to Christ. These messages are clear and often repeated on organization websites, in movement literature, and in interviews with movement elites. But do grassroots evangelical families *truly* pursue adoption or foster care for these reasons *in practice*? Do their surface accounts and the actual circumstances of their pursuits match up? Movement critics and advocates alike seem convinced that "Thousands of Christian families are adopting not because of infertility but in response to God's call."[29] In the following chapter, I consider whether the movement has been as successful at generating new missional motives to compel Christian families to adopt or foster as much as it has been successful at disseminating certain evangelical scripts or narratives through which Christian adoptive families must now justify their actions.

4

So, Why Did You Adopt?

It has been my experience that many people do not begin
thinking about Adoption theologically until they themselves
are involved in adopting (or at least considering adopting)
a child. Very often, the consideration to adopt a child precedes the consideration of the truth that God has graciously
adopted us to be His children. We usually think *adoption* before we think *Adoption*.
—Dan Cruver, "Adoption, adoption, and Caring
for Orphans" (2010)

Coming from a long road of infertility, we wanted to be all in
for Jesus and all in for the orphan, so long as we could get a
beautiful, perfect, healthy infant.
—Amanda Bennett, *In Defense of the Fatherless* (2015:85).

Sometime in 2016 while I was finishing this chapter, I visited an adoption ministry website and happened to see a video testimonial with
nearly fourteen thousand views at the time. I immediately recognized
the family in the video because they were one of the families I interviewed back in 2013, Brian and Lauren Davis and their adopted daughter
Faith. Having very much enjoyed talking with this family in their cozy
Dallas home, I eagerly clicked on the video. After introducing each family member, Brian spoke first:

> We just wanted to talk to you [the viewer] about how God brought our
> family together. We felt the calling to adopt because of the gospel. The gospel
> tells us that because of what Christ did for us, that we can have salva-
> tion. And then that Christ tells us at the end of Matthew that we are to
> go and take the gospel with us, and we thought one of the best ways to do
> that, one of the ways that we felt called to go and share the gospel is to adopt.

> And to bring our child that God had for us into our home to share the
> gospel with [them].

Upon hearing that introduction, I paused video for a moment. I remembered there being another important detail in their adoption story that I wanted to confirm. I pulled up their interview transcript, and sure enough, I had remembered correctly: Lauren had been diagnosed with endometriosis in high school. The doctors had told her that she might never give birth to children. When they started dating in college, Lauren shared her diagnosis with Brian, and so both Brian and Lauren knew going into marriage that, if they were going to be parents, adoption would most likely be the route they would have to take.

When I viewed the rest of the video, I saw that Lauren shared later on that she had endometriosis. It was not something she tried to hide in any way, and she was open about how that diagnosis got her thinking about adoption. But that is not how they began the video. What Brian *first* articulated seemed to suggest fairly clearly that they had adopted, primarily, as a response to the gospel and as a means of sharing the gospel with their adopted child. I certainly do not mean to imply that the Davis's did not genuinely feel that God called them to adopt. But when adoption had *always* been understood as something they would inevitably have to do, anyway, given Lauren's diagnosis, what compelled them to begin their adoption story with the statement "We felt the calling to adopt because of the gospel"? To better understand that question, I will introduce you to another family in the process of adoption, the Bakers.

Adoption as a Divine Calling

Frank and Mandy Baker, an evangelical couple in Georgia, are raising money to fund their domestic adoption. Because the cost to adopt children internationally or domestically through a private agency is greater than what most prospective adoptive parents can bear on their own,[1] many engage in fundraising among their friends, family, and (if religious) faith community to help defray the costs. Among the various evangelical nonprofits geared toward funding Christian adoption, several organizations allow prospective adopters like Frank and Mandy to advertise their fundraising campaign online and receive donations through their website. Within a few paragraphs on their fundraising page, they describe their journey toward adoption:[2]

God started to implant the idea of adoption in our minds some years ago, and He has never let that thought leave. Our Father has sovereignly placed us among a community of believers that are passionate about seeing children find forever families. And he has enlarged our desire to embody the teaching in James 1:27, which says: "Religion that is pure and undefiled before God, the Father, is this: to visit orphans and widows in their affliction. . . ." Now some years down the road, precisely on God's schedule, we are ready to take these steps of faith. God has brought us to the place where we are ready for adoption, and He will faithfully guide us onward. Our Heavenly Father has made it unmistakably apparent that adoption is His will for our lives. Of all the different kinds of adoption out there, God has drawn us to domestic adoption with a private agency. Children are in need in this country. The U.S. is rampant with teen pregnancy, kids being raised in the child welfare system, and tragically-high rates of abortion. Placing a child for adoption is the choice of only two percent of women with unplanned pregnancies. This grieves us, but most importantly, it grieves God Himself. We regret that we can't bring home every child in our nation that needs a family, but we will accomplish for this child what we long to see happen for the millions of orphans globally. We believe that Abba Father has lovingly selected our child and that God has waited until now—the right time for that child—to bring her or him to us. Even though the economic cost is daunting, we believe that The One who called us to adoption will supply all our needs. Ultimately, through this process our family will not only increase in size, but in dependence on our Heavenly Father.

The Bakers go on in their fundraising advertisement to ask for prayer and financial support from readers. Several points are worth noting about the messages conveyed in this excerpt. First, God is the active, sovereign author of virtually every facet of the adoption experience, from its very inception in the Bakers' minds to its ultimate accomplishment. In this brief paragraph, we see that

- God was placing the subject of adoption on the Bakers' minds years ago;
- God has continued to keep adoption in their minds;

- God has placed them with a community of believers who are passionate about adopting vulnerable children;
- God has enlarged their deep desire to live out the teaching of James 1:27 that those who are truly religious will look after orphans (and widows) in their affliction;
- God had a specific timing worked out for them to be ready to begin their steps of faith;
- God has brought them to the place where they are ready for adoption;
- God will faithfully lead them on their pathway to and through adoption;
- God has made it clear to them that adoption is his will for their lives;
- God led them to choose domestic (private agency) adoption out of other possibilities;
- God's sadness (over teen pregnancy, children in foster care, abortion, and the fact that so few women with unplanned pregnancies choose adoption) motivates the Bakers;
- God has picked out their child;
- God has waited until now when his specific child for the Bakers is ready;
- God will bring the child home;
- God called them to adoption;
- God will provide the resources to meet the extensive cost of private agency adoption; and
- an ultimate result of adoption will be the Baker's spiritual growth as they learn to trust God more.

It is little exaggeration to say that, in their description, the Bakers are almost completely without agency. It is as if God has thrust adoption upon them by indirectly commanding them in the Bible to adopt, surrounding them with a community of Christian adoptive families, and transforming their hearts to recognize his specific call and desire for adoption—implying that they would not have desired such a thing naturally on their own. Even as they take practical steps to raise donations to fund their adoption, the Bakers diminish their own role and affirm that God himself will supply their needs. Moreover, even while the Bakers also imply that their pursuit of domestic adoption is in response to the social problems they mention, the focus is ultimately on God's desires. The Bakers explain that, while the unfortunate realities of teen pregnancy, foster children, and abortions break their hearts, of paramount concern is that these situations grieve God's heart. So again, the Bakers' pursuit of adoption, though altruistic in a sense, is primarily an act of obedience—bringing the world into conformity with God's will, one child at a time. Indeed, the ultimate result that the Bakers describe ("our family will not only increase in size, but in dependence on our Heavenly Father") seems just as much about their own spiritual edification and relationship with God as it is about serving an "orphan." Through this account, the Bakers convey one overarching point unequivocally: *God himself, and his plans, desires, and actions are the beginning and end of the Bakers' adoption activities, and their own plans, desires, and actions are not.*

Beneath the Surface

When I spoke to Frank and Mandy in person about their path to adoption, the source of their motives and calling to adopt appeared to be more ambiguous. While the Bakers already had two healthy biological children over seven, Mandy had experienced a variety of pregnancy and labor complications with each. Both girls were born premature, and Mandy had been on bed rest for over ten weeks for each pregnancy. These complications likely stemmed from Mandy's own health problems. Early on in her life, doctors had recognized a polycystic disorder in Mandy's ovaries coupled with fairly severe endometriosis. After the two difficult pregnancies, Mandy recounted being in constant pain. In light of health and quality-of-life concerns, the Bakers elected for Mandy to have a hysterectomy, ensuring that she would never have more biological children. This story came up early in our conversation. Yet, as I switched the topic to the Bakers' adoption pursuits, Frank chimed in:

> Yeah, I mean, long story short . . . we are not adopting to have our third kid necessarily. I think we both wanted three kids just in general, and then by the time our medical situations, and two healthy girls surprisingly, the hysterectomy, we were not necessarily bummed that we couldn't have any more kids biologically just beside the natural kind of loss any woman would feel. We didn't necessarily desire to fill our home with a third kid. . . . I think the idea of adoption just became more familiar to us, just more stories being told. Like we heard about it more, and literally

it's a three-and-a-half, four-year process from going back today of God slowly moving it into our hearts and giving us a pretty intense value system for adoption, and it going from a really good idea to something that we really wanted to support and know more about, to something where we thought that maybe we were the ones that needed to do the adopting. But certainly that combined with the fact that we couldn't have any more kids, we generally were interested in a third, those factors helped, you know what I mean? . . . The fact that we can't biologically and generally do want a third, but it is 90 percent that little piece of God's heart for the helpless and for the orphan, and he just kind of implanted that into our hearts to where we cry about it, and we're moved by it, and we just kind of started heading down that road, and it really was just a really slow, sure slippery slope of commitment for us, and of faith.

Following on the heels of our conversations about pregnancy issues and Mandy's hysterectomy, Frank felt compelled to make it clear that, while they both wanted to have three kids in general, they were not adopting primarily because they wanted a third child. He even stated that they were not especially saddened about not being able to have a third biological child. Rather, he indicated that their desire to adopt developed as they heard more stories of adoption from those in their church and that God was "slowly moving in [their] hearts" for them to desire adoption. Frank acknowledged that God's moving in their hearts, combined with their physical limitations and their genuine desire for a third child, helped move them along. But he stresses that the desire to adopt is "90 percent that little piece of God's heart for the helpless and for the orphan" and God's implanting a burden for orphans in their hearts. As on their fundraising webpage, the Bakers wished to convey the message in person that their pursuit of adoption was best understood as a step of obedience to God's call on their lives, with God's own priorities in mind. Although they acknowledged here that they were unable to have a third child naturally, and did want a third, they did not list these reasons as a major factor in their decision to adopt. Taking from Frank's account, these factors would account for only about 10 percent of the reason for choosing to adopt. Yet, as I pressed further into their adoption pursuit, it became clear how Frank and Mandy's own desires, as well as their own practical concerns, were playing a central role in shaping their decisions about adoption.

For example, given their expressed calling to adopt the "helpless" and the "orphan," I was a little surprised that they felt "led" to adopt domestically through a private agency. Children in orphanages overseas are more likely to be "orphans" in the technical sense of both parents (or even one) being deceased, while children placed through domestic private agencies are rarely orphans in that way. Moreover, foster children who are now available for adoption are by definition coming from broken families and would ostensibly be more "helpless" than children being voluntarily placed through an agency. Further, children in foster care are available and waiting to be adopted for free, rather than at the high cost of domestic private agency adoption. Adopting from foster care would allow the Bakers to avoid fundraising entirely. When I asked the Bakers why they chose to adopt domestically through a private agency, Frank explained,

> Yeah, it came down to our desire was for an infant, so it became a matter of just practically, international adoption, you know if you adopt an infant, you're going to get—they're probably going to be around two when you get them, and then the same with adopting from the foster care system. So we decided to go with the domestic infant adoption for that reason. And then I think after doing that, we found out some really interesting statistics as far as girls who ended up pregnant and the decisions that they make and that kind of thing, and so after making the decision, I think it became more clear that it was a good decision.

Here the Bakers express that ultimately they wanted to adopt an infant and that would not have been possible if they had adopted internationally or from foster care. It was only after they started pursuing infant adoption that they learned about the statistics on young pregnant women and abortions, and this affirmed that the domestic private agency adoption was a good thing to do. Still later, when I inquired further on their decision to adopt an infant, Mandy admits, "Honestly, I think it was a selfish desire of mine [laughs], you know? Not being able to have kids myself anymore, just wanting that infant experience again, wanting our girls to have that, to be a part of that." And Frank added, "Well, and earlier in the process it was that, and we didn't want to disrupt the birth order." So the Bakers acknowledge that there were both self-interested and practical concerns influencing the decision to adopt an infant.

Moreover, the Bakers had first considered adopting overseas from China. Frank recounted, "I think we were initially really interested in the more romantic idea of—and you know, there's nothing wrong with this, but this is one of the first pictures we had in our head of just a little Chinese girl [laughs], and everybody wants a little Chinese girl. And so international [adoption] is so romantic of an idea." But the Bakers expressed that they ultimately did not feel called to adopt internationally from China or Africa, and they also acknowledged the high cost of international adoption compared to domestic. Frank explained, "Practically speaking as well, just financially, I mean, if it costs $20,000 or $50,000, it almost doesn't matter, but at some point, there is a really practical element to how much money adopting a child costs, so it certainly wasn't all about money. It wasn't all about spiritual motivations either, and it wasn't all just statistics, either. It was kind of a hodgepodge, honestly, of all of those things. A little bit of all those things, yeah." So Frank acknowledges that the decision to adopt domestically was in reality a combination of several influences: practical, spiritual, and altruistic—in his words, a hodgepodge.

Lastly, I inquired whether the Bakers were willing to adopt transracially and how they navigated issues of which "special needs" they would be willing to accept in their adopted child. When I asked about transracial adoption, Mandy said, "Yeah, we indicated that we'd be willing to accept any race. That doesn't matter to us at all." I responded by asking them whether they thought about the challenges of raising a child of a different race. Frank replied, "I would say for me personally, I would even prefer a Caucasian baby for that purpose, and I would just pray that God would bring an African American family to adopt an African American baby, just because it can be a pretty significant issue for the child." So Frank expresses that, given the challenges of raising a black child in particular, he would actually prefer a white child. Frank was later sure to explain that the race of the child would not be a deal breaker, but that his preference would be to forgo the racial challenges for the child's own sake. On the topic of special needs, Mandy explained, "As far as special needs go, we don't feel at this point just with our resources that we'd be willing—that we'd be able to give adequate care to a child with special needs or to a child that we know has special needs already. So we indicated we wouldn't be willing to accept that, and then there was all the health things for the mom that we had to decide about, too."

The health issues to consider about the birth mother were whether she had a history of drug and alcohol use, smoking, or mental illness, all of which were disqualifications for the Bakers. As they talked, the Bakers eventually said that they would be willing to accept an infant with correctable issues, such as a cleft lip, that could be repaired with minor surgery. But they reiterated that they rejected "anything that we are aware of that we really don't feel like we just make enough money to treat properly or really make a special amount of time to dedicate toward, so we have plenty of time to give our kids plenty of time as they grow up. . . . We're just realistic with what we can—just our time and our resources."

In sum, through our conversation, the Bakers communicated that both had previously wanted a third child, but they are now medically infertile and that they are quite intentionally selecting a healthy (preferably for Frank, white) infant, coming from a mentally and physically healthy birth mother. And in their own words, these preferences were shaped by self-interested and practical concerns like simply "wanting the infant experience again" or to maintain birth order and wanting to avoid the challenges of navigating racial issues with the child or not having enough time or material resources to raise a child with severe special needs while also tending to their own biological children. How do these very particular, and ostensibly self-interested or at least self-protecting, preferences jibe with the Bakers' description of their adoption pursuit as being a step of obedience to God, reflecting God's heart for the helpless orphan?

First, I must make it clear that none of the Bakers' preferences and concerns about adoption are unusual. Research shows that adoptive parents have a variety of complex motives and concerns shaping why and how they pursue adoption.[3] The Bakers appear to be adopting for reasons similar to most other adoptive families,[4] with what most would consider reasonable and appropriate concerns in mind.[5] *And that is THE critical point to understand.* If one was only reading their fundraising webpage or uncritically accepting their initial in-person account of their adoption pursuit, one would conclude that the Bakers were pursuing adoption for reasons that were almost completely ideological and devoid of any self-interest. Yet, if we look more closely at their story, it seems more that they are adopting for generally the same reasons, and with similar concerns, as most other American couples seeking to adopt a healthy (white) infant domestically—because they genuinely want another child and they would prefer to avoid excess time and material costs that would come with other alternatives (e.g., older child adoption, foster care, special needs adoption, international adoption, and/or transracial adoption). Certainly the Bakers feel that adoption is a morally good thing to do, but, by their own admission, their understanding of the social problems associated with unplanned pregnancy came *after* their pursuit of adopting an infant.

My argument is *not* to say that the Bakers do not genuinely feel that God is leading them to adopt and is active in their adoption story. Rather, I argue that, at their core, families like the Davises and the Bakers are very similar to most other prospective adoptive parents (Christian or otherwise) but that, somewhere along their experiences, they have learned to articulate their pursuit of adoption to others, and particularly to other Christians, by using what I call "evangelical vocabularies of motive," borrowing from the sociologist C. Wright Mills.[6] I propose in this chapter that the orphan care movement has not been successful at generating *new* motives among American Christians such that they pursue adoption or foster care more than they had in the past. Instead, the movement has been successful at disseminating evangelical vocabularies of motive that Christian adoptive families now feel compelled to use to articulate their adoption pursuits and experiences. These common vocabularies— one could also call them "scripts" or "accounts"—highlight God's activity and the families' own obedience to his divine calling while also suppressing the self-interested and practical aspects of the choices Christian families have made in adoption. This pattern ultimately obscures the orphan care movement's relative lack of success at motivating and mobilizing American Christian families to adopt or foster more in the last fifteen years. This also creates a strategic liability in that it conceals evangelicals' fundamental misunderstanding about culture, motivation, and social action.

Vocabularies of Motive and the Orphan Care Movement

C. Wright Mills observes that language serves an important social function in that it situates one's own behavior within a framework where others can understand it. Speaking to the topic of motives, Mills proposes that we should not think of motives as subjective springs from which action flows but, rather, as standard vocabularies that situate action within defined social situations. Social actors give an "account" of their motives for specific reasons. And those reasons are usually because those accounts, or "vocabularies of motive," are those that are socially condoned by a particular audience given the social situation. Different institutional situations call for different vocabularies of motive to account for certain lines of behavior. Mills avoids disregarding these socially approved accounts as mere lies (although some might be lies) because he believes these vocabularies of motive are often internalized by actors to genuinely shape their future action. He explains, "The long acting out of a role, with its appropriate motives, will often induce a man to become what at first he merely sought to appear. . . . Vocabularies of motives for different situations are significant determinants of conduct."[7] Mills criticizes the quest for "real" motives, as he believes this quest begins with the faulty assumption that real motives are something essential to the individual that we cannot observe empirically. Rather, he proposes that social scientists are better served by analyzing vocabularies of motive to understand the social situations in which such vocabularies are learned and expected.[8]

Related to this idea of vocabularies justifying social action, Ziad Munson, in his study of pro-life activists, considers religion's role in shaping social movement mobilization. He considers the ways religious institutions provide various resources for movements as well as the beliefs and ideas that might motivate activist's activities. Religion, he argues, also provides a "language of motivation" through which to frame one's movement participation. He writes,

> The dominant language of motivation in American society puts an
> overwhelming premium on self-interested behavior. Even participation
> in charitable, volunteer, or self-sacrificing activity is understood by
> both scholars and public alike in terms of the satisfactions it brings

to the participant ("I enjoy volunteering," or "I feel good when I give money").... This kind of language can also be found in the pro-life movement, but the language of religious faith offers an alternative to understanding one's own involvement in self-interested terms.... Mobilization into the pro-life movement forces activists to confront the question of why they do what they do, both for others and for themselves. Religious ideas offer a language through which activists' large commitments of time and resources to the movement can be understood. Altruism, because God wants it or requires it, helps make sense of social movement activity in a world where many doubt any motive not rooted in self-interest and economic advantage.[9]

While the world generally expects that persons are engaging in social activism for the cause itself or the satisfaction it provides the actor, religious vocabularies allow activists to distance themselves from self-interested motives for participation, which may be frowned upon in religious circles.

Seen in this light, Mills's idea of vocabularies of motive is helpful for understanding the accounts given by the Davises, the Bakers, and dozens of other evangelical adoptive families in their interviews. As I have already shown, pietistic idealism demands that morally right actions must be done *primarily* out of obedience to God's call and an explicit desire to glorify God. Among the most devout evangelical communities, this teaching extends to mundane daily activities, such as the clothes one wore this morning, to big life decisions, such as whom to marry, how many kids to have, and where to send them to school. Of course, pietistic idealism represents a sacred ideal or standard for what *should* guide evangelicals, rather than a statement of fact. Evangelicals, like everyone else, are influenced by the broader society and make most daily decisions with a combination of self-interested and practical concerns in mind. Most evangelicals do not go around asking each other if they ate their breakfast that morning to the glory of God. And even in the secular workplace, most American evangelicals do not feel the need to distinguish themselves from other Americans in the way they go about everyday activities. But within the context of other evangelicals, believers are expected to draw on community-approved vocabularies of motive to explain socially significant life decisions.

How do evangelical vocabularies of motive become applied to adoption and orphan care activism? This has been the primary contribution of the orphan care movement, particularly the mobilization literature disseminated by movement leaders. In my interviews with evangelical adoptive families, many stated that, *after* they began to consider adoption—usually because of some combination of (1) struggle with fertility or fecundity issues and (2) being within a network of other Christian adoptive families—they picked up a Christian book on adoption, like Russell Moore's *Adopted for Life* or Merida and Morton's *Orphanology*.[10] I have already shown how these books, as well as their authors and the orphan care organizations themselves, provide (and prescribe) the appropriate vocabularies of motive for families to employ. When I interviewed families, they, too, described how these books shaped their thinking on the topic of adoption.

Owing to the current popularity of evangelical adoption and orphan care literature, conferences, and events like Orphan Sunday, evangelical adoptive families have increasingly found themselves within a social situation in which group members are expected to give a particular account of their adoption activities that draws on the prescribed vocabularies of "orphans," "calling," "obedience," "adoption and the gospel," "God's glory," and so on, while avoiding, or at least de-emphasizing, alternative vocabularies of motive that express self-interested or practical concerns. It is unsurprising, then, that certain cultural scripts or evangelical vocabularies of motive become repeated among the evangelical adoptive families that I interviewed, like the Davises and the Bakers.

The pervasive expectation that evangelical adoptive families employ these vocabularies of motive is ironic considering that many of the evangelical leaders that articulate and promote these scripts initially pursued adoption because of fertility or fecundity issues. In fact, at least twenty-five of the evangelical leaders I interviewed stated (when asked) that they and their spouses had been unable to have healthy, biological children prior to their adoptions. Several of these influential leaders and authors, like Paul and Robin Pennington, Russell Moore, Kelly Rosati, Brian Luwis, Jason Kovacs, Rick Morton, Michael and Amy Monroe, and Jodi Jackson Tucker, as well as others I have not interviewed, like David Platt, Sara Brinton, Amanda Bennett, Michelle Gardner, and Mardie Caldwell, have described publically their own struggles with infertility either in books or on websites.[11] And while I will not list the other names because such information is highly personal, these leaders represent much of the board of directors and executive staff of the Christian Alliance for Orphans as well as the authors of the most influential orphan care literature within the last eight years.[12] By mentioning all of this, I only mean to emphasize that most adoptions—even those of leaders in the orphan care movement who promote specialized vocabularies of motive for why Christians should pursue adoption—are pursued for a variety of complex reasons. Chief among these reasons is often the deeply held, but thwarted, desire to have biological children.

The subcultural pressure to provide these evangelical vocabularies of motive, as opposed to simply acknowledging the self-interest inevitably involved in adopting a child, has become overwhelming for some evangelical adoptive families. It has even driven some to resentment. For instance, several evangelical parents who had initially posted videos similar to the Davises told me they later requested their videos be taken down. In one father's words, "We will not make our adopted daughter a mascot [for the movement]." A number of other parents described their frustration when people praise them for being so selfless to adopt their children because they resent the contemporary emphasis among Christians on portraying adoption as "rescue." One Christian mother in South Carolina who adopted in the 1990s explained,

> You know, as we've watched [other families adopt] over the last ten years, I'm mixed about the trend of even [Christian] couples adopting, because sometimes it does feel very much like the rescuing thing, and for us, people always say a thing to us about how wonderful we were for having adopted: "You did such a good thing for those kids," and really, it was *selfish*. You know [*laughs*], they did something good for us. They were a gift and blessing to us. Sometimes it feels like the way [other families] talk about it, it feels a little bit like you know, that it's a rescuing.

An adoptive mother in Georgia expressed a similar sentiment:

> It's kind of a pet peeve, when people say to me or to us, "Oh, you're such good people. You helped this baby." And I want to say to say to them what I always say to [our adopted child], that he was an answer to *our* prayers.

We, especially I, kind of selfishly just wanted another baby. I didn't want a five-year-old foster kid. I wanted a baby. . . . We didn't do it because we're so good and we have a heart for orphans. No, I wanted a dang baby, and this baby dropped in our lap, and I believe God orchestrated it all.

Both mothers believe that God was active in their adoption story, but not because they had a passion for rescuing orphans, necessarily. Rather, they adopted because they genuinely wanted children and could not have them by birth. The children were God's gift to them, an answer to prayer. Given their true motives, these mothers resent what they feel is a recent assumption or expectation that, because they are Christians, they must have adopted in order to rescue their children (in a physical and spiritual sense). Similarly, an evangelical father in Texas explained:

For me, I have kind of always struggled being in and around the culture of evangelical adoption where people talk a lot about having a heart to adopt and for these kids, because I have never really felt that personally. I mean, I love adoption. I think it's awesome. I love our daughter. Maybe we'll adopt again someday, who knows, but I don't feel personally this burden to go save kids, if that makes any sense. I feel compassion for kids who are in need, for sure, but I don't know. There are other things that I'm wired to care about. I think that adoption isn't for everybody, but I think a lot of the churches and a lot of—maybe not churches, but there are definitely nonprofits that will make it sound like [adoption] should be for everybody, and I think that if you're a believer in Jesus, you should be caring for the fatherless in some way, but that doesn't necessarily mean that you should adopt or foster. There are other ways that you can be a part of that.

As with the two adoptive mothers quoted above, this father resents messages implicit within the "culture of evangelical adoption" expressing that adoption should be done out of a motive to save children. Indeed, he rejects the notion propagated by some evangelical nonprofits that adoption should be for all Christians. While some concern for orphans should be expected of Christians, Christians can care for orphans in other ways besides adoption, such as fostering, supporting other Christian adoptive or fostering families, or mentoring orphans.

The sentiments expressed by these parents in my interviews have been echoed among Christians in more public venues. In September 2012, *Christianity Today* published an op-ed piece written by Megan Hill, a popular Christian blogger and adoptive mom. The essay was entitled "Adopting a Kid, Not a Cause: What Ever Happened to Adopting Simply Out of the Desire to Have Children?" Hill acknowledges with the movement leaders that physical adoption is "a beautiful picture of God's redemption of us, his broken children. And human adoption is a compassionate response to the divine love that we ourselves have received." However, Hill counters: "I want to propose that adoptive parents don't have to be on a global crusade. Whether they admit it or not, many Christian couples adopt simply because they want kids. And that's okay. God thinks it's good to want kids. . . . I propose that wanting children, or wanting more children, is a legitimate reason to adopt. . . . Every Christian mom I know, whether biological or adoptive, fundamentally loves being a mom to her kids. And we talk like that's an unimportant, or at least less important, impetus for adopting."[13]

It is important to highlight Hill's claim that many Christian adoptive couples "whether they admit it or not" simply want kids. Even Hill in this instance recognizes that there is pressure for Christian couples to suppress their self-interested (though legitimate) reasons for wanting kids in order to project an image of being on a selfless, global crusade. Hill goes on to argue that overemphasizing the missional aspects of adopting while minimizing the longing for children marginalizes the Christian women who struggle with infertility and calls their interest in adoption lesser, that it risks objectifying adopted children as involuntary ambassadors for a Christian cause, and that it creates a false hierarchy that places international or special needs children as more valuable than healthy, same-race infants.

In response to Hill's op-ed, however, *Christianity Today* published an essay written by Dennae Pierre, former speaker with Together for Adoption and, as of 2015, founder and executive director of Foster Care Initiatives. Pierre's response, entitled "Adoption: Not a Justice Cause but a Spiritual Reality," is emblematic of the pietistic idealism expressed by orphan care movement elites in person and through their literature. Pierre affirms Hill's statement that Christians adopt because they want children but emphasizes that Christians must ask, "Why do we want children?" Pierre points out that Adam and Eve were commanded to be fruitful and multiply "not primarily to meet the instinctual need of Eve to nurture a child [and] not primarily to secure Adam's family line [but] the primary reason was to spread God's name through the earth. From the beginning, there has always been something very missional about having children." Pierre goes on to make explicit the mission of Together for Adoption and the now-institutionalized vocabularies of motive promoted by the broader orphan care movement:

> We believe it is necessary to remind the church of the doctrine of their adoption precisely to awaken their minds to the idea of loving some of the most vulnerable children in our world. We are convinced that our message is necessary because the global orphan crisis is massive and unacceptable. . . . What should motivate the Church to social action? Every single time, it needs to be the gospel. If we remove the gospel as the main motivation for the church to take action, we are left with individuals being motivated out of works righteousness.[14]

Here, even as Hill expresses the desire of many Christians to simply say that they adopted by because they truly wanted children, Pierre (and a majority of orphan care movement leaders, organizations, and books) emphasizes the only morally appropriate motives for Christian adoption. In Pierre's words: "Every single time, it needs to be the gospel."

But as we have already seen, the orphan care movement has not been successful at mobilizing American Christians to adopt more or foster more. And my interviews with evangelical adoptive families demonstrate that, for many such families, even those who adhere to evangelical vocabularies of motive to describe their adoption activities, their pursuit of adoption begins (at least in part) with barriers to physical childbearing that would have made adoption a natural course of action, anyway. All this suggests that the movement has been less successful at generating *new* motives to adopt, as opposed to disseminating evangelical vocabularies of motive that evangelical adoptive families are now expected to use to justify their actions.

But this does not seem right. Biblically faithful, gospel-centered preaching that stresses the Christian's responsibility to serve orphans *should* motivate Christians to adopt and foster, not just justify what they were already doing. Recent research in cognitive psychology and the sociology of culture can help shed light on what the orphan care movement, and perhaps evangelicals in general, fundamentally misunderstands about social action.

How Research on Culture and Action Sheds Light on the Orphan Care Movement

Why did the Bakers' account of their motives in pursuing adoption seem so inconsistent? At some points in the conversation they said that their motive was "90 percent that little piece of God's heart for the helpless and for the orphan," while at other points they acknowledged that their hope to adopt an infant was a "selfish desire." They discussed pursuing domestic infant adoption versus international adoption as a practical, financial issue but also said that their decision "wasn't all about money. It wasn't all about spiritual motivations either, and it wasn't all just statistics either. It was kind of a hodgepodge honestly of all of those things." A hodgepodge of influences certainly seems to be the most accurate description.

To sociologists who study the interplay of culture, cognition (or thought processes), and social action, the fact that the Bakers were so inconsistent in the ways they described their adoption motivations would be unsurprising. People tend to be fairly bad at understanding themselves, much less explaining *why* they do what they do. This tendency, social scientists are learning, is because a number cognitive processes influence our decision making, and the most powerful processes are unconscious or intuitive.[15] Humans try to give consistent accounts of why they pursue particular lines of action, but they are capable only of using the available vocabularies of motive that they have received and are aware of to justify their actions.

The sociologist Stephen Vaisey has elaborated what he calls the "dual-process model" of how culture shapes social action. In this theory, culture shapes social action by influencing two modes of cognition—one fast, automatic, and largely unconscious, and one slow, deliberate, and largely conscious.[16] To illustrate how these two modes of cognition work, Vaisey employs a metaphor about a rider on top of an elephant, borrowed from the psychologist Jonathan Haidt.[17] The rider on the back of an elephant represents our deliberate conscious reasoning; it can try to explain where we are going and why. But unfortunately, a rider on an elephant is not ultimately in charge of where the two are going. The elephant represents our unconscious, automatic intuitive processes and is stronger than the rider and thus dictates the course of action, going wherever it wants on the basis of impulse. The rider pretends to be in control, or to know exactly what the elephant is doing, and may even be able to trick the elephant at times, but the rider is often ineffective at explaining why they are going in a given direction.

In terms of everyday life, dual-process cognition makes things easier on the brain. We do not have to make new decisions everyday about whether we will practice personal hygiene, or how to get dressed, or the manner in which we will relate to strangers, but these actions are done almost without thinking thanks to years of ingrained habit. So in Vaisey's theory, culture shapes our actions by (1) shaping our deeper, unconscious cognitive processes through years of socialization, which largely determines our underlying motivations for action, and (2) shaping our more conscious, rational cognitive processes, where we keep our vocabularies of motive to make sense of our actions socially and provide post hoc justifications.

Vaisey's dual-process model of culture in action helps clarify the fundamental misunderstandings of the orphan care movement when it comes to the motives driving Christian families to adopt or foster children. Here I also wish to incorporate Paul Lichterman's concept of "thin culture." Lichterman studied how Americans use self-help books. He noticed that readers genuinely shared an understanding that the words and advice in the self-help books could be read and implemented loosely and inconsistently, without lasting commitment.[18] He proposed that readers use and compare information from self-books in relation to other more deeply held cultural schemas. Thus he calls the information in self-help books "thin culture" because it does not support a deep commitment from readers but it is employed situationally and cast aside easily.[19] So, too, I argue that the "culture of adoption/orphan care" articulated and promoted by orphan care movement literature and conferences represents a thin culture in that it seldom seems to influence evangelical leaders and families to establish enduring conviction resulting in sacrificial adoption and orphan care activism, at least not initially. Rather, this thin culture provides the optional, post hoc justifications for action described by Stephen Vaisey.[20] I contrast this with forms of culture that are *deep* and reside at the level of cognitive schemas and dispositions that shape the convictions and motivations of actors. These would be shaped much less by sermons and casual reading of movement literature than by years of primary socialization, practice, and social pressure.[21]

For many of the evangelical leaders and families I interviewed, it would be more accurate to say that they were primarily driven (at least initially) by the deeply held cultural schema of pronatalism: the idea that having children is central to personhood and family life. Christians, and particularly evangelical women, are often raised with this idea that children are not only a gift from God but also a responsibility and essential aspect of a full Christian life.[22] Numerous adoptive and fostering families in my interviews described a lifelong desire for children, and many expressed that they had hoped for an especially large family. Confronted with barriers to obtaining this goal, many of the Christian families I interviewed reported being profoundly upset. One adoptive mother in Chicago, after recounting her desire for children growing up, said, "We never anticipated that we would be infertile. I mean, that was devastating. Absolutely devastating and took me to my knees. It was one of the darkest times in my life."

Moreover, families often recounted that when they first experienced trouble getting pregnant naturally, adoption was not the first alternative. Rather, they pursued a variety of alternatives, including home remedies, hormones, fertility drugs, in vitro fertilization (for a few), and ultimately adoption, often as a last resort.

In the past, Christian families might have simply justified their pursuit of adoption by stating plainly that they wanted children. In fact, in most of my interviews with families who adopted before 2000, this is exactly how they articulated their adoption pursuits. But because of the pervasive exposure of the orphan care movement through books, conferences, and Orphan Sunday, such Christian families are now equipped with new post hoc justifications or vocabularies of motive to explain their actions in socially approved ways.

Figure 4.1 illustrates the process and limited effectiveness of the orphan care movement at promoting an evangelical "culture of adoption/

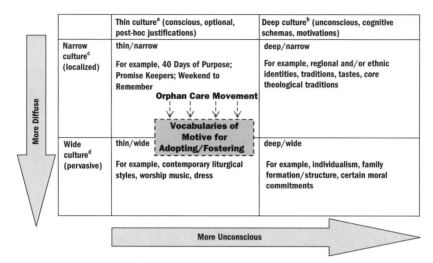

Figure 4.1. Dimensions of culture

[a] "Thin culture" refers to symbols, justifications, strategies, and practices that are optional and do not motivate action so much as they are selectively appropriated according to the social context. These may be narrow (localized) or wide (pervasive).

[b] "Deep culture" consists of cognitive frameworks and schemas that structure deep-level, intuitive motivations, values, and patterns of thought. These may be narrow or wide.

[c] "Narrow culture" refers to culture that is localized either among a particular group (e.g., certain evangelicals for whom the culture is relevant) or region of the country (e.g., the Southeast United States).

[d] "Wide culture" refers to culture that is pervasive throughout an entire group (e.g., most evangelicals in the U.S.) or region (e.g., the entire United States).

orphan care" in such a way that it generates new and compelling motives for Christians to adopt or foster. The four quadrants of the figure distinguish between forms of culture that are thin/narrow, thin/wide, deep/narrow, and deep/wide. Through Orphan Sundays, movement literature, and large conferences, the orphan care movement has successfully disseminated a thin culture (a complex of accounts or vocabularies of motive) from a narrow localized venue to a wide platform. Put simply, the movement has taken the language of adoption and orphan care and made it pervasive throughout American evangelicalism. However, the movement has been unsuccessful at shaping and moving a deep culture, consisting of cognitive schemas that influence motivation, at least among a wide enough audience to influence adoption and foster trends at the national or state level.

Mobilization in Theory and in Practice in the Orphan Care Movement

The adoption accounts that many evangelical families now regularly articulate obscure reality both for orphan care movement leaders and critics of the movement, giving the impression that the movement has been more successful than it really is, despite what the numbers suggest. In her 2013 article written for the progressive magazine *Mother Jones*, entitled "Orphan Fever: The Evangelical Movement's Adoption Obsession," Kathryn Joyce provides a diagram she uses to illustrate the process of how evangelical families are mobilized to adopt children. I have included excerpts from this in figure 4.2.[23]

Because her account builds on a superficial understanding of why evangelical families are actually adopting children, Joyce presumes that *effective* mobilization has happened in several steps: First, the influential denominations, congregations, and organizations within the orphan care

---

IT TAKES A CONGREGATION

A snapshot of the Christian adoption network

Religious Groups like the Southern Baptist Convention, keystone churches like Saddleback, and groups like Focus on the Family and Hope for Orphans implore Christians to adopt. An umbrella coalition, the Christian Alliance for Orphans, helps unite the movement.

Adoptive Parents declare themselves "serial adopters" as orphan fever sweeps through evangelical congregations. Some families adopt as many as five or six new children.

Ministries including the Abba Fund and God's Grace Adoption Ministry direct parents to Christian agencies, host conferences, promote overseas mission trips, and give interest-free loans and grants to adoptive parents.

Adoption Agencies such as All God's Children, Bethany Christian Services, and America World Adoption fund humanitarian projects, donate to orphanages, and handle the paperwork.

Foreign Governments exercise varying degrees of oversight. Trafficking and corruption have plagued adoptions in places like Ethiopia and Kyrgyzstan, where Christian agencies were implicated in unethical and/or illegal behavior.

Orphanages often cut exclusive deals to supply adoption agencies. They also take in local children who need temporary sanctuary and schooling.

Birth Parents in some cases have complained that adoption was misrepresented to them as a sort of sponsorship or education opportunity.

Figure 4.2. The process of mobilizing evangelical families, taken from Kathryn Joyce (2013a).

movement are successfully mobilizing Christian families to adopt by first imploring Christians to adopt from up front through sermons, conferences, and so forth. This is how the movement leaders see mobilization happening as well. Second, "orphan fever" sweeps through evangelical congregations, and evangelical families are compelled to label themselves "serial adopters" and adopt up to five or six new children in response to this religious frenzy. Third, this supposedly *new* evangelical impulse to adopt children is facilitated by evangelical grant and loan agencies providing money, while Christian adoption agencies handle the paperwork, foreign governments look the other way, orphanages cut special deals with Christian adoption agencies, and birth parents are duped into surrendering their children.

Aside from the fact that there is no evidence to suggest the orphan care movement has been successful in mobilizing Christians to adopt more, which Kathryn Joyce certainly implies is happening, this theorized model of mobilization completely misunderstands what has in fact taken place among evangelical adoptive families involved at some capacity with the movement.

Joyce's model, as well as that proposed by movement elites in their mobilization literature, can be illustrated with a process diagram (see fig. 4.3). First, evangelical elites implore evangelicals to adopt or foster children through various media but primarily through mobilization literature, national and regional conferences, sermons, and so on. Within this teaching, leaders convey their movement ideology, which understands sacrificial adoption as an important aspect of the Christian life and a reflection of the gospel, diminishes adoption for family growth or "Plan B adoptions," and draws boundaries around which adoptions count as most pleasing to God. Elite orphan care leaders influence congregational leaders who begin to promote adoption and foster care from the pulpit and through congregational events like Orphan Sunday. This teaching also stimulates the development of orphan care nonprofits that are geared toward facilitating Christian adoption efforts either by advocating for adoption, providing financial help, or literally placing children. As congregational leaders start to preach and teach about orphan care, the congregation develops a "culture of adoption/orphan care" in which adoption, fostering, and other forms of ministry to orphans pervades the ethos of the congregation. From this, grassroots evangelical

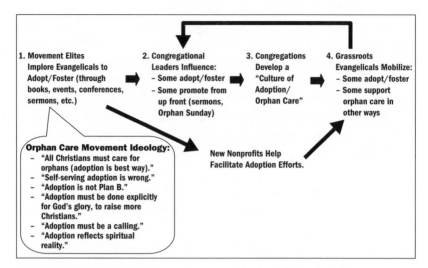

Figure 4.3. Model of adoption/orphan care mobilization held by movement critics and leaders.

families are mobilized to adopt or foster children or support orphan care in some other way, perhaps by donating money to help another evangelical family in one's congregation to adopt or providing respite care. These grassroots efforts are aided by the funding and adopting infrastructure provided by the new orphan care nonprofits.

The theorized model suggested by Joyce and movement leaders also resembles the "framing" model of mobilization in which movement elites seek to mobilize a grassroots population by extending certain collective action frames that will resonate with a particular target audience and provoke them to action. The model assumes that motivating ideas precede movement activism, and thus movement leaders need to shape the ideas and interpretations of target audiences to recruit and deploy them to achieve movement objectives.[24] The framing model has been challenged on a variety of fronts, primarily on the grounds that ideas and ideologies are not necessarily the leading contributor to successful mobilization. Recent work on pro-life activism by Ziad Munson suggests that social movement participants are often recruited to activism through relationships and begin participation in movement activities *before* they ever adopt the ideology of the larger movement itself, *not because* of that ideology. In fact, it is through participation in the activism itself that the actors begin to learn and internalize movement scripts and ideals.[25]

I found that Munson's proposed model of mobilization more accurately reflects what I observed among most evangelical families. Such families most often adopted *first* because of their own personal reasons and only later, as they read orphan care movement literature and became involved in the Christian adoption community, became activists. Indeed, this is what Together for Adoption founder Dan Cruver acknowledged back in 2010. He explained, "It has been my experience that many people do not begin thinking about Adoption theologically until they themselves are involved in adopting (or at least considering adopting) a child. Very often, the consideration to adopt a child precedes the consideration of the truth that God has graciously adopted us to be His children. We usually think *adoption* before we think *Adoption*."[26] Cruver goes on to identify this as a problem that motivates Together for Adoption to educate Christians on why the recognition of *Adoption* as a spiritual reality should precede the human *adoption* of children, not the other way around.

Figure 4.4 illustrates the process as it actually occurred for most families in my study. Evangelical families struggled with some sort of infertility or sub-fecundity. This struggle took place within a cultural context of deeply held (i.e., behavior-influencing) cultural schemas. These included

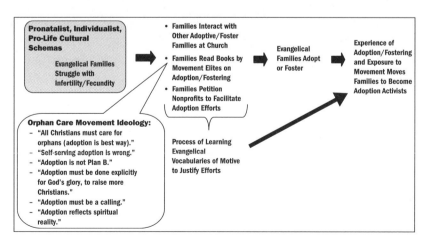

Figure 4.4. Observed model of evangelical adoption and orphan care mobilization.

pronatalism (influencing the families to want children), individualism (influencing families to seek personal fulfillment through children), and pro-life ideals (influencing families to value adoption as an alternative to abortion and to be skeptical of the most drastic alternative reproductive technologies like in vitro fertilization). The struggle of infertility/sub-fecundity within this cultural context motivates evangelical families to look into adoption. Within this process, evangelical families interact with other Christian adoptive and fostering families in their circle of friends; they begin to read popular or recommended books on Christian adoption/fostering written by movement elites; and they begin to petition orphan care nonprofits to help facilitate their adoption efforts through funding or placement.

During this process of pursuing adoption, evangelical families also begin the process of learning movement ideology and community-approved vocabularies of motives to articulate their adoption pursuit within the evangelical context. Next, evangelical families actually do adopt or foster children. Oftentimes it was this experience of adopting or fostering children, coupled with the more-or-less internalized evangelical vocabularies of motive for adopting or fostering, that led such families to become adoption or foster care activists, engaging in forms of orphan care leadership or activism beyond merely adopting.

It is important to reiterate, however, that because the observed process of mobilization often begins with Christian families struggling with fertility/fecundity issues, those who adopt or foster are often *not* doing so primarily, or at least originally, because of their identification with the movement or their internalization of movement ideals. These things did not motivate their *initial* interest in adoption or fostering; rather, identification and internalization happened *because* of their pursuit of adoption.

Aaron Klein is an adoptive father and founder of Hope Takes Root, a nonprofit facilitating a variety of orphan care activities, including adoption advocacy and support. With no biological children of their own, he and his wife adopted a son from South Korea and a daughter from Ethiopia. When I asked him about his journey to become an advocate for orphan care, he explained, "I can say with absolute conviction that we would not be involved in the cause of global orphan care today, were it not for these incredible blessings of these two kids and the way that they've changed our lives. . . . I think that adoption is often the, shall we say, the gateway drug to activism." In Aaron's account, adoption (with infertility) came first; a commitment to orphan care activism came second.

Other leaders report a similar flow of events. For example, in his book *Counter Culture*, the adoption advocate and megachurch pastor David Platt recalls the adoption of his first son, Caleb. He and his wife chose to adopt after over five years of struggling with infertility.[27] While they were aware of statistics about orphans, these numbers did not become real until they traveled to Kazakhstan to pick up Caleb. He explains,

> Everything changed when we made our first trip to the orphanage in Kazakhstan. We saw children playing outside. We walked past their rooms inside. Suddenly those numbers on a page came alive in our hearts. We realized that it was Caleb who was sleeping in one of those cribs, and it was Caleb who was included in those numbers. All at once the numbers became real . . . and personal. We learned that orphans are easier to ignore before you know their names. They are easier to ignore before you see their faces. It is easier to pretend they're not real before you hold them in your arms. But once you do, everything changes.[28]

Notice it was the personal experience of adoption that led to Platt's advocacy on behalf of orphans, not the other way around. Likewise, Sara Brinton, co-author of the 2015 book *In Defense of the Fatherless*, recounts the very process described in figure 4.4 in her own adoption experience:

> We began praying about adoption five years ago. At the time, I was pregnant with our youngest son. My pregnancy was complicated, and we knew he would be our last biological child. . . . We brought dinner to friends who had just adopted a child from Ethiopia and asked for wisdom. They gave us a copy of Russell Moore's *Adopted for Life*. This book opened our eyes to the truth that Christians are adopted by God—and left us with a deep convention that we were called to adopt. At the same time, I began reading the blogs of dozens of adoptive families.[29]

This is exactly how the process worked for most in my research. In Brinton's account, her family started thinking about adoption *because* they could not have more biological children but wanted more children.

They started asking questions of other Christians who had adopted and were influenced by a combination of their friends' experience, movement mobilization literature, and Christian adoption blogs. Yet despite the fact that her interest in adoption (as well as that of her co-author, Amanda Bennett) began with infertility, Brinton seems to forget this and credits her Christian friend, the book *Adopted for Life* (whose author also adopted because of infertility), and Christian adoption blogs with being the key influences in motivating "thousands of Christian families" to start caring for orphans.

The process described in figure 4.4 helps explain why there are not more evangelical families adopting or fostering now than they have in the past. Put simply, *the same Christians who are adopting today are generally the same Christians who were adopting thirty years ago*—that is, they are people who want more children than they can have through natural means—*but now they are articulating their choices in more distinctively evangelical ways, in large part because of the orphan care movement.* Neither the movement elites, nor the movement critics like Kathryn Joyce, seem to recognize that for many, if not most, evangelical families (even for most of the key leaders and authors in the movement!) the causal direction between movement ideology and movement activism is reversed. As Ziad Munson argues, activism (adopting or fostering because of personal reasons) precedes the ideology. This is particularly hard for many evangelicals to understand or believe because, as we have seen previously, pietistic idealism supposes that right ideas (motivations to glorify God and share the gospel) should precede right actions for those actions to be morally appropriate. Indeed, it is primarily because of this cultural expectation that many evangelical families obscure their true motives for pursuing adoption in the first place, giving the impression that they adopted *because* of their core evangelical commitments, rather than those commitments coming *after* their initial pursuit of adoption.

How this Confusion Undermines Evangelical Effectiveness at Social Engagement

Let me summarize briefly what I repeatedly observed in my interviews with evangelical adoptive families, both among grassroots families and leaders. Evangelicals who have adopted within the last ten years or so often present their adoption pursuits and experience in similar, almost scripted language, using terminology like "calling," "obedience," "adoption and the gospel," "orphans," and emphasizing their pursuit of God's will and glory. By contrast, they often downplay the self-interested or practical aspects of their adoptions. Yet, for the majority of evangelical adoptive or foster-to-adopt families I interviewed, as well as for a majority of movement leaders directly involved in adoption, their interest in adoption was preceded by some sort of struggle with infertility or sub-fecundity. Moreover, their choices throughout the adoption process (the type of adoption, the location, the child's characteristics and background) were greatly influenced by practical and self-interested concerns. None of those desires or concerns were abnormal for prospective adoptive parents to have, per se. Rather, they were consistent with what research finds among most prospective adoptive parents.[30]

My initial question was: Why is there a discrepancy between evangelicals' initial, surface accounts of their adoption journey and their actual story? I have argued that over the last decade the evangelical orphan care movement has not successfully been able to generate *new* motives to mobilize American Christians to adopt or foster more. Rather, they have been successful at disseminating certain vocabularies of motive among American evangelicals such that those who pursue adoption or fostering now feel compelled to provide these cultural scripts to justify their actions to their community and to outsiders.

This pattern limits evangelical effectiveness at social engagement in two key ways. First, it feeds into the confirmation bias discussed earlier. When evangelical families and leaders are *collectively* describing their pursuit of adoption as almost entirely about the gospel or God's heart for the orphan while minimizing the fact that they initially became interested in adoption because of infertility, it gives the impression to journalists, movement leaders, other evangelical families, and other Americans that movement efforts have been more successful than they really are. People are incredulous when the data suggest that evangelical families are *not* adopting more than they have in the past because within the last ten or so years it seems like most evangelical adoptive families are describing *new* motives for adopting, even when they initially became interested in adoption for the same reasons most other people do. This is not to say that these evangelical families are not genuinely motived at some level by a sense of God's calling and that what they are doing advances the gospel. But my point is that the pattern observed allows the movement (and its critics) to rest assured that its mobilization tactics are far more effective than they really are.

Second, the *inconsistency* between evangelicals' adoption accounts and actual experiences reveals something that evangelicals fundamentally misunderstand about how people are motivated to make drastic changes and the extent to which evangelicals are culturally locked into ineffective strategies. As I have shown in previous chapters, evangelicals are institutionally bound to preaching, teaching, and personal influence as the primary vehicle for social change. The firm conviction is that faithful gospel preaching (in sermons and conversations) will effectively call Christians to action by influencing them to embrace new beliefs and values and essentially want different things. However, research suggests that the thought processes that govern our motivations and values are not easily changed because they are based on years of primary socialization, ingrained habits, and—frankly—self-interest.

Getting average evangelical churchgoers to drastically change their desires in order to encourage sacrificial commitments (e.g., adopting children with special needs when a person already has plenty of biological children) will seldom be accomplished by pastors telling them that Christians should look after orphans or showing them statistics about children in need. *Some* may respond to such appeals (I will talk about who these people are in a moment), but average evangelical churchgoers are fairly adept at excusing their own lack of response to weekly sermons. Rather, what *is* more easily changed through preaching, teaching, and personal influence are the community-approved vocabularies of motive that people learn to justify their actions to others.[31]

At the risk of sounding like I am contradicting myself, I do not want to give the impression that *every* evangelical adoptive or fostering family I encountered had adopted because of fertility or fecundity issues. Most did, but some did not. In fact, some seemed to fit the media stereotype of a committed evangelical family that already had plenty of biological children and sought to adopt or foster because of their commitment to living out pro-life values, the Great Commission, James 1:27, and so on. These families almost always had several characteristics in common:

They were almost always pastors or elders in their respective churches. In other words, they were not average American pew sitters; none were on the periphery of their local religious community but were instead at the core. And as such, they also had compelling social reasons to adopt, particularly the fact that they served as representatives to their congregation of what a Christian family is supposed to look like. Related to this, they virtually always had adoption or fostering in their close friendship networks, sometimes in their own family growing up. They were seldom the first person they knew to adopt or foster children but were doing so within a community of equally committed believers. This is quite consistent with what we know about sacrificial forms of activism. Research shows that the strongest predictor of whether someone engages in activist activities with a high risk or cost is not ideological commitment but whether someone has a close friend who is also doing it.[32]

All of these factors are also consistent with what we know about motivation and social action. These families—again, representing a minority of evangelical adoptive families in my experience—displayed a combination of deeply held religious convictions and identity (truthfully beyond what the vast majority of evangelical Christians demonstrate), high social status within a Christian community, previous (positive) experience with adoption or fostering, and a network of other close friends or family who were adopting or fostering. These influences collectively seemed to stimulate these families to sacrificial (even radical) forms of adoption or foster care, taking on multiple special needs children, often at tremendous cost. In the following chapter, I show how certain aspects of the evangelical subculture limit the support given to these families, thereby undermining movement effectiveness in other fundamental ways.

5

Costs Not Counted

In previous chapters, I have shown how evangelical social engagement is shaped by the dominant cultural schemas of pietistic idealism as well as that of individualism and its corollary, anti-structuralism. American evangelicals largely view individual heart transformation as both the source of activism and the ultimate result. Consequently, they tend to be suspicious of activist strategies that primarily target social structures, public policies, or whole organizations rather than individuals, since these strategies do not directly address one's eternal relationship with God. A closely related aspect of evangelical culture is what some have called "populism."[1] The term is often used in a political sense—a populist presidential candidate, for example, may generate a swell of grassroots voter support by being anti-elite and anti–status quo while appealing to common fears. In reference to American evangelicals, however, scholars also believe they exhibit highly populist tendencies. They tend to be suspicious of secular elites and intellectuals (especially within the secular academy), but they are also heavily influenced by social media, lower forms of culture (popular TV, movies, radio, books, blogs), and appeals to sentimentality rather than theologically sophisticated argumentation.[2]

On the one hand, the combination of evangelical populist tendencies with their adherence to pietistic idealism and individualism/anti-structuralism has potential advantages for inspiring collective action, particularly regarding the task of mobilization. Evangelicals feel compelled to take action as individuals, and evangelical leaders have great potential to provoke masses of evangelicals to quickly take action on particular social issues by appealing to their sentimentality through sermons, conferences, seminars, books, radio, and television.[3] Indeed, these seem to be the very strategies advocated and employed by elites in the orphan care movement.

On the other hand, these potential advantages can be overshadowed by their acute collective drawbacks. First, consider the evangelical suspicion of fostering social transformation by engaging social structure rather than individual hearts.[4] Evangelical elites in the orphan care movement, for example, repeatedly stressed that believers seeking to mobilize their church toward adoption and foster care should not establish another structure or "ministry." Rather, they should create a "culture" in their congregation in which each believer recognizes the connection between the gospel and serving orphans. Moreover, these leaders were clear that Christian families and the local church were responsible for looking after orphans, not the government. The potentially negative consequence of this anti-structuralism is that (1) humans can be fickle and individual motivation may not last long, and (2) not everyone in the congregation may buy into the culture of adoption or orphan care, perhaps only a handful of the most committed believers or those who were already interested.

Second, the populist tendency of evangelicals may lead them to dive into social activism without being educated about the problems they seek to address, the communities they are trying to help, or the long-term consequences of their action for themselves or for others.[5] For example, the sociologist Elizabeth Bernstein has conducted extensive research on evangelicals' involvement in global anti-trafficking efforts over the past decade. She describes how evangelicals, and other secular individuals who partner with them, often set about "rescuing" women out of trafficking situations without considering whether there are better alternatives for those women or whether they even want to be rescued from what is often their own voluntary prostitution. Bernstein also points out how the proposed solution for such evangelicals, like those in the orphan care movement, is *individual* acts of rescue rather than dismantling structures that contribute to the demand for trafficking and prostitution (e.g., poverty and corruption).[6]

In this chapter, I show how pietistic idealism, individualism/anti-structuralism, and populism combine to inhibit the sustainability of evangelical social engagement. First, together these three factors can persuade committed evangelical couples that God demands life decisions (even potentially very costly ones) be done in faith over and above practical concerns. Second, these factors supply congregational leaders with convenient excuses for withdrawing support for particular social causes when they are deemed by leaders to be distracting from the church's primary mission—namely, glorifying God through evangelism and discipleship. In other words, some evangelical families face a situation in which they take radical and risky steps of faith to adopt or foster children with special needs or from otherwise difficult backgrounds only to be forgotten by the very community that encouraged those steps in the first place. Such was the case for a number of evangelical activist adopters and foster parents in my study. This resulted in their own family stress and brokenness and, for an unfortunate few, the removal of their adopted or foster children. The consequences of the ephemeral, populist nature of evangelical activism can thus be devastating both for the activists themselves and the individuals or communities they seek to serve.

The Reluctance of Churches to Accommodate Adopting or Fostering Families

Although most of the evangelical couples I spoke with started their adoption journey with fertility or fecundity issues, this was not the case for all. Carolyn and Kiel Twietmeyer are by all accounts an activistic adoptive family.[7] Kiel came into the marriage with four children from a divorce, and Carolyn and Kiel gave birth to three more as a couple. But even with seven children already in their home, Carolyn had felt called to care for orphans from a very young age as she recounted seeing images of hungry children in Africa on TV and knowing that she would one day adopt such children. Through a series of circumstances, they ended up adopting numerous orphans from Africa, a number of whom are HIV positive. Later, they would also adopt children both domestically and internationally with Down syndrome. After their adoption of children with HIV/AIDS, Carolyn founded a nonprofit called Project Hopeful that serves to educate families who have adopted children with HIV/AIDS and to help them care for these children and prevent the stigma that can follow from the disease.

When I came to their home in Joliet, Illinois, to interview them, they were taking a family photo that included all eight of their adopted children, along with some of their spouses or significant others. Most of these children were still living under the Twietmeyer's roof. Every room in the house (including some larger closets) were turned into bedrooms.

I was amazed to hear the Twietmeyer's story, which had been covered in a *People* magazine article, the *Today Show*, *CBS Evening News*, other news outlets.

As the interview progressed, I was curious to hear about what sort of financial and social resources they might have received to raise their now-enormous family. They explained that they had a very tight-knit adoption community and that they were also founding members of a small community church in their area. They also drew heavily on informational resources provided by CAFO. As they described the support they received from their small community church, they compared it favorably with their earlier megachurch home. I asked them to elaborate, and they explained,

CAROLYN: We went to a megachurch when everything hit with major media and stuff like that. We were at a church that was not supportive of us—they were supportive in the way of advertising as *their* family but never . . .

KIEL: They did a whole big thing about us. Like a big video and showed it all over the place.

CAROLYN: "The [church's name] very own Twietmeyer family." Like, they did all this crazy stuff really kind of exploiting what was going on with us, but never would allow us to speak about our ministry. We never, ever one time were able to speak about our ministry, when we were doing any kind of anything to raise funds to go get the kids. They were totally like, "No way, no thanks." They were like, "Good job, you guys. You go right ahead." . . . It got really kind of—yeah, what you're doing is really awesome, really cool, but . . .

KIEL: To be honest, a lot of the negative aspects that we've encountered in adoption, not so much, a little bit for ourselves, but just in the broad spectrum of everybody, all the stories, a whole lot of negative comes out of the church.

CAROLYN: Most of it comes out of the church.

The Twietmeyers felt that the large church they attended was happy to endorse their adoption from up front because it brought visibility to the church itself and symbolized that the church was involved in ministries of orphan care and mercy. But the church leadership had not necessarily bought into the vision of orphan care to the point where they would allow the Twietmeyers to raise money for their adoptions. Later in the interview, the Twietmeyers recounted how they felt abandoned and misunderstood by their church when they brought the children back from Africa. When I asked them what they meant by "most of [the negativity in adoption] comes out of the church," they explained:

> KIEL: Okay. So, people that get worked up about HIV? It's constantly coming out of the church.
> CAROLYN: Oh yeah. When I get calls . . .
> KIEL: "Oh, well, my kid's not going to Sunday School if your kid's there."
> CAROLYN: Or families being asked to not let their children into child care or Sunday School. Or having teenagers not be allowed to volunteer in the nursery because they find out the children have HIV. Crazy stuff like that.
> KIEL: The HIV stuff, that's absolute far and away number one. Negative.

Initially, the Twietmeyers interpreted these misunderstandings as ignorance on the part of families and staff at their megachurch. But over time, as they have become more connected with other parents of adopted children with similar health and ability challenges, they have heard similar stories among many of their close friends. These stories lead them to worry about whether evangelical congregations really are willing to support the families engaged in adoption and orphan care. Carolyn explained:

> [I see] a lot of lack of care for kids with special needs in general, in the church. I get a pretty good U.S. perspective because we have so many families all over the place. Thank God it's not my case because my little screaming Isaac can go in Sunday School any day. They'll take him. They don't care what he does, they're going to love him, anyway. But that's sadly not the case in most churches. So families that are adopting children with Down syndrome and multiples of kids with Down syndrome are most often shunned in a lot of ways. Mothers often can't go to church anymore, they got to stay home with their kids because there's no service available, nothing to help with kids with special needs. I see that a lot of the kids

with autism and fetal alcohol syndrome and behavioral type issues, the church is like "No thanks. It's your problem." And that's a very common heartbreak, and I see people leaving a lot of churches and church shopping as a result of that, which is so sad. Yeah, it's really sad, and I think it's cut a lot of . . . you know, when you bring your kids home, whether they have special needs or not, they all have special needs. You're bringing home kids from hard, hurt places, and the initial period of that bonding you need, and not let them go in children's church or whatever, you need to bond with your kid, then you have some churches saying, "Well, you know, they all can't be in service, they have to be . . ." You know, just all these crazy rules and stuff that can't apply necessarily to the new, modern family, which is people like us bringing these kids here. *The church, in a lot of ways, has not evolved. It's good for orphan care if we send missionaries and send people out, and we'll send them money, but the game changes when they come to us. So there's a lot of needs not being met because it's not evolving to meet specific needs*, you know what I mean? (emphasis added)

With clear frustration, Carolyn recounts the experiences of other adoptive parents of special needs children and concludes that the evangelical church in general is not "evolving" to accommodate the families who are adopting children with specific needs like HIV/AIDS, Down syndrome, autism, fetal alcohol syndrome, and so on. She points to the inconsistency that congregations are enthusiastic about sending missionaries to take care of orphans, and they will even send them money, but the church is not prepared to serve orphans when they are brought home.

These concerns have been echoed by leaders in the orphan care movement, particularly those who work in the realms of counseling. Jon Bergeron is a clinical psychologist who serves as director of family care for Hope for Orphans. While Jon is optimistic about the ability of the local church to address the needs of adoptive families eventually, he acknowledges that

one of the challenges I've heard from a lot of families is they're dealing with some kids that have pretty significant behavior issues, and a lot of churches weren't ready, and some aren't willing, to deal with those. And so you get parents that end up not going to church because they can't bring their kid. Their kid's getting kicked out of Sunday School and they're told well, sorry, we just can't . . . there's no place for your child here. Which is hugely discouraging. . . . And so I think a lot of churches can do a better job of developing special needs ministries, really, [which] is what they need within their children's program that can handle behavior problems. Because these kids aren't suddenly going to just start acting right because they're in a Christian home for a couple of months. There's a lot of growth and healing that has to happen. And they need a holding environment during that process. And churches, in general, have not done a great job of making a place for difficult-to-manage kids. So, I think that's a huge piece that the Church needs to really do a better job of.

The stories that the Twietmeyers recount of churches being support-ive and excited on the front end of adoption but unwilling or unpre-pared to accommodate their adopted children on the back end were shared by other evangelical families I interviewed. A particularly striking set of stories came from eight families who were all members of the same church in North Texas, Living Hope Church.[8] Living Hope is a large, rapidly growing church populated primarily by young families and col-lege students. The church has its roots in the Southern Baptist Conven-tion, but, like many such churches, they are no longer up front about their connection. The church is led by a relatively young pastor who is one of the rising stars in the New Calvinist tradition of evangelicalism characteristic of churches affiliated with organizations like The Gospel Coalition or the Acts 29 Network. Recently, the church grew so large that it branched off into four or five satellite campuses, each with its own campus pastor, but the sermons for the main services on the weekends are almost always from the lead pastor and streamed live or played on video at the satellite campuses.

Of the eight families I interviewed at Living Hope, some were on church staff or lay leaders. One family used to attend and serve as lay leadership but had since moved away. The eight families were evenly split in terms of having adopted or fostered-to-adopt for fertility rea-sons or primarily ideological reasons. I asked each of the eight adoptive couples to talk about the support they received from their church and the state of their adoption and foster care ministry there.

As the number of adoptive families at Living Hope grew, a group of lay leaders decided to form a ministry that would serve a dual purpose as a source of social support to adoptive and fostering families and also provide resources from other evangelical nonprofit ministries on how to parent adopted children, particularly those with special needs. The families I interviewed were all enthusiastic about this ministry, but they felt that it did not receive official support from the church. One couple explained,

> MOTHER: We didn't really have a lot of resources with [the ministry] because the [founding family] just kept hitting a brick wall with the church staff. We just could never really get it off the ground very far. I mean, we have a network of people.
>
> FATHER: Which is really what we wanted in the first place.
>
> MOTHER: Which is what we wanted, but . . .
>
> FATHER: We just don't have the monetary or space resources that we would like to get from the church.
>
> MOTHER: The church doesn't, like, tell people about us. The only way you would even know about it is if you meet somebody who already knows about it. . . . Any time we ever had an announcement, they always messed it up, every time.

I asked another adoptive mother at Living Hope to explain what was lacking from the church leadership, and she recounted that

> MOTHER: The church had, as a body, had not been supportive of this foster adoption ministry and . . .
>
> SP: What do you mean, not been supportive?
>
> MOTHER: The ministry would meet [on the church grounds] and maybe someone would forget to unlock the door, like it was not prioritized, that kind of thing. Or they would ask to do something for like Orphan Sunday, and that's not really in the plan, you know what I mean? There were other smaller ministries that could do anything they wanted, but this one was like, we don't really need this, and so they kind of pushed through and fought for space and time.

Eventually, the lay leaders who founded the adoption and foster care ministry at Living Hope were going to be transplanted because of the father's job. The church leadership apparently saw this as an opportunity for them to shut down the ministry, meaning they were no longer going to provide any pastoral oversight or direct any resources toward the group. The adoption and foster care ministry would also not be permitted to use the church building for meeting space. The lay leader families involved were discouraged by this decision because they felt that they had been marginalized and cast aside. The last mother mentioned above said,

> MOTHER: You know, as a church you're not going to support the [adoption and foster care] ministry, so instead of finding somebody else to take over, just kill the ministry, and I was actually in another planning meeting because, at the time, I was a co-leader for an infertility and pregnancy loss support group . . . and the group's pastor over these little sub-ministries said, hey, you know, the [adoption and foster care] ministry, we're going to be killing that.
>
> SP: Did they use that word? Did they say kill it? They said, We're going to kill [the ministry]?
>
> MOTHER: Yeah, we're going to kill [the ministry], unless anybody here has any different kind of idea how we can keep it alive, we're going to go ahead and kill it.

One lay leader explained that a number of the families continued to meet together to support one another, but without the church's formal support, it became more of a "mothers' coffee time," and the fathers were no longer involved.

I asked the adoptive parents who were also church staff about their decision to shut down the adoption and foster care ministry at Living Hope. Their responses were telling. I asked one staff member if removing the ministry had left a vacuum for those families, and he replied: "Yeah I think so. The main difficulty we had, and part of it was just from a structures perspective. We didn't know kind of where to put it, and so it got moved from a groups ministry, to under the recovery umbrella, to kind of a stand-alone kind of thing. It was just basically an oversight issue. So who is overseeing all of this, and I think partly that kind of burned [out] the leaders, so I definitely will say that we [the church staff] have got to own that part."

This staff member recounted how the families involved in the ministry felt shuffled around and were unable to maintain large enough numbers to justify meeting space and that the church leadership ultimately decided to make it an "organic thing" rather than something that the church staff were responsible for. He also explained how the church leadership was really emphasizing "home groups" at the time as the proper place for discipleship and social support, so they ultimately wanted to see the support for these adoptive and fostering families coming from their own home groups rather than a separate "siloed" group. So it became easier to justify getting rid of the ministry. Nevertheless, this staff member concluded,

> But I do think, man, [the adoptive families] suffered a little bit just from being shuffled around, not being able to really pinpoint what . . . if it was something like Tapestry (a large adoption support ministry at another megachurch in the metroplex) or something like that where it was just kind of a machine where they had a large group of people that were involved and participating on a regular basis, maybe things wouldn't have ended up the way they did, but I think just because of philosophy and ministry, the way we were driving things to home groups at such a high pace, that it just kind of went about the wayside.

This last point clarifies how an adjustment in church philosophy or structure—or simply a lack of sufficiently high numbers of participants—can quickly dissolve support ministries for adoptive and fostering families, leaving them to feel like they are fending for themselves or are otherwise unsupported by the congregation. Another staff member in the church who is also an adoptive father reiterated the point about emphasizing home groups over specialty ministries like the orphan care ministry:

> There was [a foster and adoption ministry], and slowly but surely, along with other sort of specialized ministries—I don't know how better I could put it—ministry-specific groups of people, went away. At least formally, where there's a staff person overseeing it or something like that, so there are organic groups that still meet, and we encourage that, and there's even venues online otherwise for that to happen. But you know, like women's Bible study, men's Bible study, so these specialized groups, not just for adoption, foster care, but that one as well, we sort of said, Hey, as a staff,

we don't have the bandwidth to oversee these and to sort of keep these going in the ways that we have historically. We'd love to support you and encourage you, but in terms of us really giving ourselves to it, we're really going to put most of our eggs in home group basket and strengthening home group, because it felt like we were spread so thin with all these specialized ministries, that we were not . . . there was no clarity. We weren't doing anything well, you know?

These two staff leaders at Living Hope illustrate how evangelical congregations—even ones with staff who are adoptive or foster parents and are sympathetic to the needs of such families—think through supporting adoptive and fostering families. Foster care and adoption are no longer structured into the functions and activities of the church in the forms of formal ministries, but churches encourage such support to emerge organically as families seek it out and interact with one another.

As is evident by the responses of lay leaders above, Living Hope's decision regarding the orphan care ministry was discouraging for families because they felt unsupported and that the church had other pet ministries that it would rather focus its resources toward. The stories recounted by the Twietmeyers and the families at Living Hope are illustrative of a common theme among evangelical adoptive parents in my study, specifically, that churches, even those that ostensibly support orphan care in principle and have adoptive parents on staff, are seldom interested in completely changing the way they organize church structure or activities for the sake of adoption and foster care. Having a "culture of adoption/orphan care" is no guarantee that the church will provide financial resources or staff oversight specifically for adoption or foster care. Rather, because evangelical congregations see decisions to adopt or foster as individual decisions, which individual believers are ultimately responsible for, they conclude that the responsibility of finding financial and social support for adoptive or fostering families lies with the families themselves. This should not necessarily be provided by the church itself but should emerge "organically," as families seek out these resources on their own.

Here we see how the combination of evangelical populist tendencies with pietistic idealism and individualism result in a situation that backfires for the orphan care movement. Owing to the populist tendencies of evangelicals, *some* committed evangelical families will be inspired through captivating sermons, videos, and Orphan Sunday events (always in combination with other personal factors) to welcome hurting and special needs children into their home through adoption and fostering. These families need all manner of support. Yet it is often the case that the very congregations that encouraged their sacrificial activism—because of their own commitment to pietistic idealism (the Church's primary focus is evangelism and spiritual discipleship) and individualism (families are units that are primarily responsible for themselves)—are unwilling to restructure to accommodate these adoptive and fostering families. Stemming from situations like these, a considerable number of evangelical families are struggling mightily with their decisions to adopt or foster.

Evangelical Populism and Its Consequences for Families in the Orphan Care Movement

Regardless of their motives in deciding to adopt or foster—whether it was primarily out of desire for family growth or because of divine calling, or some of both—more and more families are having to adopt children with special needs internationally or domestically from foster care. With this trend comes tremendous challenges. Special needs children may require medical attention, but perhaps even more difficult are those special needs cases that affect day-to-day behavior and interpersonal interactions, like Down syndrome, fetal alcohol syndrome, autism, or the reactive attachment disorder that comes as a consequence of emotional trauma. Adoptive families with children who are affected by these issues are often unprepared to deal with them and need special help. Tom Davis, adoptive father and author of *Fields of the Fatherless*, expressed his frustration with the unfortunate consequences of evangelical populist tendencies related to orphan care and adoption:

> American [evangelicals] have big hearts. They want to help. I think that
> our problem is that we want a quick fix. . . . You know the classic example,
> even for adoption, are people who think that they're going to take this
> kid who has lived in an orphanage all their life, whose never learned to
> bond, and they're just going to adopt them at ten, eleven, twelve years

old, and they're going to come into their family, and this kid is going to be so happy because they're loving them. They're going to thank them the rest of their life. You know, here's this kid who's never had anything. And they show up with this beautiful room, with tons of stuffed animals, and an Xbox video game system. And this kid is like completely freaked out. They've never had *anything*. The person never thought anything about how do you transition them into a family. How do you help address the issues? And then they wonder why three, four, five months down the road, they've stolen everything from them, and all of their friends, and they're fighting. And they're saying they want to kill the mother. I mean, if they would have stopped and done the research and talked to the experts and found out what they could do to help, you know, create healing. But we don't do that. We're just very much, bam, we want to see something happen, we want to see it happen fast, we want to change it fast.

Even more alarming—and potentially dangerous—than the "quick fix" tendency of American evangelicalism Tom Davis describes are situations in which families are tempted to adopt children as a new evangelical status symbol. While I did not personally interact with grassroots families whom I perceived to have adopted for status-seeking reasons, leaders in the orphan care movement pointed out that this happens enough to be cause for concern. Paul and Robin Pennington, both pioneers in the orphan care movement, described how it had suddenly become fashionable to adopt a black (African or African American) child among evangelical couples, to the point where there was often a waiting list for such children. When I asked them why this might be the case, they explained:

ROBIN: I'm afraid it might be . . . I think it might be that the black child signifies to your world out there that you've adopted and it draws attention to your family as . . .

PAUL: This new phrase Robin read to me today from an article is "missional narcissism." That when it becomes kind of a semi-Munchausen, or there's always something new and cool in the church. You know, when we were younger, it was making bread, wearing jumpers, homeschooling. Things like that.

ROBIN: Yeah, kind of a litmus test for how serious you were at that time, how well you were disciplining your children and how you are schooling your children. Are they in a Christian school? But I'm afraid that adoption has become that new litmus test for Christians and especially, you know, in the twenty- and thirty-year-old range. I was speaking at a conference, and one of the men told me he had a new baby, and he was holding the baby and I said, "Is your baby adopted?" and he goes, "No, no. But my wife, she's just dying to adopt." And I said, "Really? So like from what country?" And he goes, "Oh, I don't know what country, but she just keeps saying 'I can see on our Christmas card a black child right there—right there with us.'" And that is concerning because they [adoptive children] are not a project. I mean, it's a life, and they become you and you become them, and so if whatever their culture is, that becomes part of your family and your identity as a family. But it's so much deeper than a Christmas card, and I think that we've seen a whole lot of that now where it's—I mean, I had someone tell me a couple of weeks ago one of the couples in their missional group hasn't adopted yet and they have all kinds of reasons for not adopting, but she says, "But I feel bad because they're the only ones that haven't adopted yet." And I'm going "No. No." [laughs] And that's probably one of our biggest concerns at this point, especially because we help families post-placement, where you see all the issues and all the husbands were dragged into it and all the well-meaning adoptions that hadn't really been well thought through.

Several times throughout our conversation, Paul and Robin reiterated their concern that adoption had become a new status symbol for Christians. Paul repeated that "some Christians want to use [adopted children] as trophy kids to elevate their spirituality." In trying to explain this phenomenon, Paul pointed to messages coming from well-meaning megachurch pastors who happen to be vocal advocates for orphan care. The implicit message is that Christians, if they really love God, should take on the hardest possible children in adoption and foster care:

PAUL: We've done stuff with Francis Chan. We helped launch foster care ministry in David Platt's church, and so we love those guys. I mean, there's some great things, but Francis and David are kind of preaching this new message that if you're going to be really serious about

Christianity, you give it up—you take the hardest child. You know, it's that extreme missional thing, and if you're not doing that, you're kind of a loser, you know? Well, it's kind of like the A-Team and then the B-Team, and if you're out adopting and getting the really hard kids and you're traveling then you're on the A-Team. And if you're just helping orphans, or you're helping support the families who are adopting, or you're helping financially for other families, I mean, that's a good thing, but it's kind of B-Team.

ROBIN: And that's really how it's seen, and that's got to end. That's got to end.

As others have pointed out, these sorts of situations, as described by Tom Davis and Robin Pennington, have led to adoption "disruptions" (when the adopted child is returned to the agency) or even illegal "re-homing" (when an adoptive family unofficially places their adopted child with another family), potentially causing even more trauma for such children.[9] In other situations, marriages and sibling relationships are severely harmed. Carolyn Twietmeyer concluded her interview on a positive note by acknowledging that "there's a couple of ministries starting to fire up to help enable churches to better care for kids with special needs and adoption considerations." Such ministries have emerged within the last ten years to start addressing the needs of Christian families in these situations.

The most well known ministry that provides resources for (Christian) parents with special needs children is Empowered To Connect and its associated church ministry, Tapestry of Irving Bible Church (IBC), an evangelical megachurch in Irving, Texas. Tapestry is led by Michael and Amy Monroe, who are adoptive parents of four children from Guatemala. Michael is a successful lawyer. Amy stays at home with their school-aged children while also taking on much responsibility with Tapestry and Empowered To Connect. Tapestry was started in another church in the Dallas–Fort Worth area, where Monroes attended at the time. Tapestry was basically a small support group for adoptive families in that church that had little momentum until the Monroes took over in the early 2000s. Eventually, the Monroes left their other church and took Tapestry with them. It is now a thriving sub-ministry of IBC that provides resources to families with adopted or foster children, regardless of whether they are Christian. Though many of the resources are geared toward Christians, the Monroes see the ministry of Tapestry as seeking to help any adoptive and fostering families. It has gained a national reputation within the orphan care movement as an important resource, and Tapestry even holds a national conference each year in October in which adoptive and fostering families and social workers come to learn about helping children from difficult backgrounds. Empowered To Connect is a ministry that the Monroes helped to found, and it could be understood as the national wing of Tapestry. Empowered To Connect publishes and distributes certain books, workbooks, and resources written by the Monroes and an evangelical child psychologist, the late Dr. Karyn Purvis, at Texas Christian University. Empowered To Connect also holds regional conferences around the country, often housed in large megachurches.

In 2013, I was able to attend a Tapestry leadership meeting at the Monroes' home, a Tapestry national conference at IBC, and an Empowered To Connect conference in Houston, Texas, held at the enormous Second Baptist Church of Houston. I was also able to interview the Monroes (together once, and with Michael alone a second time) and Dr. Purvis (twice) about what they view as the challenges facing the evangelical orphan care movement and where they feel the answers lie.

Michael recounted how, in the early days of Tapestry, there was very little support within his own church. They had no budget and were seen as a "tack-on ministry" that ministered to a rather marginalized population of the congregation. He described his interaction with the church staff overseeing Tapestry: "We got a new staff person, and his interest could not have been less than it was. I mean, if there's disinterest, his was negative interest. I mean, it was just like 'I don't care. I will meet with you guys and just pacify you because I have to, because you're on my roster.'" It took them three years to get their first announcement made from up front at the church. The announcement was to recruit to Tapestry's first full-fledged conference, and the church was so lackadaisical about the ministry that they announced the conference one week before it was taking place. Eventually, Tapestry was placed under the oversight of another church staff person who had more vision for the ministry, and from there it took off. Even though Tapestry now has a ministry budget from IBC, Michael still doubts whether some leaders in the church really understand their ministry or why it is important. He still feels that he has to fight for influence within the church to educate and get the word out.

As an evangelical adoptive family, the Monroes love adoption and love serving adoptive and fostering families. Moreover, they remain committed to the idea that the local church is really the best solution confronting vulnerable children and adoptive/fostering families. However, because of the problems they have seen among Christian adoptive and fostering families, they hold a somewhat ambivalent (even critical) opinion of the orphan care movement, Michael especially. Michael's main criticisms of the movement are with reference to its populism, that is, what he perceived as its anti-intellectualism and its adherence to sentimentality and shallow theology based on easily digestible catchphrases.

For example, Michael explained that the movement was strong in its emphasis on theology but fairly weak on data and social science that might help inform the practices of organizations and practitioners:

> Within this movement there's a very strong intellectual theological element. But there's not been a very strong intellectual social science, and developmental psychology, there's been a real suspicion. There's a lot that's embedded in that, but what's unfortunate is that, somehow along the way, I believe, that the theological bent and this kind of practical bent have been pitted against each other, and they shouldn't [be]. I think they fit hand in glove, but we want to see more of these science, evidence-based tools brought in and integrated into what we understand, how we understand. God's created us to relate, and what he says in his word—we don't see them in competition. We don't see them in, you know, in friction with one another. We need more data in this movement. There's no data in this movement.

Michael here sees a populist trend in the orphan care movement that is suspicious of intellectualism and science and wants to keep the focus on the theological aspects of orphan care and adoption. Michael's role as someone serving struggling families or hurt children, however, inclines him to want as many evidence-based tools as possible to help. Michael recapitulates and reiterates the overemphasis on theology to the neglect of data:

Who's going to produce the data that we can actually learn about ourselves and improve? And then there seems to be like, "Why would we do that?" Well, why *wouldn't* we do that? You know, I mean we can mine the scriptures for adoption coded into Leviticus, or we can also look at some hard data, and I think both are important. And we're doing a good job as a movement on the theological side, I think. Maybe even *too* good a job—and that's probably controversial, but . . . too good because if it means to the exclusion of the other, right? It's got to be both/and. And so we feel like in a lot of ways the theological side's covered up [the data side].

Speaking to the theology of the movement, Michael was also critical of what he thought was "hypertheologizing" of adoption and orphan care:

Some of our theology surrounding this [movement] is just bad, you know? We talk about vertical adoption, as it's been talked about, and this idea that God—we obviously can't reach up to God, God reaches down to us. He rescues us out of our sin and brings us into relationship, and then somehow along the way—with, in my opinion, little scriptural justification—we make the pivot and we become God and we become the rescuers, and all of that language and all of that motive and all of the implications that flow out of that, we start talking in this rescue language. Well, you know, I'm comfortable with a lot of things, but making the pivot and becoming God is not one of them, and yet we've quickly done that.

To Michael's point, it is difficult to deny the prevalence of "rescue" language in the orphan care movement, especially earlier on. Russell Moore's cover story in the July 2010 issue of *Christianity Today* carried the subtitle, "Why Every Christian Is Called to Rescue Orphans."[10] And movement authors often draw explicit parallels between Christ's spiritual rescue of his children and the Christian's rescue of orphans in adoption. Dan Cruver writes, "Adoption and our care for the fatherless provide a visible demonstration of the gospel. Our adoption of children serves as a window into Christ's rescue of us."[11] And Johnny Carr states, "Often, we forget that we were once orphans. Jesus Christ endured the horrors of the cross to rescue us from an eternity in hell. How far are we willing to go to rescue orphaned children from a living hell?"[12]

While it can be true that some vulnerable children are in dire circumstances and, thus, placing them in a safe, loving family does constitute a rescue of sorts, Michael and others have pointed out that Christ's spiritual rescue and adoption of the elect and child adoption by Christian parents are inappropriate theological parallels to make. In Christian theology, Christ's death and resurrection rescues sinners from the consequences of *their own* sin and sinfulness. Analogizing Christ's salvific rescue with child adoption implies things about Christian parents (gracious, God-like), adoption (salvation, heaven), vulnerable children (wretched, deserving judgment), and often their own birth parents and native communities (sin, hell) that many are uncomfortable with. While movement leaders and organizations have (wisely) backed away from "rescue" language in recent years, interested Christians are still reading movement literature in which these terms and ideas are pervasive.

Michael also argues that the movement has been too focused on the stories and experiences of adoptive parents and is thus wrongly neglecting the voice of the adopted child. He explains,

> We've not invited the honest, unfiltered, uncensored, completely welcome on its own voice of the adult adopted person. We have spent so much time talking about our families to our families, about our kids to our kids, we've never let our kids have a voice in this whole thing. In response to this need, Tapestry has recently started to create intentional space to let the teen and the adult adopted person speak, tell their story, give their perspective. We run around talking about the word "orphan," or the rescue theme, and we never ask these kids what they think about that. Well, guess what, as we ask them, they've all got a lot of things to say.

Michael believes these oversights are another indication of the populist tendencies of the orphan care movement, focusing on sentimentality and highlighting feel-good rescue accounts in order to mobilize Christian families to adopt and foster. Because ministries like Tapestry and Empowered To Connect have had to deal with the consequences of uninformed adoption and fostering for both parents and their children, Michael feels the best corrective would be a larger focus on real-life experiences, data, best practices, and listening to adult adoptive children.

An associate of Michael Monroe, the late Dr. Karyn Purvis, was director of the Institute of Child Development at Texas Christian University until her death from cancer in April 2016. She was also the author of a popular book for adoptive or fostering families with children from what she describes as "hard places." Her 2007 book, *The Connected Child* (co-authored by David Cross and Wendy Lyons Sunshine) diagnoses problem behavior as a response to cognitive trauma and provides strategies to develop bonds of affection and trust, deal with behavioral disorders, and even discipline children without provoking more problem behavior or greater trauma.[13] The popularity of this book among adoptive parents was the primary catalyst for the Monroes founding the Empowered To Connect ministry, where Dr. Purvis served as the headliner. Purvis was also a devout evangelical Christian and, despite her social science education and vocation, her casual speech was always peppered with biblical and spiritual references. This manner of speaking, in combination with her charming Texas drawl, made her come across as delightfully folksy and disarming.

Dr. Purvis also had strong opinions about the orphan care movement. Like Michael Monroe, Dr. Purvis expressed concern over what she perceived as the shallow-but-popular theological reasoning of the movement that lacked nuance and scientific backing. In my conversation with her, she recounted her first experiences with the orphan care movement at an early CAFO Summit meeting in the mid-2000s. In these early days, the leaders of the movement were already starting to develop and articulate a theology of adoption that saw child adoption as a response to and visual representation of the gospel. She described her experience coming in as a keynote speaker at the CAFO Summit:

> It was traumatic and horrifying for me. What I saw made me sick, physically, and heart sick. The little children's African choir was there to sing and belt out about the children in Africa, and you could tell that they had been told they had to smile and sing it loudly, and I considered it abuse, what was being done to those children. They were smiling phony smiles and screaming at that top of their lungs as though they were joyful. It was so inauthentic that it repelled me, and then the children were required to come off the platform and go through the crowd, hugging necks. My God, the last thing in the world you want to do is teach a child who's an

orphan to be indiscriminate and touch strangers, and I went to the leadership of that movement—those that I could get to, I couldn't get access to
the high level of leadership, but I went to those who I could access, and I
said, I want you to know that I have been here three days and three nights
and I believe that what you're doing here is immoral and unethical and
ungodly. What I believe you're doing is an abomination. That if you say,
"If you love Jesus, you adopt," you violate everything that I understand
about a sovereign God—and you're calling people out, telling them if they
love Jesus, they've got to adopt.

In our conversation, Dr. Purvis qualified that Christians are indeed
called to look after vulnerable children, but she specified that this did
not necessarily mean adoption, and she recounted the tragic consequences of this misunderstanding for some families in the movement:

It is our DNA as believers to minister to and to nurture and to protect and
to care for the vulnerable, but that does not mean I adopt. That does not
mean I'm prepared to adopt. It does not mean I'm called to adopt. There
are ten thousand ways that you can identify in a heartbeat that people
can serve and can express this part of their Christian DNA, but you can
never say that everybody who loves Jesus should adopt, that if you love
Jesus, it's proved by the fact that you adopt and they called out the church
at that time to adopt.

Dr. Purvis later recounted what happened to a number of Christian
leaders' families, which she seemed to feel was a result of undue and
uninformed pressure in Christian circles to adopt children from difficult
backgrounds:

And then the following year, many leaders in the Christian movement
crashed and burned. Their little children were sexually molested by foster
kids if [the parents] weren't prepared to help heal [foster kids]. Foster kids
in their homes were going psychotic because they didn't understand the
needs or the fear, and parents were using discipline, spanking and other
harsh punitive measures with children who had been beaten and sodom-
ized and harmed in unspeakable ways, and they wondered why the kids
went psychotic.

As I concluded our interview, I asked Dr. Purvis whether she felt that the evangelical fervor and enthusiasm about adoption and fostering would ultimately fizzle out and end up being a fad that took off quickly and is never heard from again. She answered:

> The less success our families have, the more sour this thing goes, which is why I advocated so unkindly the first time I went to one of those [CAFO Summit] meetings, you know? We've got myriads of families suffering alone, and myriads of little children knowing that they're unloved in these homes where women brought them as a mission and despise them now because they can't meet the need that the woman thought she needed filled. Yeah, I really do."

Dr. Purvis was not alone in that prediction. Paula Freeman is founder and former CEO of Hope's Promise, a Christian adoption and orphan care agency in Colorado. When I asked her about where the orphan care movement would end up, she replied,

> Oh, I love your question, Sam, I just don't know. . . . I do think adoption and orphan care [are] very clearly a piece of our Father's heart. I think, if churches come up short, and they can't fix the brokenness of the families around them, they may lose heart. . . . I think there will be a time where we'll see [adoption] portrayed differently than we do now. I don't know what that means. But I think where we are is pretty unsustainable."

Karyn Purvis and the Monroes have seen firsthand in their own ministries the consequences of evangelical families adopting or fostering children from difficult backgrounds—some because they almost feel required to—and floundering because those who encouraged them to do so did not equip them or properly support them through the process. These problems were repeatedly recounted by evangelical adoptive and fostering families in my interviews. I propose that these situations reflect the broader evangelical cultural commitment to individualistic activism (in that both activism and "family issues" are individual problems to be solved on one's own) and populism (in that the activism was often based on popular sentiment and lacked careful thought and nuance to prepare evangelical families for the challenges).

Why Evangelical Activism Is Difficult to Sustain

As we saw earlier, evangelical families adopt and foster children for a variety of reasons, often for a variety of reasons simultaneously. Although most of the evangelical families and leaders I interviewed initially became interested in adoption and foster care because of fertility or fecundity issues, not all of them did. A number already had biological children and, in combination with other important life circumstances, genuinely internalized the messages of the orphan care movement. They subsequently adopted or fostered other children, often ones from difficult circumstances and troubled backgrounds. Moreover, as I indicated in the previous chapter, a number of Christian families who initially adopted for self-interested, family-growth reasons eventually internalized the movement's message and would later adopt or foster more children as a form of obedience-activism.

Regardless of reason that evangelical families adopt and foster, such families often need variety of resources for support. Many of the families I interviewed, however, recounted that their congregations, which were initially supportive of adoption and fostering on the front end, were unwilling to accommodate these families and their practical needs. Foster and adoption ministries could be terminated at a moment's notice, and families would be encouraged to find resources and support networks "organically." At other times, families like the Twietmeyers, who had adopted children with Down syndrome or HIV/AIDS, would be made to feel unwelcome since few evangelical congregations are equipped (or even inclined) to deal with such children. Ironically, while the orphan care movement and CAFO explicitly believes that the solution to the orphan crisis is rooted in the "local church,"[14] it is the local church that depends on affinity groups to naturally emerge among its members, or on parachurch organizations, like Empowered To Connect, and ministries at other churches, like Tapestry, to serve their adoptive and fostering families.

This is why evangelical activism is difficult to sustain and why the problem lies within the evangelical subculture itself. Evangelical populist tendencies in combination with the evangelical commitments to pietistic idealism and individualism create the following situation: Some movement leaders and pastors want to stimulate action quickly. Using a variety of media, they draw catchy but tenuous theological connections between Christ's spiritual adoption of his children and every Christian's responsibility to rescue vulnerable children. Some individual Christian families, before they are well informed or emotionally prepared, may be provoked to rash action, perhaps adopting or fostering children from difficult circumstances. Evangelical congregations promote these sorts of things in theory. But because congregations are committed primarily to evangelism and spiritual discipleship over addressing practical concerns, and because family issues are the responsibility of individuals, these congregations may be unwilling to change the structure and activities of the church to accommodate those who adopt or foster, leaving families to struggle alone. This is why Paula Freeman, when I asked her what would ultimately become of the movement, said, "If churches come up short, and they can't fix the brokenness of the families around them, they may lose heart . . . I think where we are is pretty unsustainable."

But this situation eventually creates a mobilization problem as well. Evangelical families who may have otherwise been inclined to adopt or foster will hear the stories of those who feel burned by the church. They may fear that they will not be supported in their efforts, that they will suddenly be unwelcome, or that they will have to fend for themselves when it comes to finding resources or information. As many evangelical families have struggled through adoption and fostering alone, or at least with what they feel like is limited support from their congregations, it becomes less and less surprising that evangelical families would be disinclined to adopt or foster children *unless* they had to owing to fertility or fecundity issues.

Put simply, evangelical populism promotes rash action. Churches often embrace evangelical fads, show emotional videos, and encourage such rash action. Some evangelicals step up. Pietistic idealism and individualism at the organizational level guarantees most churches cannot or will not adjust for these families, who must then fend for themselves. In terms of long-term action on behalf of vulnerable children, this situation is unsustainable. Such flurries of rash activism are short-lived and may actually cause more harm than good for all parties—the families, their adopted/foster children, and the movement itself. Recent evangelical writers have drawn similar conclusions regarding Christian efforts to alleviate hunger and poverty in African nations.[15]

Partly in response to criticisms raised by the Monroes and Dr. Purvis, as well as those of Kathryn Joyce and other vocal critics of the movement, CAFO and the wider orphan care movement have been evolving rapidly within the last few years. New emphases are emerging, with new language being adopted by principal leaders. In the following chapter, I consider the consequences of this evolution for the movement and what it signifies about evangelical social engagement more broadly.

6

What Will a Mature Evangelical Movement Look Like?

American stuff comes and goes because we like to think that we can help Jesus, and we think that if we use business principles and use a strategic plan and fleshly driven things, there can be some results from that, but sustainability is only possible when it is genuinely spirit led and engineered. Do I think that CAFO and the American orphan ministry movement in America [will be sustained]? I think that depends on whether we want to take the steering wheel.
—Paul Pennington

The Ephesian philosopher Heraclitus is famous for having said, "Everything changes and nothing remains still . . . you cannot step twice into the same stream." This certainly applies to studying social groups. They are *always* changing. In truth, the orphan care movement I have been describing in these pages no longer exists. Religious and social movements live in a perpetual state of change, always evolving in response to various factors. The orphan care movement was evolving during the period I conducted my research from 2012 to 2016, and the movement I have described based on those interviews and observations will not be the same movement when readers finally hold this book in 2017 or later.

But the fact that religious groups and movements are always evolving does not mean they are entirely unpredictable. In fact, one of the oldest observations in the sociology of religion is that religious groups and movements tend to evolve in very similar patterns. In the first half of the nineteenth century, scholars of religion like Max Weber, Ernst Troeltsch, H. Richard Niebuhr, and subsequent others, developed the idea of the "sect-church continuum" or "process" to describe these common patterns of religious evolution.[1]

First, a religious sect emerges as an offshoot of an existing religious tradition, usually in protest against liberalizing trends in the parent religion and in the hopes of returning to the way religion was originally attended to be. Sects are often quite zealous and action oriented but disorganized and made up of poorly educated masses. There is also often great tension between religious sects and the state or other secular powers (think early Christianity as a Jewish sect under Roman rule). As sects attract participants and develop in their organization, they start to become what Niebuhr called a "denomination." A denomination is larger, more highly developed, and on better terms with secular authorities than a sect. It is often led by professional (i.e., trained, ordained, and paid) second-generation leadership, and it tends to attract more educated, sophisticated membership. It also tends to be more relaxed about maintaining doctrinal purity and is more tolerant of internal diversity compared to sects (think most Christian denominations in the United States). If a denomination continues to grow in a society, it may eventually become an established church, which can be viewed as a group that holds a religious monopoly on society and has essentially merged with state power. In such a situation, members are no longer converted into the religion but are born into it by virtue of their citizenship; apostasy becomes illegal (think the Catholic Church in the Holy Roman Empire, Puritanism in early New England colonies, or Islam in some contemporary Middle Eastern nations).[2]

So what these scholars observed is that religious groups and movements start off highly ideological, voluntary, disorganized, and in tension with secular society, but over time, they gradually become more pragmatic, professionalized, organized, and accommodating to society. This evolutionary process has both benefits and drawbacks. On the positive side, the religious group or movement grows in numbers, resources, organization, and even strategic effectiveness at accomplishing practical objectives. For example, research shows that modern megachurches are more effective at a number of practical tasks than smaller, upstart church plants. They can recruit (or train) better-quality communicators and strategists in their leadership, attract a more diverse membership, purchase (or even create) better educational curricula, and offer a wider array of social services both to members and the community.[3] The downside to this evolutionary process, however, is that, as religious groups or movements grow, diversify, professionalize, and accommodate, they inevitably lose something in terms of their religious zeal and doctrinal purity. The boundaries of group membership become lax (or virtually non-existent), and volunteerism starts to wane as the group becomes dependent on professional clergy and overrun with free riders.[4]

Another way to think about this progression so that we broaden the categories out to include religious organizations beyond congregations is to think of the evolution as a transition from a movement, to a ministry, to a machine, and eventually to a monument.[5] We could call this the "4M" model of group evolution. Like sects, movements start off disorganized, volunteer-driven, ideologically motivated, and zealous to take action on behalf a particular cause or religious priority (ostensibly one that others have been neglecting). As they recruit participants and grow in size, they develop in their organization and become ministries. They develop divisions of labor, hire professional leaders and staff, and perhaps even purchase buildings or equipment, which allows them to become more effective at confronting the religious or social issues they initially sought to address. Eventually they become so organized, professional, focused, and efficient at addressing those particular issues that they could be called "machines." By this point, the majority of those running the organizations are paid professionals, and, for groups targeting a particular social issue, the organizations could address their issues almost entirely without even holding to the original ideals of the groups' founders. The organizations truly run themselves. In the last stage, the groups, once passionately devoted to a set of ideologies, have now become monuments. Everyone working for the organizations is a professional, and most who are served by the organizations will not even remember *why* the groups were originally founded, only that they now exist solely to bring about some practical objectives.

There are countless examples of religious groups or movements in the United States that have followed this 4M pattern. Once devoutly religious movements, they have become monuments with little connection to the ideological roots of their founders. The most obvious examples would be the Ivy League universities like Yale, Brown, and Princeton or the YMCA or even the Salvation Army in some part of the country. But there are other examples in child placement circles such as Holt International and Gladney Center for Adoption, both of which were fervently evangelical in their founding but have since removed formal connections with Christianity.

In this chapter, I want to describe a tension that exists for the Christian Alliance for Orphans and the orphan care movement more broadly. All movements—not just some, but *all*—evolve and change over time. Some die off, but the ones that live on do so by changing in response to various internal and external pressures. The orphan care movement has already changed a good deal since its founding. Most of these changes have been natural, necessary, and I believe, for the better. But these changes have been *in spite of* dominant evangelical cultural schemas like pietistic idealism and individualism, rather than because of them. As I have explained above, the evolution of religious groups tends to follow a consistent pattern with groups growing and becoming more strategically effective while most often losing much of their original emphasis and commitment. For movement leaders, the cultural schema of pietistic idealism makes such an outcome unacceptable. Evolution for the sake of strategic effectiveness, while important, has never been their primary concern, and certainly never at the cost of compromising the founding ideals. Indeed, based on my observations, I expect that movement leaders would rather see CAFO and the movement cease its activities entirely rather than watch it develop into a "machine" or "monument" as I have described above. This is yet another instance, then, of how evangelical social engagement is self-limiting. We see that pietistic idealism is fundamentally conservative, oriented toward *preserving* rather than innovating or evolving, even when necessary to grow in strategic effectiveness.

The Evolution of CAFO and the Orphan Care Movement

In truth, much of CAFO's development already resembles the common patterns forecast in the sect-church process or the 4M model described above. This is certainly not to imply that the movement will inevitably become an empty monument. Rather, as orphan care organizations have grown and professionalized, they have diversified and lost some of their *overt* religious identity and expression. They have also become more accommodating to the secular state and child welfare system. There are at least four factors that have contributed to this evolution.

Increasing Size, Organization, and Scope of the Movement

The orphan care movement started off resembling a sect, or movement, as described above. Paul Pennington was convinced that the church had abdicated its responsibility to look after the orphan. The collective that grew from Paul's initial efforts was unapologetically driven by the commitment that vulnerable children should be adopted into Christian families where they can be physically rescued, but ultimately spiritually rescued, as they are adopted into Christ's family. It was rather disorganized and volunteer driven. It started to gather steam and attract the interest of more powerful movers and shakers within mainstream evangelicalism, and with their involvement came increased organization. The Christian Alliance for Orphans coalesced as an organization, and eventually the movement hired professional staff and a president, Jedd Medefind. Jedd was a trained leader who held influence in Washington, DC, but had been uninvolved in the movement at its inception.

The Christian Alliance for Orphans has also grown in the number of orphan care emphases it hopes to promote and facilitate. For example, while there were four categories of member organization until 2015 (advocacy, global orphan care, adoption, and foster care), by 2016 that number had grown to twenty-two (see fig. I.4 in the Introduction), ranging from adoption to camp programs to child sponsorships, and so on. Corresponding to CAFO's growth in numbers and variety of orphan care possibilities, their staff team has quickly grown over the years to provide oversight for the growing number of orphan care emphases CAFO wishes to promote (adoption, foster care, Orphan Sunday, global orphan care, church initiatives, etc.).

Last, CAFO has removed some of the overt emphasis on adopting or fostering explicitly to convert children. In an earlier chapter, I quoted from the CAFO website back in 2015, where member organizations who oversaw adoption placements had to agree that they would "place children only in Christian families" and that they would "affirm a commitment to evangelism and discipleship" as the ultimate end of orphan care activity. Those sorts of statements are no longer found on the website, most likely because the growth and visibility of CAFO requires the organization to more carefully nuance their public statements.

In all of these respects, CAFO has followed the typical pattern of a growing organization or movement—numerical growth, professionalization, increased organization, and diversification, while also softening their hard ideological edge, at least formally.

Criticisms Coming from Outside the Movement

Growth has not been the only factor contributing to change in the orphan care movement. The Christian Alliance for Orphans, and the movement more broadly, have had to respond to criticisms leveled against evangelical adoption and orphan care by critics outside of the movement, like the journalist Kathryn Joyce, law professor David Smolin, and others. Two watershed events in the orphan care movement that provoked change were the Haiti kidnapping scandal and the publication of Joyce's *The Child Catchers*. Following the devastating earthquake in Haiti in 2010 that killed over one hundred sixty thousand people and displaced almost two million, a team of Christian activists from Idaho were arrested by Haitian authorities trying to extract thirty-three children from the country, many of whom had families looking for them. While CAFO and the mainstream orphan care movement were not to blame for the illegal actions of the Idaho team, this event threw public scrutiny on evangelicals and adoption and thus provoked public statements from movement leaders like Jedd Medefind decrying adoption activism done illegally or in haste.[6]

This negative publicity was followed by other accusations from outside the movement, most prominently from David Smolin and Kathryn Joyce. A professing evangelical and adoptive parent himself, Smolin is a law professor at the Cumberland School of Law at Samford University in Birmingham, Alabama. Smolin's family was the victim of child trafficking (his adopted daughters had been stolen from their birth parents in India), and this experience incited him to research and write about the corrupt international adoption system. In his writings, he argued that the evangelical orphan care movement had misinterpreted scripture to promote adoption as the primary means through which God wants Christians to look after orphans. He pointed out that "orphans and widows" are almost always included together in scripture as a unit, and thus Christians would be more responsible to serve vulnerable single mothers and their children (and keep them together), rather than focusing on adopting those children to the neglect of their mothers. Joyce's book *The Child Catchers* compiled her years of research on the orphan care movement to argue that the supposedly new evangelical "obsession" with adoption had unwittingly contributed to child trafficking and the oppression of single, pregnant women in crisis pregnancy centers.[7] While Joyce's criticisms were not necessarily new, the visibility of her work sparked a media frenzy in the United States, scrutinizing evangelicals and their adoption pursuits.[8]

These sorts of criticisms from Smolin, Joyce, and subsequent others required a response from movement leaders, defending the theology and intentions of the orphan care movement.[9] But these criticisms also contributed in no small part to the efforts made by CAFO to promote "best practices" and ensure that it was encouraging Christians to think carefully about the adoption process and how they could help serve orphans beyond adoption, which has simply become less of an option at the international level. Jedd Medefind and other Christian leaders thoughtfully framed the outside criticisms as opportunities for the movement to grow in the right directions.[10]

Criticisms Coming from Inside the Movement

While criticisms from outside the movement focused primarily on the negative consequences of evangelicals' adoption pursuits for birth mothers or vulnerable communities, criticisms from within the movement focused on the negative consequences of rash or uninformed adoption or foster care activities for adoptive families and their children. Tragic situations involving disrupted adoptions or rehoming among evangelical parents, or simply widespread struggle with parenting challenging adopted or foster children, became well known within the movement. In light of these trends, a variety of leaders, including Michael and Amy Monroe and Karyn Purvis, expressed their concerns directly to CAFO leadership and others about the undue pressure evangelical families may feel to adopt children without being prepared for the challenges ahead.

The Christian Alliance for Orphans has responded to these criticism from within the movement to provide greater emphasis at CAFO Summits, on the CAFO website, and within other communication tools to highlight organizations like Empowered To Connect and Tapestry or written resources like *The Connected Child* by Karyn Purvis. These changes have signaled a shift away from pushing adoption and foster care among evangelicals generally to equipping such families who do feel called to adopt or foster with the resources they need to be successful. In doing so, the movement has become a greater conduit of information for adoptive and fostering families and their churches who wish to support them in their efforts.

Growing Ties and Accommodation to the Secular State

Last, CAFO and its constituent organizations have had to evolve in response to the changing nature of adoption in the United States as well as to their greater connection to the secular state. As CAFO and their member organizations have become more involved in foster care and family preservation or reunification, this has entailed a connection to the child welfare system, which requires a number of adjustments. For example, it would be illegal for Christian adoption or foster placement agencies to receive money from the government while actively discriminating against gay or lesbian couples who wish to participate in adoption or fostering. Some Christian agencies opt to close down rather than compromise on this issue,[11] while others choose to accommodate for a variety of reasons. While these ministry leaders assure me that their organizations seldom have to deal with gay or lesbian families wanting to adopt or foster with them, this is nevertheless an area where these organizations have had to compromise and become more accommodating to the secular society.

Another example would be the forms of discipline that Christian organizations and their foster parents would be allowed to administer to their foster children. While some evangelicals may be proponents of spanking for their own biological children, and perhaps for the children they have adopted through a private agency or from overseas, this is not allowed for foster children under the state's care. Indeed, for many foster children, that sort of corporal punishment could trigger great trauma owing to their past experiences, as Karyn Purvis pointed out in an earlier chapter. Thus, Christian placement organizations have had to accommodate to the state's views on discipline. Relatedly, CAFO more generally has also begun to advocate and facilitate a "best practices" approach to adoption, fostering, and orphan care that draws on established research done by clinical psychologists and child welfare professionals, which has been another area of accommodation. These adjustments have also made CAFO itself a resource for professional social workers and clinicians, who may obtain continuing education credit through CAFO Summit meetings or events run by Empowered To Connect or Tapestry.

This brief history highlights some of the major developments and transitions in the orphan care movement in response to various internal and external pressures. While much of the original emphasis remains the same, CAFO and the movement have grown in the ways predicted by the sect-church process or 4M model. It has increased in numbers, organization, diversity, and professionalization. Along the way it has had to soften its hard ideological edge and accommodate to secular society in formal ways.

Ultimately, these changes have helped CAFO and the movement become more effective in several respects. They appeal to a broader (Christian) audience, they communicate more thoughtfully about orphan care activism like adoption and fostering, and they are better conduits of counseling resources for adoptive and fostering families. But how do movement leaders interpret this trend? While these changes would suggest that CAFO should continue down this path to become more effective at accomplishing practical objectives, there is an ongoing tension between this evolution and a concern about becoming unmoored from the movement's founding ideals and values.

Pietistic Idealism and Movement Growth

As I spoke with movement leaders, I found they are generally aware that movements evolve over time and that the tension exists between adjusting to become more effective and maintaining core ideological commitments. But there was some disagreement about what change would look like going forward in order for the movement to be successful and enduring.

While leaders like Karyn Purvis, Michael and Amy Monroe, and others stated that Christian adoption is a good thing and that vulnerable children do indeed need loving families, they have been critical of the theological underpinnings and explicit or implicit messages about Christian identity and adoption. As evangelicals, they, too, believe that the gospel should orient social engagement and inform Christians' approach to serving vulnerable children. But they are outsiders in the sense that their role has been primarily to equip and counsel adoptive and fostering families, rather than to mobilize Christians to action, as CAFO and the authors of mobilization literature do. Their orientation to change has thus been uniquely practical and forward thinking among evangelical leaders in the movement.

Specifically, Dr. Purvis and the Monroes stressed that the movement must continue to evolve in several key ways: (1) They must avoid making irresponsible statements (or implying) that God wants all Christians to adopt or foster or even that child adoption is somehow analogous to God the Father's adoption of believers into his family. (2) More education needs to be provided to Christian communities about the needs of adopting and fostering families, and support structures need to be developed within churches to help meet those needs. And (3) adoptive and fostering parents themselves need to be better equipped with resources to holistically serve their children, particularly those from difficult backgrounds. Short of those sorts of changes, these leaders were skeptical about the ability of the movement to sustain itself. That is why, when I asked Karyn Purvis if she thought the orphan care movement would eventually fizzle out, she stated that "the less success our families have, the more sour this thing goes. . . . Yeah, I really do."

It is safe to say that all other leaders in the orphan care movement would affirm that greater theological nuance, community education, and preparation for adoptive and fostering families are necessary and good things. Indeed, within the last few years the movement has already begun to make those changes. Yet most other leaders I spoke with also maintained a different emphasis about what factors would be *most* crucial in sustaining the movement. While some leaders emphasized the need to make tactical changes in order to cultivate greater practical effectiveness in promoting responsible activism and support for families, most others saw the key to movement longevity and success through the lens of pietistic idealism, that is, while practical effectiveness and "best practices" are certainly important, these things cannot be the *ul-*

timate goal. Rather, the goal must be obedience to God's calling, as a response to the gospel. To miss that point is to miss everything. Consequently, other leaders stated that the key to movement sustainability was not necessarily to change in certain ways but to avoid change of the wrong sort. Wrong change meant any loss of focus from the ultimate goal—faithfulness to the gospel—in exchange for embracing modern techniques and practical results.

For example, Jon Bergeron, director of counseling with Hope for Orphans, proposes that staying gospel centered will be the key to the longevity of the orphan care movement: "I think the big challenge is if we keep the gospel at the center of what we do, then I don't think [the movement will become a fad]. I think those kinds of flashes in the pan and trendy things happen when we get caught up in a very Western view of marketing and sales pitches and all the stuff that we kind of do in a consumer-based society, and we lose really the gospel center of whatever it is." Certainly Jon, among all leaders, being a counselor of families who adopt and foster children, advocates for greater equipping and provision for such families. Nevertheless, he emphasizes that organizations and movements become temporary fads, not when they are strategically ineffective, but when they replace the gospel, which should be at the center of their activities, with Western marketing techniques and focus on attracting consumers.

Other leaders reflected Jon's sentiment completely. At the 2013 CAFO Summit in Nashville, Tennessee, Russell Moore gave a talk entitled, "How the Orphan Care Movement Could Wreck Itself . . . and What's Needed to Avoid It." Like Bergeron, Moore preached that the movement must be rooted in gospel truth, or else it will lose its effectiveness and ultimately be replaced by God. He concludes, "[Our adoption in the gospel] ought to free us then from the fear of what's going to happen in our future, and it ought to free us from the pride that becomes so easily settled with the sort of success that the rest of the world can honor. But if we go into this with worldly methods and with worldly goals, then the orphan care movement in your church, in your home, around the world will wreck itself. And God will raise up something new." In Moore's view, happy families and thriving ministries are good things, but these cannot be the goal or foundation of the orphan care movement because they can become a source of worldly concern and pride. Rather, it is their position as adopted children in God's family that can free Christians to embrace the risk of adoption and orphan care.

Leaders outside of adoption placement ministry held a similar concern about not losing sight of the ultimate goal. Matt Storer is a long-time board member with CAFO and has served as president and CEO of VisionTrust International, an education and discipleship ministry for children in developing nations. Consistent with pietistic idealism, Matt emphasized the distinction between commitment to a cause in and of itself and serving orphans as a part of living biblically. "Sometimes people like a cause, and [the orphan care movement] is not a cause. I have a bunch of people who want to talk, and a lot of them are interested in causes. [*laughs*] I'm like, I think this movement needs to be just about biblical living, not a cause that gains momentum and then disappears someday, like a fad. It's got to be biblically based about how you live out your life, and you can kind of start to see how all this fits in with the concept of living for God." For Matt, social causes gain momentum and then fizzle out, but enduring movements are built around the idea of living completely for God in every area of life, according to scripture.

Jason Kovacs co-founded (with Dan Cruver) Together for Adoption in 2008 in order to highlight the theological foundations of adoption and orphan care. In his interview, he expressed that they were motivated to start Together for Adoption was because they felt that CAFO Summits were already becoming too focused on practices and practical aspects of orphan care to the neglect of theological truth:

> Summit at that point—and even to a degree it still is—very practical focused, very much, you know, best practices. A lot of the main sessions, especially back then, were just very practical in nature. So we said, Well, now what would it look like if we just explicitly laid this foundation of the gospel underneath this movement? And we really felt like that was going to be critical if this movement was to sustain. It needed to be not driven by a passion to help children. It needed to be a spirit-driven passion that was rooted in our understanding of God's great plan of adoption, and we felt like, if we can do that, then, you know, we have hope that this can last not just, you know, five years because it's this fad.

Certainly, Kovacs is not criticizing the need for practical equipping regarding adoption and foster care and "best practices." As a pastor of care and counseling at the Austin Stone Community Church, he values those things, too. But again, what Kovacs and Cruver felt was *most* necessary for the movement's longevity and impact was a deeper theological foundation, rooted in the gospel. This would be "critical if this movement was to sustain."

Perhaps the clearest representation of pietistic idealism came from the father of the orphan care movement himself, Paul Pennington. When I asked him about what could sustain the movement over time, he responded:

> There've been many American-based movements that flash in the pan and then recede. Christianity has lasted for twenty centuries. It didn't fizzle out. We don't do anything for God or for Jesus. We only have the privilege to join him where he's working. Sometimes we join in where he's working, and then we want to take over. My biggest problem in my life is that the older I get, the more I realize that the most important item in my life is me, and that I want Jesus to be a spare tire most of the time and I wanted to drive. Whenever we make Jesus the spare tire and we want to start driving, that's when we start running out of gas. But if Jesus is driving, it's not a hybrid, it's—it's solar power and—and that's why the church exists, because there was a real Jesus who really rose from the dead, and there is a real holy spirit who really thinks and who knows and who searches the hearts of men, who has all power, who knows everything, and he keeps his promises, and he loves these children, and he loves the widows, and [orphan care] isn't anything new. This is just something that the Western church forgot how to do the last hundred years. It was sustained for nineteen centuries because of the reality of the gospel, the power of the spirit through following people. So, yeah, American stuff comes and goes because we like to think that we can help Jesus, and we think that if we use business principles and use a strategic plan and fleshly driven things, there can be some results from that, but sustainability is only possible when it is genuinely spirit led and engineered. Do I think that CAFO and the American orphan ministry movement in America [will be sustained]? I think that depends on whether we want to take the steering wheel.

What sustained orphan care in the Christian church for almost two thousand years? In Paul's view, it was "the reality of the gospel, the power of the spirit" in obedient believers. More than this, Jesus will sustain those things where he is completely in control. The human tendency is to take control from Jesus, by beginning to incorporate fleshly principles and business techniques and to make the work ultimately about ourselves. So Paul concludes that CAFO and the orphan care movement will be sustained to the extent that it keeps Jesus himself at the center of its efforts. This is another way of saying that Jesus' priorities—God's glory and the salvation of lost souls—must remain the focus of movement efforts and not necessarily a cause for its own sake.

Oftentimes as I asked about the longevity of the orphan care movement, I would compare it to another evangelical movement that was wildly popular during its time, Promise Keepers.[12] Promise Keepers is an evangelical ministry that targets men, particularly fathers. It exploded onto the scene in the late 1990s, drawing thousands of men and boys to fill up football stadiums and listen to evangelical pastors talk about masculinity, leadership, family, racial reconciliation, and other principles. The Promise Keepers movement declined rapidly after its early popularity and has since become famous in evangelical circles as a flash-in-the-pan ministry that many remember but that no one has heard from in years. In my conversation with Elizabeth Styffe, director of orphan initiatives for Saddleback Community Church, I asked her whether the orphan care movement would eventually become like Promise Keepers. She laughed and affirmed that Promise Keepers was an exemplar of what most Christian movements would not like to end up as. In her response she expressed concern that the movement had already begun to make the same mistakes:

> ES: Now let me tell you, because Promise Keepers is a great example. Promise [Keepers] first started as a church movement. It became an organization. And it died. And Rick Warren said to them, "Guys, don't hire staff." And he said, "It needs to be churchy, you're serving the church instead of the church serving you. . . ." And so I think that would be a really good analogy.

SP: Yeah, so how do you make sure the movement doesn't become Promise Keepers? Because there are professional staff already running CAFO and these other organizations.

ES: Yeah. Oh, there's a million ways. And you know, we talk about it a lot. The *pastor* should be speaking, not the president of organizations. Their job is to promote the local church—the local church is the hero. You know, of the leaders you've talked to so far, how many of them were in churches?

SP: Yeah, not a lot.

ES: Right. So besides the fact that [the movement] is not producing results yet . . . I mean I think things like Orphan Sunday, that's the outside telling the inside what to do, and it doesn't work that way.

So for Elizabeth Styffe, the orphan care movement (which she thinks has not produced the sort of lasting results she would hope for) has already fallen into the same trap of Promise Keepers. In hiring full-time staff and promoting nonprofits and parachurch organizations, they have underemphasized the central role of the local church. She went on to reiterate the power of the local church to address the needs of vulnerable children, over and against other organizations:

[The church] is the longest-lasting organism. It's not a fly-by-night organization. It doesn't go away. You know, and the big idea is that has the greatest distribution. So, if there are 2.3 billion believers in the world, and there are 153 million orphans. . . . This is such a doable issue, it's not even funny. It's not even on our list of global giants because it affects millions, not billions. But [Saddleback] is tackling it because we believe it's what the church needs to do, but we're really interested in not medicating and educating but curing. Because there *are* enough families.

Like Paul Pennington, Elizabeth is convinced that the local church (and local churches globally) hold enough human potential to wipe out the orphan crisis. But also, like Paul Pennington and other leaders, her concern is that the movement has started to professionalize, become an organization for its own sake, and move away from one of its initial core commitments, which is giving primacy of place to the local church. This is an initial step toward dying out.

How Pietistic Idealism Limits Strategic Effectiveness Long Term

Describing a religious movement is like painting the portrait of a marathoner while she is still running. When something is constantly in motion, the best one can do is faithfully capture the most recent snapshot, which I have tried to do in these pages. Yet movements, like runners, move according to patterns, and the orphan care movement has followed a familiar course since its inception in the mid-2000s. Like many groups over the years, CAFO and the broader movement began as largely voluntary, loosely organized, and ideologically committed to a "biblical" approach to social engagement that put them at odds with secular society—in this case, the approach that vulnerable children whenever possible should be adopted into Christian families so they could be physically rescued but, more important, so they could be spiritually rescued. Over time, however, CAFO and the movement have evolved in many ways sociologists would expect. They have grown numerically in terms of membership; professionalized their leadership; diversified in their appeal, emphases, and resources they provide for families; softened the tone of their public theological stance; and have genuinely accommodated to the secular state in meaningful ways. All of these changes, I believe, move CAFO toward greater strategic effectiveness in terms serving vulnerable children.

Yet *none* of these changes have been the result of evangelical cultural schemas like pietistic idealism or individualism. Rather, they stem from a number of other factors, including necessity, internal and external criticisms, and partnership with the state. It would be more accurate to say that the evolution of the movement toward greater strategic effectiveness has taken place in tension with those cultural schemas, if not in spite of them. Pietistic idealism curbs the strategic effectiveness of evangelical social engagement, not because it holds that Christians ought to honor God through orphan care, but because it is fundamentally *conservative* in its orientation. I do not mean "conservative" in the political sense that it promotes traditional family values or morality. I mean that it is fundamentally oriented toward the *preservation* of earlier ideals and is therefore suspicious of innovation or progress, even when they are both practically necessary.

Certainly, I do not mean to suggest that movement leaders have been personally resistant to changes that see the movement make more nuanced theological arguments, broaden their vision to encourage other non-adoption forms of orphan care, and promote a "best practices" approach to help vulnerable children and the families who adopt or foster them. All leaders see these things as positive developments, I believe. But when leaders think about what sort of factors give a movement sustainability over the long run, pietistic idealism does not lead their thoughts toward tactical revision in order to maximize strategic effectiveness in a changing world. Rather, pietistic idealism leads their thoughts toward preserving something sacred—for example, the ultimate value of God's glory reflected in the obedience of Christ-centered churches and believers, or the adherence to "biblical" strategies to address the orphan crisis, like preaching sermons about orphans/adoption, placement with married heterosexual Christian parents, or local church-level activism. Only then, will a movement be blessed with sustainability.

In the evangelical view, worldly movements seek to sustain themselves by being man-centered and focusing on practical results and innovation. Christ-centered movements are sustained by God himself when—and only when—believers are faithful. Evangelical efforts at social engagement like the orphan care movement are fundamentally self-limiting because they will tend to be oriented more toward preservation of an ideal than continually evolving to more effectively accomplish a practical task.

To put this another way, imagine that one of the key leaders in the orphan care movement is given three hypothetical options. The Christian Alliance for Orphans and the movement can take *only* one of three paths from this point forward:

A. be gospel-driven and theologically sound but ineffective at serving vulnerable children in tangible ways;
B. become cause-driven and secular but highly effective at serving vulnerable children (at least in terms of getting them in families and meeting their physical needs); or
C. shut down operations completely.

Most would probably demand a fourth option for the movement: "D. be gospel-driven and highly effective at serving vulnerable children." But suppose I removed that option and they were genuinely forced to choose one of the hypothetical options available. Based on my observations and interactions with movement leaders, I would venture that most—not all, but most—would choose options A or even C before considering B.[13] In fact, what is basically implied in some of the leaders' quotes above is that God himself would rather the movement shut down completely rather than see it become something secular, man-centered, or cause driven. Russell Moore said that much in his address: "If we go into this with worldly methods and with worldly goals, then the orphan care movement . . . will wreck itself. And God will raise up something new."

In fact, some Christian agencies have already chosen option C, deciding to shut down rather than compromise with worldliness. Take, for example, the Christian placement agencies who have chosen to shut down their foster care program rather than place children with same-sex couples. Diane Lynn Elliot describes examples of this in Illinois:

> The state, through the Department of Child and Family Services (DCFS), had formerly subsidized foster care in both public and private agencies. A new law was instituted in 2011 stating that all agencies, regardless of their religious affiliation, have to accept and license people who are in same-sex relationships if they are to work with DCFS. Agencies unwilling to license people who do not meet their biblical criteria have chosen not to compromise their moral integrity and have forfeited their licenses to place children in foster care. It is a sad day when a quality private foster care and adoption agency can no longer serve vulnerable children because a state agency dictates their moral beliefs.[14]

It is instructive how Elliot frames the situation. Regardless of the fact that the majority of parents looking to foster children through an obviously Christian agency would be themselves Christians and that relatively few would be same-sex couples, these agencies would rather withdraw from foster placement *entirely* rather than compromise. But Elliot does not even acknowledge the choice. To her, there is no choice. The real tragedy, in her view, is that "a quality private foster care and adoption agency can no longer serve vulnerable children because a state agency dictates their moral beliefs." Placing vulnerable children into loving, stable families is not the ultimate goal. Obedience is.

Christian Smith aptly described the dual commitment of evangelicals to maintaining biblical integrity and engaging their world in tangible ways as "engaged orthodoxy."[15] It is a helpful phrase. But the positioning of words must not be mistaken to mean that being "engaged" takes precedence over "orthodoxy" for evangelicals. For those most committed to pietistic idealism, it must always be orthodoxy first, engagement second. More than this, engagement is not for its own sake, but must flow out of orthodoxy. As Jason Kovacs said, the orphan care movement should not be "driven by a passion to help children" if it has any hope of enduring. Helping children is a great thing, but it is not the *ultimate* thing. The goal is therefore, not to advance in strategic effectiveness (however necessary that may be), but to stay focused on Christ, in spite of pressures to evolve as the organization grows. To the extent that Christian movements are influenced by pietistic idealism, then, they are self-limiting by definition.

Conclusion

The social forces that can unite a people into a movement can also paradoxically undermine their attempts at effective social influence in the public square. In the case of American evangelicalism, we find a religious tradition which, ironically, is often for the very same reasons, yet in different ways, both strong and ineffective.

—Christian Smith, *American Evangelicalism* (1998:217)

Almost twenty years ago, Christian Smith described a paradox within American evangelicalism—while evangelicals' subcultural characteristics gave them tremendous strength as a religious movement for itself, the same characteristics were also a hindrance to accomplishing distinctively Christian social change. Specifically, Smith argued that evangelicals' subcultural strengths alienated them from non-evangelical Americans; their relationalism and individualism blinded them to the ways supra-individual social factors shaped social problems; and their "voluntaristic absolutism" (itself being a contradiction) hindered them from articulating a coherent social policy. As important as these observations were, Smith's analysis was unfortunately limited to general public opinion data and interviews with evangelicals *about* engaging social issues and politics, rather than focusing on groups of evangelicals actually engaged in addressing particular social problems. This book has sought to redress those limitations to better understand how the evangelical subculture not only stimulates collective action around various social issues but can also ultimately hinder evangelical efforts to accomplish practical social change.[1]

Using the orphan care movement as a test case, this book has elaborated the ways in which evangelical cultural schemas like pietistic idealism and individualism/anti-structuralism, and other cultural characteristics like populism, influence evangelical social engagement. As we have seen, first, evangelicals by and large are committed to the idea that the motivation for social action is only morally appropriate when it is explicitly oriented around God's glory and the gospel and that the ultimate result of social action *must* go beyond practical results to the transformation of sinful hearts. Otherwise, the material benefit to individuals or society is in vain. This perspective requires evangelical groups to draw boundaries around what sorts of social engagement count as pleasing to God and who can justifiably be recruited to such activities. Relatedly, because of their focus on individual motivations and heart transformation, evangelicals have become institutionally locked into forms of engagement that have some sort of biblical precedent or analog (e.g., child adoption by married heterosexual couples, or serving "orphans") and mobilization techniques that involve each individual's ideas and intentions (e.g., preaching and teaching, interpersonal conversations, mobilization literature), regardless of whether they practically work.

Second, in addition to pietistic idealism and individualism, evangelicals are also particularly susceptible to populist appeals in the form of shallow theological reasoning, sentimentality, and to some degree peer pressure or status concerns (e.g., adopting or fostering difficult-to-parent "trophy kids" as a marker of spiritual status). While not necessarily changing individuals' deep-seated motivations, in combination these influences can provoke rash activities among well-meaning evangelicals—activities that their faith communities may not have the inclination or the resources to support long term.

Last, pietistic idealism is fundamentally conservative in that it is oriented toward preserving the original founding ideals of the movement and holds faithfulness to these ideals as the key for longevity. While not necessarily opposing positive practical changes for the better, pietistic idealism is suspicious of incorporating "worldly" ideas and methods, however strategically advantageous they may be. Further, it is not oriented toward innovation or progress for its own sake since all activities should ideally be oriented toward God's glory, for the advance of the gospel, and with biblical methods in mind.

To be sure, there are some strategic benefits to these cultural schemas and characteristics of American evangelicalism. First and foremost, as Christian Smith pointed out, these qualities serve the primary purpose of uniting evangelicals around a common "orthodoxy" and ensuring that the boundaries of evangelical identity are vigilantly defended. For example, the evangelical suspicion toward wrong motivations (e.g., seeing orphan care as a cause for its own sake) keeps them from watering down their message of salvation or banding together with those who would challenge their worldview and methods. Seen in this light, social engagement for evangelicals is less about accomplishing practical objectives and more about religious renewal and preserving group solidarity. In this regard, evangelical social engagement may be very functional *for evangelicals*, even while being of limited help for society at large. This corresponds perfectly to what sociologist Émile Durkheim observed long ago, and what psychologist Jonathan Haidt has argued recently, that religious activities, however altruistic and selfless in appearance, ultimately serve the purpose of group cohesion and growth.[2]

Related to this last point, the cultural commitment to individualism and populism helps evangelicals to stimulate flurries of collective action quickly in response to public appeals from pastors or other evangelical personalities. Despite some of the unfortunate consequences of the rash actions provoked by these appeals, these instances have nevertheless drawn public attention to evangelicals and their adopting or fostering efforts. The public notoriety of evangelical orphan care activities has contributed to a broader cultural narrative about American evangelicals being people of compassion rather than simply being known for their opposition to abortion, gays, pornography, liberalism, and so forth. Though not without controversy, people have certainly taken notice, and this may help with the "public relations problem" Christian Smith described.[3]

Another potential benefit brought about by distinctively evangelical social engagement is that, in *some* instances, it can deliver on its promises. Some vulnerable children *do* get adopted or fostered by loving, established Christian families—*occasionally* it may even be a direct result of the movement's message about loving orphans—and these children's lives are better for it. While there is no evidence to suggest that this is happening more often than it has in the past or anywhere near as often as what is portrayed by movement critics or advocates, it should be celebrated when children who would have otherwise aged out of institutional care are embraced by loving families. This is not to say that adoption and foster care themselves are not rooted in tragic circumstances and, to a large degree, social injustice. Evangelicals should do their part to build a society in which there are not only fewer children in institutions or foster care but in which there are fewer unplanned pregnancies and fewer women who are in desperate enough circumstances to relinquish or lose their children. Yet that does not change the fact that there are vulnerable children *now*, especially in American foster care, who need loving families. Society should applaud those who wish to be a part of their lives.

Beyond their strategic benefits, however, this book has shown how evangelical cultural schemas and characteristics can be strategic drawbacks for effective social engagement in at least six ways. First, they limit the mobilization repertoires at evangelicals' disposal. Pietistic idealism sees morally acceptable social engagement as springing from explicitly God-honoring motives, and thus, evangelical leaders cannot simply rally believers to action around an injustice or cause for its own sake. Moreover, leaders must rely on institutionalized (what they see as "biblical") techniques for shaping the beliefs, values, and ultimately, the motivations of believers in order to stimulate actions—namely, preaching and interpersonal conversations about the gospel. Sermons and conversations are not simply rallies to address a particular social issue like vulnerable children or poverty; they must start with God himself, his purposes for the world, and his redemptive plan. Within the institutionalized evangelical mobilization strategy, the expectation is that preaching or talking about the gospel, when properly understood, will necessarily and inevitably result in God-honoring social engagement. Evangelicals are thus limited to a set of mobilization strategies regardless of whether they work or not.

Second, and related to the first limitation, evangelical cultural distinctives limit the strategies for addressing social issues to those dealing with *individual* heart change rather than changes in *social structure* or public policy. Christian Smith observed this primarily as evangelicals discussed their views on political change and how Christians would influence business and the economy.[4] Elsewhere, Michael Emerson and Christian Smith showed how these (predominantly white) evangelical cultural perspectives shaped their strategies for addressing racial divisions and racial inequality in the United States.[5] In both cases, the authors point out how individualism/anti-structuralism and relationalism blinded evangelicals to possibilities for addressing social problems beyond the "personal influence strategy" targeted toward improving society by changing hearts and then behavior.

This was also clearly seen in the orphan care movement. Evangelical leaders repeatedly expressed a suspicion of government intervention as a substitute or alternative to individual Christians responding to God's call to serve orphans. Moreover, the particular strategies for which the movement has most strongly advocated—adoption and, to a lesser extent, foster care—all rely on individual Christians making faith-based decisions. This emphasis causes evangelicals in the movement to ignore the possibility that structural conditions share *most* of the blame for the problem of vulnerable children, and these structural conditions are changed through public policy, and not by Christians adopting. Indeed, child adoption or foster care, while laudable and necessary in many circumstances, are horribly inadequate to address the problem of vulnerable children worldwide. While orphan care leaders are increasingly acknowledging the limits of child adoption as an answer to the global orphan crisis,[6] the individualism/anti-structuralism of evangelicals inclines them to be suspicious of—or at the very least, disinterested in—other solutions that do not involve direct personal contact with a child or mother, most preferably with the possibility of sharing the gospel. This severely limits the ability of evangelicals to provide much more than quick-fix, Band-Aid solutions to social problems.

The individualistic solutions that evangelicals often favor for addressing social problem are also disconnected from reality in another important way. Evangelical leaders have the unfortunate habit of overestimating the religious commitment of the average American churchgoer, even in their own pews. (Those needing a good dose of reality should consider what percentage of evangelical churchgoers actually tithe or share their faith.)[7] Leaders also overestimate the extent to which the average evangelical congregation is interested in directing energy or resources toward activities that do not directly benefit the congregation itself. As we have seen, it is often repeated that Christians should try to cultivate a "culture of adoption/orphan care" in their congregations, in which God's heart for the orphan grips each believer, spurring him or her toward action involving vulnerable children. Other individual leaders, and CAFO itself, have emphasized that the solution for the orphan crisis can be found only in the local church, through adoption, fostering, and other activities. But these ideas mistakenly assume that average American pew sitters are inclined to respond to whatever messages are given from leaders to drastically change their lives on behalf of others. That simply does not happen very often. Inertia is a more powerful influence on most American Christians than evangelical leaders are willing to acknowledge. This makes any strategies involving hundreds of thousands of individual Christians drastically altering their lives in response to sermons, conversations, or Orphan Sunday celebrations overoptimistic.

The sociologist Mark Chaves has demonstrated the inconvenient truths about American congregations and their limited social engagement. Based on data from the National Congregations Studies, Chaves showed that congregations typically only engage in social services in minor and peripheral ways, and this usually involves a small group of volunteers engaged in a specific task on a temporary basis. Moreover, when congregations do engage in social services, they are typically meeting peoples' emergency needs. They are not particularly relational, holistic, or even religious in their approach to providing social services. Chaves also points out that—despite what evangelical leaders like to think about the church's historical role in providing social services to the vulnerable—congregations in the United States have *never* served as alternatives to government agencies or religious nonprofits. In fact, congregations most often depend on such agencies in their service activities. Chaves concludes that, not only is it misguided to build a strategy for addressing domestic social problems on the assumption that congregations, and the Christians within them, will change their patterns of behavior, but, even if congregations were significantly motivated to meet the needs of the vulnerable, they also would not be able to provide the sorts of services they think they are capable of. They would ultimately need to depend heavily on nonprofits and government support, as they always have.[8]

Third, the cultural schema of pietistic idealism limits the mobilization targets that evangelicals can justifiably recruit to engage in orphan care activism. If motivation is paramount, and if God is only pleased with social engagement where the gospel is reflected and he gets the glory, then evangelical organizations are wasting time mobilizing unbelieving parents to adopt or foster available children. Unbelievers may be adequate parents, but God gets no explicit glory, and the children are no closer to becoming Christians. This is why leading evangelical agencies like Bethany Christian Service, America World Adoption, Lifeline Children's Services, and others do not recruit unbelieving parents despite the tremendous need for adoptive or fostering parents, particularly within the child welfare system. Indeed, a number of organizations like the ABBA Fund demand that Christian parents themselves be adopting with a missional intent, otherwise they will direct their resources elsewhere. Moreover, if God has provided the married two-parent family as the ideal situation in which to raise children, single Christians, regardless of their motives to adopt are not ideal mobilization targets. They may be acceptable as parents, and some organizations are willing to work with them in lieu of other options, but they are never the target of movement mobilization efforts. And if single Christians are the lowest group on the preference hierarchy of adoptive and fostering families, homosexual couples are not even on the scale. These couples are assumed to be unbelievers outright and wholly incapable of adopting in a way that God would be pleased with. Some Christian agencies have preferred to close down their foster adoption ministry entirely rather than be forced to place children with gay or lesbian couples in compliance with federal regulations.[9]

Thus, the schema of pietistic idealism limits the targets for evangelical mobilization efforts to married heterosexual Christian families who are adopting primarily (or at least ostensibly) for missional reasons. Consequently, evangelicals forfeit an enormous amount of human and political capital that could otherwise be mobilized to serve vulnerable children domestically and abroad. The mainstream movement's unwillingness to compromise in this area literally exchanges strategic effectiveness at getting vulnerable children into stable, loving homes for the sake of overt evangelism and faithfulness to a "biblical" ideal of what a family should look like.

Fourth, the formal evangelical commitments to pietistic idealism, institutionalized in the standards of CAFO organizations and mobilization literature, create a situation in which evangelical couples, regardless of what initially got them thinking about adoption or foster care, now feel compelled to publically articulate their pursuit in gospel-driven terms. Pietistic idealism is not necessarily a reality in *all* evangelical activities, but it is the standard or ideal that evangelicals are expected to live by. Thus, in numerous interviews I conducted for this study, grassroots families began by articulating their adoptions in terms of God's heart for the orphan and how adoption is a means of fulfilling the Great Commission and serves as a reflection of the Christian's adoption in Christ. But as I probed deeper, it became clear that most initially started thinking about adoption, not because of the gospel or their pro-life values or even pietistic idealism at all, but they were attracted to adoption for the same reasons most families in general consider adoption—because they desperately wanted children and adoption represented the best or only option available. Moreover, I found that this is also the case for most evangelical leaders and writers involved in adoption. Pietistic idealism, then, can hinder evangelical effectiveness at social engagement by stigmatizing those who adopt or foster primarily, or at least initially, for the purposes of family growth (as most do) and by creating a situation in which the movement feels it has been more successful than it has been at generating new motives to adopt children.

Fifth, in combination with pietistic idealism and individualism, the evangelical tendency toward populism creates a situation in which evangelicals are quickly provoked to rash activism when there may be little support in their own faith community or little preparedness among the parents themselves. Pietistic idealism and individualism leads churches to focus on preaching the gospel and meeting people's spiritual needs while treating each family as a unit responsible for its own functioning. Certainly church leaders hope that families within the congregation will engage with one another, and they promote structures like "life groups" or "community groups" to facilitate this. But even in these situations, average middle-class families are busy with their own lives and responsibilities, and the support these families can supply to adopting or fostering families pales in comparison to the needs many of those parents may have. Consequently, churches may at some point promote orphan care and sacrificial forms of adoption and fostering with no real commitment or resources to support participating families beyond what can be provided by their small community groups. Some even decide to outsource the job of congregational support to other churches with stronger adoption ministries like Tapestry.

Movement leaders have also pointed out that the populist tendencies of evangelicalism have created a situation in which numerous families, spurred on by shallow theological reasoning and community pressure, have gotten in over their heads without the necessary parenting or counseling resources to support them. This has required the movement to essentially double back and revisit their theology of orphan care and earlier emphases on urgent action. In this regard, the evangelical tendency toward populism limits strategic effectiveness in that it makes social engagement difficult to sustain in the long run.

Sixth, and last, as the movement grows in numbers and evolves as all social movements do, it is guided by pietistic idealism. Certainly, leaders would unanimously affirm that positive tactical changes are necessary and, indeed, have already been made to maximize the effectiveness of the movement. Even so, those most influenced by pietistic idealism would reject the idea that strategic effectiveness at serving vulnerable children is a goal for its own sake. Rather, the goal must always be the glory of God in the physical representation and proclamation of the gospel. To lose sight of this truth is to miss the point entirely. Pietistic idealism then is fundamentally conservative in its orientation, focusing on preservation rather than innovation and advance. If given the choice between either strategic change for greater practical effectiveness or remaining faithful to "biblical" ideals, pietistic idealists will choose the latter, even if that means strategic ineffectiveness or shutting down entirely (as several ministries have already done). Pietistic idealism is therefore fundamentally self-limiting.

How Does This Argument Extend to Other Evangelical Efforts at Social Engagement?

While this argument extends to evangelical social engagement generally, there are a number of factors about the specific empirical case of orphan care that make it unique. As far as forms of social engagement or activism go, adoption and, to a lesser degree, foster care are about as personally invested as one can get. Adopting and, to some degree, fostering children come with a number of significant risks and costs that other standard forms of activism (voting, signing a petition, handing out brochures, writing letters to congress, protesting in the streets) do not. International and private agency adoptions are incredibly expensive and time-consuming, and there is obviously the emotional investment one makes in loving and caring for an adopted child or children. But with adoption also comes the long-term commitment to raising that child into adulthood and, for most adoptive parents, passing on their possessions in death to those children. To the extent that some evangelical families are adopting or fostering primarily out of obedience to God's call to care for orphans, few other practical forms of social engagement could hold a candle to such commitment. In fact, the only forms of activism that might express greater commitment would be the kinds that result in permanent harm to one's body (e.g., self-immolation, suicide bombing) or long-term imprisonment.

Conversely, the benefits that one receives from adoption and foster care are also unique relative to other forms of social engagement. Even if primarily faith-based reasons influenced evangelical families in their decisions to adopt or foster children, such families were almost certainly eager to invite children into their home and share love with them. As evangelical families repeatedly recounted in my interviews, these children, even the ones who came with significant health and/or behavioral challenges, were "a blessing" and source of great joy to these families. Few forms of activism would be quite as gratifying as a long-term parent-child relationship, and especially if a desire for that relationship was a major motivating factor, as it was for the vast majority of evangelical adoptive or fostering families I interviewed.

Despite these particularities about evangelicals and orphan care activism, the arguments outlined above extend to other examples of evangelical social engagement. The broader argument that transcends the issues of adoption and foster care is that evangelical social engagement is fundamentally self-limiting because of the cultural distinctives I have described. On the one hand, evangelicals are compelled to engage their society and culture and bring about change, and there are elements within contemporary evangelicalism that lead them to want to address practical social issues like vulnerable children, poverty, sex trafficking, racial conflict, environmental degradation, or all of the above.[10] But because American evangelicals are often compelled by the cultural influence of pietistic idealism along with individualism/anti-structuralism and populism, I contend that evangelical efforts at addressing these issues are rendered practically ineffective. Consider the research on two such attempts, one domestic and one international.

Evangelical Efforts at Addressing Racial Issues

Evangelical engagement with domestic racial issues provides a clear example of the cultural limits of evangelical activism I have described. Moreover, because issues of race and class the United States are so closely linked, the challenges confronting evangelicals in their attempts to address racial divisions and racial inequality in the United States can be extended to their approach on domestic poverty as well.

Michael Emerson and Christian Smith's award-winning book *Divided by Faith: Evangelical Religion and the Problem of Race in America* was a watershed book for evangelicals, and their arguments became the focus of an entire issue of *Christianity Today* in October 2000.[11] Emerson and Smith propose that white evangelicals and black Protestants, while very similar in terms of their religious convictions and practices, hold to different views about racial inequality and social change that drive them apart socially and politically. Emerson and Smith focus acutely on white evangelicals' adherence to individualism/anti-structuralism and relationalism as solutions to social problems, often ignoring the reality of supra-individual factors that contribute to racial injustice in the United States.

In terms of fostering racial reconciliation, Emerson and Smith argue that the dominant white evangelical cultural view drives a wedge between them and black Protestants. Rather than seeking to understand the experiences of black Americans in the United States, white evangelicals tend to minimize the importance of race as a shaper of social outcomes and highlight the importance of individual responsibility and personal influence through relationships. In this view, racism is the result of individual whites being prejudiced and discriminatory rather than a system that disproportionately awards benefits to some groups over others. Therefore racism can be almost entirely eradicated by preaching the gospel and changing individuals' hearts, thereby changing their actions.

This perspective fits perfectly with statements made by orphan care movement leaders about racial injustice. Johnny Carr, for example, in his book *Orphan Justice*, explains that racism in the American culture is a matter of the heart and thus cannot be remedied by government intervention. Rather, hearts can only be transformed by the gospel: "If racism is a heart issue, no amount of education or government reform will change our culture. This is not the kind of change that comes merely from human effort—from 'trying harder' and 'doing more.' Confronting the racist in each one of us starts with a new understanding of the gospel that begins to transform our often-hard hearts."[12]

Emerson and Smith show that, at its most extreme, the individualism/anti-structuralism of white evangelicals can lead them to blame black Americans themselves for racial inequality rather than consider how the historical legacies of white racism continue to shape life chances for blacks. Rather, black Americans must make better decisions and work their way out of poverty. This perspective also leads white evangelicals to be suspicious of government interventions on behalf of black Americans, believing that it not only absolves individual Christians of their social responsibility but also incentivizes sinful laziness and family dysfunction for poor blacks.

Ultimately, Emerson and Smith conclude that the dominant white evangelical cultural schemas of individualism/anti-structuralism and relationalism lead them to propose solutions for racial divisions and racial inequality that do not practically work. The evangelical perspective often "mistakenly presumes that multilevel problems can be solved by unilevel solutions."[13] Moreover, it directs churches to be so consumed with converting souls that they teach new converts that Christian maturity means evangelizing to the neglect of taking social responsibility—a mistake neither Jesus nor the apostle Paul made in their own ministries. While Emerson and Smith never refer to pietistic idealism as I have outlined it here, the evangelical commitment to converting souls—potentially to the neglect of redeeming society in ways that extend beyond, but are not excluding, spiritual well-being—are another way evangelical attempts at addressing racial issues are self-limiting.

While Emerson and Smith focus primarily on evangelicalism and racial divisions within society at large, their findings have been confirmed by a number of subsequent studies that explore how evangelicals seek to overcome racial tensions at the congregational level.[14] For example, Gerardo Marti and Michael Emerson have recently written about various evangelical attempts to promote racial reconciliation and develop diverse congregations. They first identify a populist tendency within evangelicalism regarding racial issues. Within the evangelical subculture, racial diversity has become a status symbol for congregations, indicating that a congregation is creating a welcoming environment for a diverse audience. The authors call this the "badge of diversity." Yet Marti and Emerson point out that evangelical notions of racial problems, and how to solve those problems, are inevitably influenced by evangelical schemas of individualism/anti-structuralism. They explain, "Evangelical discourse involves a complex of assumptions regarding agency and structure that underlie their religiosity. Evangelicals see change as personal and individual; conversion and repentance are generic tools for transformation that are believed to be able to conquer all forms of social ills. The local church is the site in which personal transformation occurs. It would be difficult to overstate this miracle motif: Social change comes from individual conversion, promoted by the ministry of the church, one heart at a time."[15]

Marti and Emerson go on to explain how evangelical approaches to racial reconciliation all flow out of their commitment to individual heart transformation (e.g., people repenting of racial prejudices or even seeing race) and personal reconciliation. However, they explain, "The pervasive focus on individualism, free will, and personal relationships renders racial injustices invisible and thereby perpetuates racial inequality."[16]

Within the rise of the diversity emphasis among evangelicals, and the attendant rise of "diversity experts" who serve as consultants to promote racial diversity and reconciliation in congregations, Marti and Emerson identify a paradoxical situation: "What is most interesting is that the same evangelical framework criticized by scholars for its inability to address race relations is the same framework used by diversity experts to describe their successes. That is, successfully diverse evangelical congregations access their individualist and personalist theological language to explain their successes."[17] Stated in the reverse, Marti and Emerson argue that the very strengths evangelicals identify in their attempts to promote racial reconciliation and racial diversity within their congregations (individualism and personal relationships) are the very same aspects of the evangelical framework that researchers have criticized as hindering their ability to address race relations in a deeper way. This is consistent with this book's argument that the very aspects of the American evangelical subculture that stimulate flurries of social engagement (pietistic idealism, individualism/anti-structuralism, populism) are the same factors that ultimately hinder their efforts at accomplishing significant social change.

Evangelical Efforts at Addressing Human Trafficking

Elements of this book's argument can also be found in research on evangelical anti-trafficking efforts. Evangelical Christians and organizations have been increasingly active in working against human slavery and sex trafficking for the last decade.[18] While some of this effort has taken place at the level of local congregations, most of it has been done through explicitly evangelical anti-trafficking organizations like Project Rescue; Rescue: Freedom; Freedom's Promise; and most prominent, International Justice Mission. There even exists a CAFO-like organization that serves as a hub and resource to connect Christian anti-trafficking organizations called FAAST (Faith Alliance Against Slavery and Trafficking).

Evangelicals have become so involved in anti-trafficking efforts that leaders in the orphan care movement often cited this work as a defense against accusations that they were unwittingly contributing to child trafficking overseas. For example, Russell Moore explained to me that, "from the left, you have the concern that [the orphan care movement] is empowering human trafficking. Well, evangelicals—and especially those in the evangelical orphan care movement—are at the forefront of combating human trafficking. The same people who are concerned about orphans are concerned about trafficking and are bringing the attention of the church to this in really remarkable ways over the past several years." Other movement leaders like Tony Merida and Rick Morton saw orphan care and anti-trafficking efforts as closely related in their minds and both suggested that the growing anti-trafficking emphasis among evangelicals should motivate the orphan care movement to ensure that it demands ethical practices in international adoption. Other evangelical authors promoting orphan care echo this argument.[19]

While far less attention has been paid to evangelical anti-trafficking efforts than their pro-life activism or even their efforts at orphan care or racial reconciliation, sociologists have begun to consider their approach. Elizabeth Bernstein has studied the anti-trafficking efforts of evangelicals for the last decade. Her work shows how these efforts are often strongly shaped by several cultural characteristics inherent within evangelicalism, which are roughly analogous with what I have described as pietistic idealism, individualism/anti-structuralism, and populism. In her various studies, she explains how young American evangelicals are often highly motivated to address the issue of prostitution and trafficking of women in foreign countries but that their engagement is often constrained and rendered unsuccessful by several factors.

First, they are often uncompromisingly committed to a "biblical" ethic of sexuality that sees paid sex work as synonymous with human trafficking and the sex trade, all of which they view as hopelessly immoral and worthy of vigorous legal opposition, regardless of whether young women are "willingly" engaging in the practice. Bernstein identifies this as a problem in that many of the young women whom evangelicals seek to "rescue" from the sex trade are not kidnaped or forced into slavery but are doing sex work "willingly." (Note that I use "willingly" in quotation marks because I do not mean to suggest that these women do this work happily; rather, they may participate voluntarily if they have no other options owing to of a lack of education, skills, or opportunities. This is not necessarily the same as sex trafficking.)

Related to this issue is the evangelical commitment to individualistic interventions on behalf of vulnerable populations. Bernstein points out that the evangelical anti-trafficking groups follow essentially the same pattern described by Emerson and Smith and what we have seen in the orphan care movement. The view is that social problems like human trafficking should be addressed by individual Christians engaging in activism on behalf of other individuals (women being trafficked) and against other bad individuals (men doing the trafficking). This is akin to Emerson and Smith's accusation that this perspective "mistakenly presumes that multilevel problems can be solved by unilevel solutions."[20] Bernstein points out that this individualist approach ignores the fact that structures of poverty and injustice in these nations have contributed to a system in which the economic situation is so dire that many women have no other options for survival outside of sex work. To "rescue" these women may in fact be to doom them to starvation. In fact, many return to sex work for lack of better options.[21]

And what of the men involved in human trafficking and the sex trade? While the evangelical narrative has often been to frame them as villains, there may be better solutions to redirecting their activities away from participation in human trafficking. Bernstein points out that the evangelicals in her study were more enthusiastic about prosecuting and imprisoning men involved rather than changing social structures in those nations to eliminate poverty and provide better alternatives to sex work for both women *and* men.[22]

While Bernstein does not give explicit attention to the evangelical tendencies toward populism, her narrative is full of examples of how well-meaning evangelicals may be spurred on to engage in rash activism without considering the consequences. This tendency regarding human trafficking activism was also identified by leaders in the orphan care movement. Tom Davis, for example, has done extensive work with anti-trafficking ministries. He expressed his deep concern about the pattern of evangelical ministries jumping from international adoption or orphan ministry to human trafficking ministry without sufficient preparation. This eventually led to some of his disenchantment with the orphan movement itself:

> And you'd get [to the CAFO Summit] and there were tons of booths, tons and tons of booths. And every single one of them says we do some form of child trafficking. Child trafficking had become very hot at that point, as far as people knowing about it. You know, sex trade and all of this. I was dumbfounded, because I'm like, wait a minute, this is an adoption conference that people are supposed to be talking about. How to adopt, what it looks like. And yet you have all of these organizations who are there. And now here they are saying that they all do sex trafficking. Which you know isn't true, because if you're involved in sex trafficking and any issue, prevention, restoration, rescue, it's a long, laborious, very difficult process. You don't wake up one day, because you can raise money and tell people you're doing some form of trafficking, and all of a sudden, you're on the trafficking radar. And so I was just grieved.

The patterns that Bernstein and Davis describe in evangelical anti-trafficking efforts are consistent with what this book has described in the orphan care movement. Evangelicals are compelled to engage with social issues, but pietistic idealism and individualism compel them to work uncompromisingly for "biblical" ideals and individual transformation to the neglect of larger structural factors. The tendency toward populism emphasizes immediate and often rash action over sufficient preparation. All these factors ultimately limit the strategic effectiveness of their efforts.

Recommendations for More Effective Evangelical Social Engagement

There is a parable I have heard evangelicals throw around (not often, but on occasion) when confronted with their own seemingly insignificant contribution to the global orphan crisis—the starfish on the beach.[23] In this story, thousands of starfish are littered across a beach after a storm. Determined to save as many starfish as possible, a little boy begins throwing starfish back into the ocean one by one. A curmudgeonly old man scoffs and tells the boy that his efforts do not matter because he will never save all those starfish. The boy holds up a single starfish and heroically declares "It matters to this one," and goes right on throwing.

Kathryn Joyce actually said that this story "has been widely adapted as the driving parable in the Christian adoption movement" and that the little boy's phrase "It matters to this one," has become "the anthem of the movement."[24] I would not go that far. In truth, orphan care movement leaders do not really like that parable because they are smart enough to know it makes the movement sound naïve, and childishly so. But the reason I share that story is to acknowledge that, thus far, I have been more like the curmudgeonly old man in that story than the kindhearted little boy, critiquing evangelical orphan care efforts for being ineffective while not necessarily offering a better strategy. No one likes that old man. So I want to end this book by offering some recommendations for the orphan care movement based on my observations.

But first, I want to provide some initial clarification. The sociologist Max Weber insisted that social scientists who study culture draw a sharp distinction between making empirical observations (about what *is*) and value judgments (about what *ought to be*). He argued, "It can never be the task of an empirical science to provide binding norms and ideals from which directives for immediate practical activity can be derived. . . . An empirical science cannot tell anyone what he *should* do, but rather what he *can* do. . . . To judge the validity of [a society's] values is a matter of *faith*."[25] In Weber's opinion (and my own), scientists cannot tell society what ultimate ends they should desire. That is the realm of moral philosophy and religious ethics. But scientists can and should tell society whether the means they use to obtain their desired ends are effective or not.

I preface my recommendations with these thoughts because I want to be clear about what I am *not* doing and what I *am* doing. I am not in any way criticizing evangelicals' desire to glorify God with their lives, nor am I criticizing the orphan care movement's desire to serve vulnerable children (and increasingly, their families and communities). The former desire is a moral imperative, an *ultimate* value for evangelicals, and I am in agreement with movement leaders that the latter desire ought to be. So I am *not* critiquing the ends, but I *am* critiquing the means. My observations of the orphan care movement over the last four years along with other studies of evangelical attempts to address social problems leads me to conclude that evangelicals are bound to means that undercut their ability to obtain their desired *practical* ends.

My recommendations are threefold. I propose evangelicals should (1) walk away from the theology that wrongly sacralizes adoption and fetishizes orphans, (2) reconsider the connection between social engagement and God's glory, and (3) consider the power of social structures to bring about lasting social change. These recommendations will not necessarily be novel. In fact, leaders in the orphan care movement may feel that influential voices are already calling for these sorts of changes. If that is so, I happily add my voice to theirs.

Biblicism and the Misreading of Adoption, adoption, and Orphans

At some level, asking evangelicals to relax their desire to connect the Bible to all human activity or to tone down the pietistic idealism is essentially like saying, "Just stop being so evangelical." The belief that Christians ought to submit their lives to biblical authority and glorify God by communicating the gospel are really the sine qua non of evangelicalism.[26] But my first two recommendations here involve a critique of particular strains (and extremes) of Biblicism and pietistic idealism and a plea for evangelicals to consider alternatives within their own tradition.

The first change the orphan care movement must make if they desire to succeed in their efforts is to walk away from (1) sacralizing child adoption by wrongly comparing it to the Christian's spiritual adoption in Christ and (2) fetishizing "orphans" and thereby orienting an entire campaign almost solely on their behalf. Both of these situations are wrong, not only strategically, but exegetically. The apostle Paul makes several statements in his epistles regarding the Christian's adoption into God's family (see Romans 8:14–17, 23; Galatians 4:4–7; Ephesians 1:3–6). I will not dive too deeply into these passages, but the respective contexts of each leave no doubt that Paul is strictly speaking about *spiritual* realities—estranged sinners being awarded the privileges of belonging to God's family through Christ. Any reading of twenty-first-century American-style child adoption into these passages is baseless, completely. Moreover, no plain reading of these texts would lead to the practical application that believers should somehow reflect their own spiritual adoption in the physical adoption of children. As Michael Monroe pointed out earlier, this theological move equates adoptive parents with the Father and the Son; adoption with salvation; vulnerable children with sinners deserving judgment; and birth parents or native communities with Satan, sin, and hell. Those who are familiar with the complexities of child adoption know better.

Even the human referent that Paul is using in these passages, the first-century Roman practice of adoption, does not fit the American context. As the historian Hugh Lindsay explains, Roman adoptions tended to involve upper-class parents who needed a legal heir adopting adult males (almost never minors or women) who had already proven themselves worthy.[27] While this makes perfect sense in Paul's spiritual analogy (Christians are sinners who are made worthy by Christ and have become co-heirs with Christ), it is hardly a parallel to the sort of adoption American evangelicals are envisioning.

I believe this misreading of child adoption into spiritual adoption has more to do with the evangelical tendency toward strict Biblicism—requiring biblical precedent, metaphor, or analog for every activity that evangelicals deem important. But this Biblicist tendency can unfortunately be connected to evangelical populist susceptibility to shallow theological reasoning. My reading of this development in the orphan care movement is that key leaders wanted American Christians to consider serving vulnerable children primarily through adoption. Needing biblical, gospel-oriented justification, they developed an entire theology connecting the practice of child adoption to the Christian's adoption in Christ, thereby sacralizing it. This is essentially how Jason Kovacs recounted the beginnings of adoption theology earlier. With CAFO and the summits already well under way, Jason Kovacs and Dan Cruver thought (as they stated in chapter 6): "Well, now what would it look like if we just explicitly laid this foundation of the gospel underneath this movement. . . . It needed to be not driven by a passion to help children. It need to be a spirit driven passion that was rooted in our understanding of God's great plan of adoption."

The consequences of this theology have been wholly negative. Much of the tendency for evangelical couples to suppress their family-growth motivations to adopt and fabricate a missional adoption narrative stems from this theology. This also contributes to the unfortunate tendency described by Paul and Robin Pennington, in which child adoption becomes a new status symbol for evangelicals—a sign that a Christian *really* understands her or his own adoption in Christ.

Related to this problem is the evangelical fetishizing of "orphans." A fetish is an object that is set apart or held sacred by a group for its supposed magical powers or divine significance. The populist-Biblicist tendencies of evangelicals have created a situation in which "orphans" have become singled out, sacralized, and made the explicit focus of activism beyond what either the Old or New Testaments would justify. This is evidenced by the fact that the movement has been so willing to extend the term "orphans" to *all* vulnerable children, regardless of whether they have one or both parents still living. Calling a child an "orphan" can be a rhetorical move to place religious significance on that child and to mobilize religious activism (adoption) on their behalf.

While there is ample evidence throughout the Bible that God's people are called to look after those who are vulnerable (including the poor, the stranger, the foreigner, the widow, the orphan, the sojourner, the oppressed, the prisoner, the sick, the lame, the leper, etc.), the "orphan" is not singled out as worthy of singular attention. Rather, as David Smolin correctly points out, almost all Old Testament references to "orphans" are included in conjunction with "widows."[28] Even the key verse in the orphan care movement from James 1:27 ("Religion that is pure and undefiled before God, the Father, is this: to visit orphans and widows in their affliction, and to keep oneself unstained from the world.") would imply that "orphans and widows" are a unit. Either they should be helped together or, at the very least, should receive equal attention. The biblical idea was never that "orphans" would be singled out for help to the neglect of anyone else, and certainly not that they would be taken from their mothers, kin, or communities and adopted into a family of strangers. Rather, God's people were to provide for single mothers and their vulnerable children because they apparently did not have a husband and would not have been provided for otherwise.

Children are indeed vulnerable globally, and *some* do need adoption (e.g., children in U.S. foster care). But the orphan care movement needs to acknowledge that connecting child adoption with the Christian's adoption in Christ or singling out "orphans" for special attention over and above their vulnerable birth mothers and communities is not only ineffective but exegetically irresponsible. Ultimately, it is my hope that evangelicals in the orphan care movement will transition from a focus on children to a focus on calling the Christian church to serve all manner of vulnerable people worldwide. Adoption may be a part of that, but it will not be a big part.

God's Glory and Social Engagement

My second recommendation for the orphan care movement is to avoid the unhelpful extreme of pietistic idealism that creates an unnecessary dualism between spiritual and physical redemption. It is exemplified in a quote shared earlier from a representative of America World Adoption:

> Our biggest goal is to get these orphans, not just to give them a home here in this world—but to give them an eternal home in heaven. If all we do is just get them adopted here and they still live and die in their sins and they don't accept Christ as their savior, we've helped them a little bit, but we've missed the big picture. The big thing is to get them adopted into Christian families who will bring them up as God says, in the nurture and admonition of the Lord, in hopes that they'll get saved—ask Jesus Christ into their hearts and then go to heaven.

This form of pietistic idealism is not distinctively evangelical, or even Christian in an orthodox sense; it is in fact gnostic. Gnostic interpretations of Christianity emerged shortly after Jesus' death. In simple terms, this teaching saw an antagonism between physical matter and spirit and taught that the spirit was really all that mattered. The physical body was worldly, lesser, and essentially irrelevant. In orthodox Christian theology, the unregenerate spirit is dead and the flesh is corrupt, but Jesus came in the flesh to redeem them both. In the gospels, Jesus' ministry was characterized by meeting individuals' physical needs as well as their spiritual needs. Oftentimes he preached the gospel and met physical needs together (Matthew 4:23). But it is critical to note that sometimes he did not do both at the same time. Sometimes Jesus simply told women and men about the Kingdom or the forgiveness of sins (often in the Gospel of John). But there are other times where Jesus seemed to provide for peoples' physical restoration without any indication that he preached the good news to them (e.g., Mark 5:21–43; Luke 5:12–14; 7:11–15).

It does not seem that Jesus only met people's physical needs as a strategy to get to the spiritual needs that *really* mattered. Nor did Jesus teach that approach to his disciples. Rather, he instructed his followers that they were expected to give to the poor (Matthew 6:3–4; Mark 10:21) and share whatever they had with those in need (Luke 6:30); that they were to invite the poor, the crippled, the lame, and the blind to their feasts, expecting nothing in return (Luke 14:13); and that the worst hypocrites were those who maintained pious reputations while neglecting the more important matters of justice and mercy for others (Matthew 23:23).

This is not to dismiss the importance of bearing verbal witness in Christian theology (Matthew 28:19–20; Acts 1:8). But the gnostic extreme of pietistic idealism I am describing here is mistaken in that it wrongly sees the endgame of *all* Christian ministry as about saving souls rather than bringing about God's redemptive purposes in a more holistic sense. In much of Christian theology, particularly the more reformed versions, Christians are taught to participate in God's grand plan of redemption, which not only involves bringing about spiritual restoration but also involves making *all things* new. As the New York pastor Tim Keller has often repeated, God's people are to "seek the peace and prosperity of the city" (Jeremiah 29:7), and that involves more than converting unbelievers; it also includes feeding the hungry, breaking the chains of injustice, and lifting the yolks of oppression (Isaiah 58:1–14, 61:1–4).[29]

The extreme of pietistic idealism that suggests that orphan care ministry can only be God honoring if the gospel is explicitly communicated in a personal way ignores the reality that getting children out of potentially harmful situations (orphanages, domestic foster care) is a moral imperative for Christians simply because God wants children out of harmful situations, period. The point of the parable of the Good Samaritan is that God is glorified when believers love and tangibly serve their neighbor. That may involve meeting a person's physical needs, even when there is no clear indication that the gospel has been explicitly communicated (Luke 10:25–37).

My plea to evangelicals in this regard is not to abandon pietistic idealism, per se, but to reject the extreme of pietistic idealism that causes them to take a myopic view of ministry to the marginalized—one that rejects opportunities to improve the lives of the vulnerable because they assume "true ministry" must involve explicit, individual communication of the gospel by certain kinds of people. As a practical example, I would suggest that all Christian ministries in the orphan care movement rethink their policies about recruiting only mission-minded, married heterosexual Christian parents to participate in adoption and foster care. The alternatives of couples or singles adopting for family growth (whether heterosexual or homosexual) would be eminently better than a child aging out of an institution overseas or domestically in foster care.

A Plea to Consider the Power of Changing Social Structures

Many Christians resist the idea that social systems need to be dealt with directly. They prefer the idea that "society is changed one heart at a time," and so they concentrate on only evangelism and individual social work. This is naïve. . . . [The vulnerable] need help, but it can't come merely in the form of relief and development. Someone must resist and change the legal, political, and social systems.
—Timothy Keller, *Generous Justice* (2010:127)

In truth, adoption is not a real solution to the global orphan crisis or even the problem of vulnerable children domestically. Movement leaders know this, and it is time to move on. Certainly, thousands of children in foster care are available for adoption now, and the orphan care movement has been wise to direct much of its domestic adoption focus to foster care initiatives. I sincerely hope they can become more successful than they have been at finding stable, loving homes for these children. But ultimately, any solutions to the problem of vulnerable children will have to look beyond adoption, or beyond *individual* acts of activism in general, and this is where I believe the movement and evangelicals themselves are most limited.

In spite of their individualist/anti-structural commitments, evangelicals must come to grips with the reality that changing social structures at the level of congregations, states, or nations can accomplish more, practically speaking, than mobilizing hundreds or even thousands of individual Christian families to essentially plug the dikes with their fingers. Let me make two recommendations about where changes in social structure could be most effective regarding vulnerable children, their parents, and communities.

AT THE LEVEL OF CONGREGATIONS

If evangelicals want ministry to the vulnerable (orphans included) to be a lasting part of church life, they should not seek to talk about it in sermons or hold an Orphan Sunday. Rather, they should do exactly what they do for those activities they truly feel are indispensable to the identity and functioning of their church—they make it part of their *structure*. They put money and organizational resources behind it. Churches *hire* individual pastors whose sole responsibility is to preach the Bible, lead worship, or lead the youth ministry. Some even have pastors who oversee families or outreach or missions. If orphan care—and more accurately, ministry to the vulnerable broadly—*really* is essential to the Christian identity, it is completely inconsistent for it to be an optional part of the budget or to have volunteers solely responsible for overseeing it.

Evangelical congregations should hire a pastor (or pastors) whose sole focus is to teach, recruit, and oversee efforts to address the needs of the vulnerable populations in the city and, to the extent that resources allow, around the world. Moreover, the pastoral staff (as well as elders and lay volunteers) must receive the sort of training and resources necessary to support those families who are in fact adopting or fostering children with special needs in order to accommodate these families. Better yet, training in ministry to vulnerable populations should be structured into discipleship itself. In practice, promoting a "culture of orphan care" in one's church means little more than "we talk about it every now and then" if it is not built into the hiring, resource allocation, and even the official mission and vision of the congregation.

An example of why this is necessary can be found in the research on multiracial congregations. One of the most consistent findings in research on stable multiracial congregations is that there is a need to *hire* diversity, not just talk about it. For predominantly white middle-class congregations seeking to open themselves up to believers of color, hiring an African American, Latino, or Asian pastor is an essential step. It signifies that those who are in the congregation are willing to adjust to accommodate others who may have different experiences and cultural preferences.[30] The same must happen for Christian families who are embracing vulnerable populations. Otherwise, those families will go elsewhere, as I found over and over again in my interviews.

AT THE LEVEL OF GOVERNMENT POLICIES
ALLEVIATING DISADVANTAGE

My final recommendation is for evangelicals to "look upstream" in their approach to addressing social problems. By this I mean they must consider how broad policy changes can provide more robust, long-term solutions to the problem of global and domestic vulnerability than individual activist efforts. Not only are evangelicals influenced by individualism/anti-structuralism, but they have also become more closely connected to fiscal conservatism over the last few decades. Consequently, they tend to be suspicious (or opposed outright) to solutions for poverty and inequality that involve governments and their dreaded "redistribution of wealth" measures. This perspective was reiterated throughout the movement mobilization literature. But focusing on individual activism to the neglect of enacting broad policy changes is hopelessly short-sighted, as Tim Keller pointed out in the epigraph to this section.

Consider the domestic problems that are most concerning for evangelicals in the orphan care movement: vulnerable children in institutions, abortion, and to some degree, disadvantaged single mothers. What unites all of these situations is unplanned pregnancy. Research on unplanned pregnancy shows that young women from disadvantaged backgrounds most often become pregnant before they are married or financially ready to take care of children for several reasons: They have not been educated about safe sex; they lack access to educational opportunities; they do not feel they have any future career prospects and thus see no reason to delay childbearing; and their male partners are also without education or employment opportunities and thus are not strong marriage candidates.[31] Adoption and foster care are not a solution to *any* of these problems. Neither are other forms of individual activism that target the symptoms rather than the disease.

Rather, research suggests that more promising solutions to the underlying causes of unplanned pregnancy are for both disadvantaged women and men to have access to better educational opportunities, better career prospects, and education about the risks associated with sex and about the use of contraceptives.[32] These interventions have done more in the last twenty years to contribute to declines in teen pregnancy and abortion than anything related to children post-partum.

Within the last few years, CAFO has begun in earnest to promote family reunification and mentoring for unwed mothers so that children can stay with their birth families and communities. I applaud that as a positive step. But if evangelicals are genuinely concerned about improving life for vulnerable populations, CAFO and other leaders need to challenge evangelicals in the pews to advocate for public policies that target the broader societal factors that require pregnant women to relinquish their babies or have them forcibly removed. This kind of change comes with greater access to opportunities and resources, and it can most effectively be administered by the state, not local churches. My hope is ultimately that American evangelicals in the orphan care movement will broaden their vision of *whom* to serve and *how* to serve them, and the result will be a society and world with less vulnerability, not only for children, but for all.

APPENDIX A

Data and Methods

In broadest terms, the initial goal of this research project was to understand how culture shapes the mobilization strategies of movement elites and activist outcomes of families participating in the evangelical orphan care movement. This goal required an inquiry into the backgrounds, ideological commitments, and experiences of orphan care movement participants across all levels of participation, including leadership, grassroots activists, and relevant actors outside of the movement, as well as the congregations and nonprofits serving these communities. To obtain this sort of data, I conducted 157 in-depth, semi-structured interviews with a grand total of 223 persons involved in adoption or serving vulnerable children (both evangelical and non-evangelical) as well as adoption/orphan experts across the United States. I supplement data from these in-depth interviews with ethnographic data from participant observation at orphan care movement events, data from movement publications and online content, and quantitative analyses of data from a variety of sources. In this methodological appendix, I elaborate more fully on my research methodology, giving particular attention to data collection and analysis.

INTERVIEWS

Recruiting Participants
The first leg of my research involved identifying and interviewing elite leaders in the orphan care movement. I was able to identify the most central leaders through a variety of means. First, I read all of the books written since 2000 promoting adoption and orphan care among evangelicals (see those listed in chapter 3). I also read books and articles by authors who were explicitly critical of conservative Christians or

evangelicals participating in domestic and international adoption.[1] As I read these works, I paid careful attention to the names and positions of individuals who endorsed the books as well as authors who were cited or the individuals and ministries that were offered as examples. The Christian Alliance for Orphans also lists their executive leadership and board of directors on their website. I contacted many of these authors and leaders prior to the 2013 CAFO Summit in Nashville, Tennessee, and set up appointments with them to conduct interviews. At the end of every interview with movement leaders, I always asked my interviewees if they could recommend at least five other leaders in the movement who they felt I should speak with. Leaders often responded to my request by giving me names of both leaders that they felt were mainstream as well as leaders they felt that were critical to the movement but might fly under the radar. Many leaders I interviewed were so kind as to provide email introductions that connected me with leaders whom they recommended. The president of CAFO, Jedd Medefind, was especially gracious in brokering access to other elite leaders in the movement. Additionally, I spent time in informal conversation with most of these leaders, and almost all of the leaders I interviewed expressed interest in the project and agreed to make themselves available for follow-up questions and additional interviews. Several even sent follow-up emails to me to ask how the research was developing or to clarify comments made on record. At the 2014 CAFO Summit at Willow Creek Community Church in Chicago, I was able to interact with many of these leaders who were eager to hear about my research progress.

Figure A1 illustrates the geographical diversity of the movement leaders I interviewed. Although leaders represent nearly twenty states across the United States, a majority of the leaders resided in four regions: the Dallas–Fort Worth metroplex; Chicagoland; Washington, DC, and northern Virginia; and central Colorado around Colorado Springs and Denver.

Table A1 lists the leaders who I interviewed for the study with relevant information about their title and involvement with adoption, foster care, or global orphan care; residence; interview date; and the nature of the interview itself. Although I have changed the names of all families who participated in my study to protect their anonymity, I have kept the

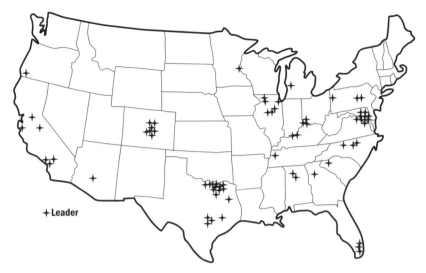

Figure A1. Map of leaders interviewed ($N = 72$).

names of leaders since they have already made themselves, their roles, and their activities public through their involvement with adoption and orphan care.

The second leg of the research focused on families involved in various forms of orphan care, but particularly adoption, foster care, and foster care alternatives such as Safe Families for Children. This was done through a combination of snowball sampling and purposive sampling. To maximize diversity of experience, I conducted interviews with families primarily within four regions: Texas, Illinois, Ohio, and areas around the Georgia–South Carolina border (see fig. A2). Following interviews, I generally asked respondents to share with me a few names of families in their church or community who were also engaged in adoption, fostering, or Safe Families who might be willing to talk. These families typically contacted their friends first to ask permission and then either made email introductions or passed along email addresses for me to request an interview.

In order to draw conclusions about the ways in which culture shapes evangelical families involved in activistic forms of orphan care, it was necessary to compare these families with others who were either non-evangelical or non-activistic in their adoptive or fostering activities.

TABLE A1. Leaders Interviewed

Name	Title(s)/ Organization(s)*	Residence	Interview Date	Interview Location
David Anderson	Founder of Safe Families for Children; executive director of LYDIA Home	Chicago, IL	July 10, 2013	Chicago, IL
Curtis Artis	National director of partnerships, Christian Alliance for Orphans	Fort Lauderdale, FL	October 28, 2013	Video Call
Phillip Aspegren	Founder and executive director, Casa Viva	Costa Rica	July 23, 2013	Telephone
Mark Barret	Founder and CEO, Parental Care Ministries	Tyler, TX	September 11, 2013	Telephone
Daniel Bennett	Senior pastor, Bethany Community Church; author of *Passion for the Fatherless*	Washington, IL	May 2, 2013	Nashville, TN
Jon Bergeron	Director of Family Care, Hope for Orphans (ministry of FamilyLife, subsidiary of Campus Crusade for Christ International)	College Station, TX	July 10, 2013	Chicago, IL
Larry Bergeron	Founder and executive director, A Child's Hope International; author of *Journey to the Fatherless*	Cincinnati, OH	May 2, 2013	Nashville, TN
Bill Blacquiere	President and CEO, Bethany Christian Services; board member, Christian Alliance for Orphans; board member, National Council for Adoption	Grand Rapids, MI	May 29, 2013	Video Call
Johnny Carr	National director of church partnerships, Bethany Christian Services; author of *Orphan Justice*	Pittsburgh, PA	May 2, 2013	Nashville, TN

TABLE A1. (*cont.*)

Name	Title(s)/ Organization(s)*	Residence	Interview Date	Interview Location
Lisa Castetter	Founder and CEO, Teen Leadership Foundation	Newport Beach, CA	August 30, 2013	Telephone
Gerald Clark	Founder and CEO, Home for Good Foundation	Grants Pass, OR	July 11, 2013	Video Call
Dan Cruver	Co-founder and president of Together for Adoption; editor and contributing author to *Reclaiming Adoption*	Greenville, SC	May 2, 2013	Nashville, TN
Amy Curtis	Director, Tapestry, Irving Bible Church; social worker	Dallas, TX	June 24, 2013	Dallas, TX
Tom Davis	CEO, Children's Hope Chest; author of *Fields of the Fatherless*	Colorado Springs, CO	September 12, 2013	Video Call
Mike Douris	Founder and president, Orphan Outreach; board member, Christian Alliance for Orphans	Dallas, TX	July 8, 2013	Telephone
C. H. Dyer	President and CEO, Bright Hope; founder, Better Orphan Care; leadership council, Faith to Action Initiative	Chicago, IL	June 13, 2013	Chicago, IL
Diane Lynn Elliot	Author of *The Global Orphan Crisis*; stateside operations administrator, Oasis for Orphans	Chicago, IL	February 7, 2014	Chicago, IL
Sharon Ford	Manager of permanency services, Colorado Department of Human Services***; board member, Christian Alliance for Orphans	Denver, CO	June 14, 2013	Telephone
Paula Freeman	Founder and executive director, Hope's Promise; author of *A Place I Didn't Belong*	Denver, CO	November 4, 2013	Telephone

TABLE A1. (*cont.*)

Name	Title(s)/ Organization(s)*	Residence	Interview Date	Interview Location
Frank Garrott	President and CEO, Gladney Center for Adoption***; board member, Joint Council on International Children's Services***; board member, Children's Home Society of America***; board member, Both Ends Burning***; board member, Bravelove***	Austin, TX	June 21, 2013	Telephone
Sarah J. Gesiriech	Founder and principal, 127 Global Strategies***; advisory board, Congressional Coalition on Adoption Institute***; advisory board, Equality for Adopted Children***; coordinator, Faith to Action Initiative	Washington, DC	July 31, 2013	Telephone
Beth Guckenberger	Co-founder and co-executive director, Back2Back Ministries; author of four books on orphans and orphan care	Monterey, Mexico/Cincinnati, OH	May 31, 2013	Video Call
Dwain Gullion	President, the ABBA Fund; North Carolina state director, Lifeline Children Services	Greensboro, NC	June 20, 2013	Video Call
Kerry Hasenbalg	Co-founder and former executive director, Congressional Coalition on Adoption Institute***; advisory board, Congressional Coalition on Adoption Institute***; advisory board, Equality for Adopted Children***	Danville, PA	July 9, 2013	Video Call
Scott Hasenbalg	Co-founder and executive director, Show Hope	Danville, PA	July 16, 2013	Telephone

TABLE A1. (*cont.*)

Name	Title(s)/ Organization(s)*	Residence	Interview Date	Interview Location
David Hennessey	Director of global movements, Christian Alliance for Orphans	Atlanta, GA	May 24, 2013	Video Call
Chuck Johnson	President and CEO, National Council for Adoption***	Baltimore, MD	June 25, 2013	Telephone
Craig Juntunen**	Founder and president, Both Ends Burning Campaign***; executive producer, *STUCK* (documentary)	Scottsdale, AZ	June 6, 2013	Telephone
Bruce and Denise Kendrick	Co-founders and executive director (Bruce), Embrace Texas	McKinney, TX	September 27, 2013	Video Call
Aaron Klein	Founder, Hope Takes Root; board member, Lifesong for Orphans Ethiopia	Sacramento, CA	September 4, 2013	Telephone
Jason Kovacs	Pastor, Austin Stone Community Church; co-founder, Together for Adoption; director of ministry development, the ABBA Fund; Contributing author to *Reclaiming Adoption*	Austin, TX	May 3, 2013	Nashville, TN
Daniel LaBry	CEO, the ABBA Fund	Dallas, TX	June 20, 2013	Dallas, TX
Andy Lehman	Vice president, Lifesong for Orphans; board member, Christian Alliance for Orphans	Gridley, IL	May 4, 2013	Nashville, TN
Tabitha Lovell	Adoption travel manager; co-founder and owner of Adoption Airfare and Cheap Mission Trips***	Louisville, KY	August 29, 2013	Video Call
Tom Lukasik	Executive director, 4Kids of South Florida; Florida Faith-Based and Community-Based Advisory Council	Miami, FL	June 17, 2013	Video Call

TABLE A1. (*cont.*)

Name	Title(s)/ Organization(s)*	Residence	Interview Date	Interview Location
Brian Luwis	Founder and CEO, America World Adoption; board member, Christian Alliance for Orphans; board member, National Council for Adoption***	Washington, DC	May 3, 2013	Nashville, TN
Ruslan Malyuta	Founder and former president, Alliance for Ukraine Without Orphans; founder and president, World Without Orphans	Kiev, Ukraine	July 10, 2013	Video Call
Jedd Medefind	President and CEO, Christian Alliance for Orphans; advisory board, Congressional Coalition on Adoption Institute***; advisory board, Faith to Action Initiative; board member (chair), Paradigm Shift	McLean, VA	May 23, 2013	Video Call
Tony Merida	Founding pastor, Imago Dei Church; associate professor, Southeastern Baptist Theological Seminary; co-author of *Orphanology*	Raleigh, NC	May 13, 2013	Video Call
Michael and Amy Monroe	Co-founders of Tapestry, Irving Bible Church; contributing speakers, Empowered to Connect Conferences; co-authors of *Created to Connect*	Dallas, TX	June 24, 2013	Dallas, TX
Russell Moore	President, Southern Baptist Ethics and Religious Liberty Commission; former dean of the School of Theology, the Southern Baptist Theological Seminary (until 2013); author of *Adopted for Life*	Louisville, KY	May 2, 2013	Nashville, TN

TABLE A1. (*cont.*)

Name	Title(s)/ Organization(s)*	Residence	Interview Date	Interview Location
Rick Morton	Associate pastor, Faith Baptist Church; co-author of *Orphanology*	Bartlett, TN	May 9, 2013	Telephone
John M. Neese	Founder and executive director, Strategic Angel Care	Dallas, TX	June 24, 2013	Dallas, TX
Herbie Newell	Executive director, Lifeline Children's Services	Birmingham, AL	June 19, 2013	Video Call
Kerry Olson	Co-founder and chairperson, Faith to Action Initiative; founder and president emeritus, Firelight Foundation***	Santa Cruz, CA	November 7, 2013	Telephone
Katie Overstreet	Program director of adoption and orphan care, Focus on the Family	Colorado Springs, CO	May 22, 2013	Video Call
Paul and Robin Pennington	Co-founders and executive director (Paul), Hope for Orphans (a ministry of Family Life, a subsidiary of Campus Crusade for Christ International); former board member, Christian Alliance for Orphans (until 2011)	Austin, TX	June 27, 2013	Austin, TX
Ellen E. Porter	Founder of Bravelove***	Dallas, TX	July 23, 2013	Telephone
Karyn Purvis	Co-founder and director, Texas Christian University Institute of Child Development and the Hope Connection***; contributing speaker, Empowered to Connect conferences; co-author of *The Connected Child*	Fort Worth, TX	August 19, 2013	Video Call
Kelly Rosati	Vice president of community outreach, Focus on the Family; co-author of *Wait No More*	Colorado Springs, CO	July 3, 2013	Telephone

TABLE A1. (*cont.*)

Name	Title(s)/ Organization(s)*	Residence	Interview Date	Interview Location
Scott and Kathy Rosenow	Co-founders and directors, The Shepherd's Crook Ministries	West Chester, OH	December 30, 2013	West Chester, OH
Maridel Sandberg	President, the MI-CAH Fund, Bethlehem Baptist Church; board Member (Chair, 2005–2011), Christian Alliance for Orphans; Twin Cities director, Safe Families for Children	Minneapolis, MN	August 20, 2013	Minneapolis, MN
Doug Sauder	President, 4Kids of South Florida; family pastor, Calvary Bible Church	Miami, FL	July 17, 2013	Telephone
David Smolin	Professor of law, Samford University***	Birmingham, AL	July 17, 2013	Video Call
Matthew Storer	President and CEO, VisionTrust International; board member (chair), Christian Alliance for Orphans	Colorado Springs, CO	July 7, 2013	Video Call
Kathleen Strottman**	Executive director, Congressional Coalition on Adoption Institute***; former legislative director for Senator Mary Landrieu (D-LA)	Washington, DC	August 23, 2013	Telephone
Elizabeth Styffe	Director, Orphan Care Initiatives, Saddleback Church	Saddleback, CA	September 10, 2013	Telephone
Bruce Thomas	Founder and CEO, Livada Orphan Care	Dallas, TX	June 20, 2013	Dallas, TX
Jodi Jackson Tucker	International director of Orphan Sunday, Christian Alliance for Orphans; board of directors, Project Hopeful; author of *Fasten Your Sweet Belt*	Durham, NC	May 13, 2013	Video Call

TABLE A1. (*cont.*)

Name	Title(s)/ Organization(s)*	Residence	Interview Date	Interview Location
Carolyn and Kiel Twietmeyer	Co-founders and executive director (Carolyn), Project Hopeful	Joliet, IL	September 2, 2013	Joliet, IL
Scott Vair	President, World Orphans	Castle Rock, CO	May 2, 2013	Nashville, TN
Michael Wear	Former faith-action advisor to the Obama administration***	Washington, DC	July 24, 2013	Telephone
Rebecca Weichhand	Director of policy, Congressional Coalition on Adoption Institute**	Washington, DC	August 5, 2013	Telephone
Jason Weber	National director of foster care initiatives, Christian Alliance for Orphans; author of *Launching an Orphans Ministry in Your Church*	Plano, TX	October 10, 2013	Video Call
Elizabeth Wiebe	Director, outreach and member services, Christian Alliance for Orphans; former associate director, White House Office of Faith-Based and Community Initiatives	Washington, DC	June 21, 2013	Telephone
Lynn Young	Director, Local Orphan Care Initiative and Extraordinary Family Institute, Saddleback Church	Saddleback, CA	September 18, 2013	Telephone

* Though not exhaustive, these were the official titles and organizations for each leader when I conducted interviews between May 2013 and November 2013.
** Does not consider oneself an evangelical.
*** Not an explicitly evangelical nonprofit or firm.

Thus, I purposively sampled families across both religious affiliation (evangelical vs. non-evangelical) and their orientation to orphan-care activism (activistic vs. non-activistic). Table A2 presents the breakdown of families across their religious commitment and participation in activistic orphan care.

Figure A2. Map of families interviewed ($N = 85$).

TABLE A2. Families in the Sample by Religion and Relationship to Orphan Care Activism

Religion/Type of Orphan Care	$N = 85$
Evangelical/activistic orphan care	$n = 43$
Evangelical/non-activistic orphan care	$n = 21$
Non-evangelical/activistic orphan care	$n = 8$
Non-evangelical/non-activistic orphan care	$n = 13$

Note: "Activistic" indicates that the family explicitly engaged in activities promoting orphan care beyond adoption, including attending promotional conferences, campaigning for orphans, starting or serving as a leader in an orphan care ministry in their church, etc. "Non-activistic" indicates that the family did not engage in any form of orphan care activism beyond adoption or fostering to adopt, primarily with the purpose of growing their family. "Non-evangelical" referred to any interviewees who were both unaffiliated with an evangelical denomination (Steensland et al. 2000) and did not hold beliefs typically associated with evangelicals (D. M. Lindsay 2007).

Interview Sample

Table A3 presents descriptive statistics of leaders, families, and individuals whom I interviewed for this study. Although about half of my interviews were conducted with couples, I treat these members of the couples as individuals in order to provide an idea of the demographic makeup of those I interviewed.

TABLE A3. Descriptive Statistics of Interview Sample (*N* = 223)

Sociodemographic Measures	Leaders % or Mean (SD)	Grassroots Individuals % or Mean (SD)
Age	47 (12)	42 (10)
Male	74	45
Race:		
White	97	98
Black	3	1
Asian	0	0
Latino	0	1
Other	0	0
Educational background:		
High school degree	5	10
Some college	3	5
College degree	80	80
Post-graduate work/degree	12	5
Region:		
South	47	33
Northeast	15	0
Midwest	21	60
West	17	7
Married	95	90
Religious affiliation:		
Evangelical Protestant	95	75
Mainline Protestant	2	10
Catholic	3	5
Jewish	0	2
Other	0	0
None	1	8
N	72	151

Note: Not all families or leaders had adopted or were necessarily involved in adoption or fostering directly. Thus I have not included percentages about how many leaders or individuals had adopted or fostered children. SD = standard deviation.

Conducting the Interviews and Data Analysis

Interviews were conducted in a variety of settings, including coffee shops, restaurants, churches, in hallways during large conferences, respondents' offices, and most frequently in respondents' homes. The majority of interviews were conducted in person, with a large percentage conducted face-to-face in a video call (using Skype or FaceTime), and a small percentage were conducted over the phone. Although I always sought to interview respondents in person whenever possible, I concluded that the technology of video calling made it unnecessary to fly out to, say, California for a single interview if I could make a Skype call at the respondents' convenience. Whether the interview was conducted in person, by video call, or by telephone did not seem to alter the quality or depth of information I received, although in-person interviews were understandably somewhat longer, mostly owing to the simple courtesies expected when someone is physically in your presence. Interviews lasted anywhere from around thirty minutes to almost three hours, with the average interview lasting about seventy minutes. All interviews were digitally recorded and transcribed by a professional transcription firm that signs a confidentiality agreement. I approved all transcriptions myself. The result was over twenty-five hundred pages of content. I coded and analyzed all the transcribed interviews using ATLAS.ti qualitative data analysis software (http://atlasti.com).

PARTICIPANT OBSERVATION

As pointed out by sociologists who criticize using interviews for the study of culture,[2] focusing exclusively on interview data would have had a number of drawbacks. Not only is culture fragmentary, incoherent, and often poorly articulated by even the sincerest of interviewees, it is possible that the orphan care movement participants I interviewed— and particularly the movement leaders who would naturally want to paint their organizations and the movement itself in the most positive light—might have neglected to give me information that could be unflatteringly publicized. For the researcher, observational data with research participants is critical in order to cross-check information that is explicitly given in formal interview contexts with the casual conversations, remarks, and interactions that take place in other settings. To provide this sort of data, I sought to observe how movement participants speak and interact with one another at large events, small groups, and other unguarded settings. Table A4 lists the various evangelical orphan care conferences, seminars, and events where I engaged in participant observation.

At these events, I took copious notes concerning what was said from up front and interactions with people and was able to conduct dozens of informal conversational interviews with volunteers and attendees. Beyond attending these conferences or seminars, I sat in on leadership planning meetings, conference calls, and volunteer-deployment meetings.

TABLE A4. Participant Observation Events in Chronological Order

Month/Year	Event	Location
March 2013	Both Ends Burning, Chicago volunteers meeting*	Conference Call
April 2013	America World Adoption, "Adopted by Design" seminar	Chesterton, IN
April 2013	Both Ends Burning, presentation at the University of Chicago School of Social Service Administration*	Chicago, IL
April 2013	Both Ends Burning, showing of *STUCK* documentary*	Chicago, IL
May 2013	Christian Alliance for Orphans, Summit conference	Nashville, TN
May 2013	Both Ends Burning, "Unstuck" March on Washington*	Washington, DC
August 2013	Safe Families for Children, national conference	Chicago, IL
September 2013	Tapestry Ministry, leadership meeting	Dallas, TX
September 2013	Empowered To Connect, conference	Houston, TX
October 2013	Tapestry, national conference (Irving Bible Church)	Dallas, TX
November 2013	Orphan Sunday service, Willow Creek Community Church	Chicago, IL
May 2014	Safe Families for Children, national conference	Chicago, IL
May 2014	Christian Alliance for Orphans, Summit conference	Chicago, IL
November 2014	Orphan Sunday service, First Presbyterian Church	Augusta, GA
September 2015	Foster care information session, Providence Road Church	Norman, OK
November 2015	Orphan Sunday service, Providence Road Church	Norman, OK

* Not an explicitly evangelical event but heavily attended and promoted by evangelicals and the Christian Alliance for Orphans.

In some cases, I took on a more active role, volunteering in several movement events by selling tickets to documentary showings, getting petitions signed, and arranging tables and equipment. Participating in these activities solidified bonds of trust with movement leaders and participants and provided more opportunities to engage in informal conversational interviews with volunteers and attendees.

CONTENT ANALYSES

Data for content analyses included a variety of sources. At every orphan care conference, seminar, or event, I collected free brochures, advertisements, DVDs, and any other promotional and informational materials that were distributed by orphan care organizations. Many orphan care conferences, and particularly the CAFO Summit conferences and the Together for Adoption national conference, allow adoption and orphan care agencies to set up booths from which appointed delegates (and sometimes the founders and executive officers themselves) distribute materials and engage attendees with information about the organization. This made collecting materials fairly easy. The executive staff of CAFO also provided me with programs for all CAFO Summits since 2004, from which I was able to make observations about common themes addressed in all these meetings. I also made use of the online postings from CAFO and other key orphan care organizations including weblogs, webinars, and all information posted on the CAFO website since 2013.

The various books that have been written by evangelicals promoting adoption and orphan care also served as important sources of information. These books provided critical insights into the mobilization strategies utilized by movement leaders and gave me a valuable means by which I could cross-check the accounts that movement leaders articulated to me, the sociologist, about their motivations and strategies, compared to what they said when they were writing to an evangelical audience. I also analyzed the content of various blog entries, online articles in venues like *Christianity Today* or *WORLD* magazine, and talks these leaders had given over the last few years for the same purpose.

Similarly, many of the evangelical families I interviewed, particularly those who embraced an activistic approach to orphan care or adoption (either initially or over time), kept blogs about their experiences. I always asked families if they kept a blog or online diary and if they would grant me access to their blog. Overall, I was able to obtain access to about twenty online blogs from evangelical families I had interviewed, and I was able to analyze the content of these blogs to compare interview accounts.

QUANTITATIVE DATA SOURCES

Scholars of child welfare in the United States agree that reliable data on adoption and foster care can be difficult to come by.[3] Although data on foster care, and to a limited degree, international adoptions, are collected by the U.S. government, data on domestic private agency or third-party adoptions are not collected. Consequently, the majority of research on adoption historically has relied on non-random samples of birth mothers, adoptive parents, or adoptees. National-level data based on probability samples have been few and far between. Valuable national-level data have included the 1973–2010 National Survey of Family Growth (NSFG) panel surveys, the 2004–2007 National Survey of Fertility Barriers, the 2007 National Survey of Adoptive Families, the Adoption and Foster Care Analysis and Reporting System reports (nos. 1–21), the 1983–2013 Survey of Income and Program Participation panel studies, and the U.S. Censuses, which in 2000 began collecting adoption data.[4] Though important for understanding aggregate adoption trends, these national data sets are limited in the questions they ask about adoptive parents' personal lives, and only the NSFG studies have asked about both adoption *seeking* and *completion* as well as parents' religious backgrounds. The Panel Study of Income Dynamics and the National Longitudinal Survey of Youth also contain questions about adoption, as well as the religious background of respondents. However, because of the nature of these studies, they are typically used to understand adoptive relationships and outcomes rather than trends in adoption seeking. Researchers in public opinion toward adoption and fostering have also made use of surveys conducted by interest groups such as the Evan B. Donaldson Institute, the Dave Thomas Institute for Adoption; and the National Council for Adoption.

Given the lack of a single comprehensive quantitative data source on adoption and foster care, in this study I draw upon a variety of quantitative data sources to provide descriptive information regarding trends in child welfare in the United States and overseas as well as within the orphan care movement itself. These sources consisted of (1) national and international data collected and published by government agencies regarding domestic and international adoption and foster care, (2) national surveys, and (3) a database of the 195+ CAFO member organizations. Below, I discuss each one of these data sources in turn.

National and International Data on Adoption and Foster Care
Numbers on adoption from the U.S. foster care system are taken from the Adoption and Foster Care Analysis and Reporting System (AFCARS) reports, published by the Children's Bureau of the U.S. Department of Health and Human Services' Administration for Children and Families.

Statistics on intercountry adoptions are taken from the Bureau of Consular Affairs, U.S. Department of State. These statistics are posted on the departmental websites and are updated annually. Last, statistics and numbers of adoptions in the aggregate are taken from the 2000 and 2010 U.S. Censuses.

National Surveys on Adoption and Foster Care Experiences and Attitudes
Statistics on various issues regarding adoption and foster care are taken from six different national surveys, most of them referenced in chapter 1. These included several waves of the National Survey of Family Growth, 2007 National Survey of Adoptive Parents, the 2007 and 2012 National Foster Care Adoption Attitudes Surveys, and the two 2013 Barna FRAMES Surveys.[5]

Database of Christian Alliance for Orphans Member Organizations
As of Spring 2016, there were over 195 organizations that listed as members in the Christian Alliance for Orphans. Membership requires an annual donation, financial transparency as demonstrated through one's approval by the Evangelical Council for Financial Accountability (ECFA; requiring the disclosure of all financial records), affirmation of an evangelical doctrinal statement (taken directly from the ECFA doctrinal statement), and agreement with a number of statements provided by CAFO. Because all of these organizations have websites, I was able to compile data on each of the 196 organizations into an organizational database. This database provides me with descriptive information about the background, characteristics, and activities of orphan care organizations affiliated with CAFO.

APPENDIX B

Interview Guides

DEMOGRAPHIC QUESTIONS (ASKED OF EVERYONE)
Can you give me a little bit of background information?

1. How old are you?
2. What does your educational background look like?
3. What do you do for a living?
4. [If married] How long have you been married?
5. How many biological children do you have?
6. How many adopted children do you have?

RELIGIOUS BACKGROUND QUESTIONS
(ASKED OF EVERYONE)
7. Do you have any sort of faith background?
8. What sorts of churches have you found yourself attending over the years?
9. Where do you attend now?
10. Would you say that you [both partners if married] are faithful attenders?

INTERVIEW GUIDE (FOR ADOPTIVE/FOSTERING OR PRE-ADOPTIVE/ FOSTERING PARENTS)
11. Okay, I'd like you to take a few minutes to describe your own family growing up.
    a. Did you know any family members or friends who were adopted/fostered?
    b. Do you recall any opinions expressed about adoption/foster care by your family or friends when you were growing up? What were these?

12. Adoption/fostering seems like a really big decision. How did you decide to adopt/foster? Describe the process.
    a. Where did the idea come from? What was the most important factor in your decision?
    b. Who did you talk to about adoption/foster care? How did you get information?
    c. Have you read any material or books that shaped your thoughts on adoption/foster care?
    d. What were the practical resources or support available?
13. What were some of the main obstacles either in your mind or actually?
    a. What kept you going despite these concerns or obstacles?
14. [If the individual or couple identify as conservative Protestant] You've described yourself as a pretty committed Christian. What role if any did your faith play in your decision to adopt/foster?
15. [If the individual or couple identify as conservative Protestant] What role did your personal religious community play in the process?
    a. Do any of the pastors/staff at church talk about adoption/foster care? Has that influenced you?
    b. Do you know people at your church who are adopting/fostering? (Pastors, elders, friends) How did that influence the process for you, if at all?
    c. Does your church have an adoption/orphan care ministry? Did you use this ministry?
    d. Did you get information or help of any kind from any other Christian adoption/orphan care organizations outside of your church?
    e. What about other Christian resources? (movies, articles, Christian speakers, adoption/orphan care organizations, Bible studies)
16. What was your larger family's role in the process?
    a. When did you tell them/talk to them about it? What were their reactions?
    b. What were their concerns, if any?
    c. What kind of practical help did they offer, if any?

17. [If respondents adopted] Adoption can be pretty expensive. If it's okay for me to ask . . .
    a. How much did each adoption cost in your situation?
    b. Where did you get the money to adopt?
18. [If the couple adopted internationally, domestically, or through foster care] So why did you decide to adopt [path chosen] rather than [alternative]?
19. Do you think adoption/fostering is something important for others to do to? If so, why?
20. Have you ever encouraged anyone else to adopt/foster? If so, how did you encourage them?
21. What about same-sex couples adopting? Would that help the problem of unwanted children finding families?
22. Have your thoughts/beliefs about adoption and orphan care evolved along the way? How so?
23. What is your opinion about the way adoption and foster care is done in the United States?
    a. Do you feel positively or negatively about current adoption policy?
    b. How do you think it could be improved?
24. [If openness in adoption has not come up yet] How do you feel about open adoptions?
25. [If an adopted/fostered child is a different race] Talk to me about how you approach (or plan to approach) racial issues with your adopted/fostered children.
    a. How do/will you explain racial differences to your adopted/fostered kids? How do you plan to explain it in the future?
26. [If an adopted child is of a different nationality/ethnicity] How do you think about your adopted child's national or ethnic heritage?
    a. What are your thoughts on incorporating cultural elements from their native culture?
27. Is there anything else that you feel would be important to know about the experience of adoption that would be helpful for me to know?
28. Can you recommend other families who have adopted or are going through the process of adoption that I could interview as well?
29. Would it be okay for me to contact you again if I had some questions later?

INTERVIEW GUIDE (FOR ORPHAN CARE
ORGANIZATIONAL LEADERS)

[Following demographic and religious background questions 1–10 above]

1. How long have you been [working or volunteering] for this organization?
2. Can you describe the goals and priorities of your organization?
3. Can you describe your role with this organization?
4. How did you come to [start/found/work for] this organization? Describe the processes leading up to that.
5. [If the interviewee has also adopted/fostered themselves] How has your own experience with adoption shaped the way you understand the role of your organization?
6. Please tell me about all the activities your organization does to facilitate and promote orphan care and adoption.
   - What are some specific examples?
   - What are the motivational goals behind these activities?
   - How do these activities fit into the overall goal of the organization?
7. Can you give me an idea of where most of the resources come from to support this organization?
8. [If this is not mentioned in the response above] You've described yourself as a pretty committed Christian.
   - What role if any did your faith play in shaping the way you think about adoption and orphan care?
   - What role if any did your faith play in your decision to [work for/ start/ found] this organization?
   - Have your thoughts or beliefs about adoption and orphan care evolved along the way? How so?
9. What are some reasons why you feel adoption and orphan care should be the concern of more people?
   - What's the strategy? What needs to be done to make that happen?
10. Are you involved in any activities promoting or facilitating adoption and orphan care outside of adopting yourself and working for your organization?
    - Do you teach church/seminary/college courses on adoption or orphan care?
    - Are you a part of any congregation that promotes or facilitates adoption or orphan care? What are the activities this congregation does to promote or facilitate adoption or orphan care?

- Can you list any other nonprofit organizations you're involved with that promote or facilitate adoption or orphan care? Can you describe your role with this organization?
- [If not mentioned in the previous questions] Are you associated with the Christian Alliance for Orphans, Together for Adoption, National Council for Adoption, or any other such organization? If so, can you describe the nature of your association?

11. Obviously both domestic and international adoption are important, but if you could encourage couples to consider one over the other, which would you promote and why?

12. How do you feel about alternatives to the adoptive families Christians are most comfortable with?
    - Non-Christian families?
    - Single-parent families?
    - Same-sex families?
    - Would the participation of these families in adoption and orphan care help the problem of unwanted children finding families?

13. What is your opinion about the way adoption and foster care is done in the United States?
    - Do you feel positively or negatively about current adoption policy?
    - How do you think it could be improved?

14. How do you feel about open adoptions? Does your organization have a policy on the issue?

15. Orphans have always been around in the United States and around the world. Why do you think this awakening of Christians toward the needs of orphans is happening now?

16. Is there anything else about your experiences with adoption and orphan care that would be helpful for me to know?

17. In your opinion, who are the top five most influential leaders in promoting, advocating, educating, and facilitating adoption and orphan care among Christians that I should be talking to? Can you connect me with these leaders?

18. Would it be okay to contact you again if I had some questions later?

[Additional questions if leaders are also authors of books on adoption or orphan care]

19. Can you summarize the argument and goals of your book [title of the book]?
20. What are some reasons why you feel adoption and orphan care should be the concern of more people?
    - What's the strategy? What needs to be done to make that happen?
21. [Assuming the interviewee has also adopted themselves] How did your own experience with adoption motivate your writing on adoption?

NOTES

PREFACE AND ACKNOWLEDGMENTS

1 See, e.g., various works by Elizabeth Bartholet, Chris Beam, Laura Briggs, Sara Dorow, Karen Dubinsky, Ellen Herman, Heather Jacobson, Barbara Melosh, Sandra Patton, Adam Pertman, Pamela Anne Quiroz, Gina Miranda Samuels, Jane Jeong Trenka, and numerous others. This of course does not include the scores of evangelical thinkers and advocates writing on adoption or foster care from a distinctively Christian viewpoint, most of whom have also had their lives shaped by adoption.

2 For *The Child Catchers*, see Joyce (2013b).

3 Haidt (2012).

4 Early on my research, several of the movement leaders I spoke with expressed to me that Kathryn Joyce had approached them about an interview and that they were reluctant to speak candidly with her for fear that she would twist their statements to paint the movement in a negative light. Others expressed to me that Kathryn Joyce engaged in practices that they considered "sneaky," even to the point of feigning support for the movement to get movement leaders and activists to speak with her.

INTRODUCTION

1 In some of these accounts, authors appear to consider "evangelicals" as virtually synonymous with the "religious right." While evangelicals do tend to espouse politically conservative views, this is changing somewhat among younger cohorts (Bean and Martinez 2014; Farrell 2011) and has never been the case for *all* evangelicals (e.g., Campolo 2009; Wallis 2006). Moreover, I would argue that it is simply inaccurate conceptually to assume that "evangelicals" (a term describing a subculture of religious beliefs, values, and practices) are synonymous with the "religious right," which is almost always a pejorative term referencing a religiopolitical group that includes non-evangelicals like politically conservative Catholics, Jews, and Mainline Protestants.

2 Joyce (2013a).

3 Barcella (2014).

4 See Barcella (2013, 2014); *Indian Country Today Media Network* staff (2013); Joyce (2009b, 2011, 2013a, 2013b, 2013c, 2013d, 2013e); Kerry and Niels (2009); Riben (2007, 2010, 2012); Schwarzschild (2013); Smolin (2012b); and Springer-Mock (2013).

5　Joyce's earlier work also focused on evangelicals and family issues. In *Quiverfull: Inside the Christian Patriarchy Movement* (Joyce 2009a), she described how conservative Christian families were promoting patriarchal authority and unbridled fertility for the purposes of world evangelization.

6　See Joyce's (2009b) article in the *Nation*, "Shotgun Adoption."

7　"Orphan care" is an umbrella term used by evangelicals themselves to refer to activities geared toward alleviating the plight of vulnerable children through adoption (primarily), fostering, mentoring, and other forms of aid (Carr 2013; Merida and Morton 2011). For evangelicals, the term "orphan" symbolically connects their activities to biblical commands to look after orphans in distress (Isaiah 1:17; James 1:27). The use of the term "orphan" is controversial, however. First and foremost, it is often technically inaccurate, since the children evangelicals seek to help are not necessarily orphans in the traditional sense that one or both of their parents might be deceased; they might instead be children in vulnerable situations for whatever reason (M. Davis 2011; Morton 2014). The term is even more problematic when used of foster children in the United States, the vast majority of whom have not lost either parent to death but have been removed from their parents because of neglect or abuse. Relatedly, because the term can be technically inaccurate, there is concern that the label "orphan" is used to frame the children as "parentless" in a way that serves those interested in adopting rather than addressing the problems that led to the vulnerable status of those children (most often, the poverty of their parents). Moreover, the term is potentially demeaning and hurtful to a child, as "orphans" are in most cultures given the lowest status, and thus the adoption of such children can be framed as a rescue of sorts. While I acknowledge these problems, I use the terms "orphan care" and "orphans" in this work because they are the terms used by the group I am studying, not because I think they are technically accurate.

8　C. Smith (2000:1).

9　C. Smith (2000:193).

10　Greeley and Hout (2006:1).

11　Meyer (2014); Snow and Soule (2010); and Tilly (2004).

12　Smelser (1963).

13　McAdam (1982); Tarrow (1983); and Tilly (1978).

14　McCarthy and Zald (1977).

15　For a review, see Williams (2004).

16　See the essays in Johnston and Klandermans (1995). Contrasting emerging social movement theory in the 1980s to its previous incarnations, Williams writes, "Thus the cultural component of new social movement theory had to do with the *content* of movement ideology, the *concerns motivating activists*, and the *arena* in which collective action was focused—that is, cultural understandings, norms, and identities rather than material interests or economic distribution" (2004:92; emphasis his).

17　Benford (1997); Benford and Snow (2000); Snow and Benford (1988); Snow, Rochford, et al. (1986); and Snow and Soule (2010).

18 Sewell (1996:842). See also Sewell (1992); Vaisey (2009); and Young (2006).

19 Sewell (1992, 1996); and Young (2006).

20 In this regard, cultural schemas are analogous to the inculcated dispositions described in the theories of Bourdieu (1984) and Giddens (1984) and, more recently, Haidt (2012) and Vaisey (2009).

21 Haidt (2012); McAdam (1986); and Willer (2009).

22 See Hackett and Lindsay (2008).

23 Greeley and Hout (2006); and Steensland et al. (2000).

24 For example, one can quickly look at the names of churches that are registered as members at the "The National Church Alliance Network" web page (Christian Alliance for Orphans, n.d.-d) and see that a variety of denominations are represented.

25 C. Smith (1998).

26 See Emerson and Smith (2000); and D. M. Lindsay (2007). This is certainly not to give the impression that American evangelicals are monolithic in their religious beliefs or other cultural ideals and practices (see Farrell 2011; Greeley and Hout 2006; C. Smith 1998; and Steensland and Goff 2014). But these shared commitments describe the core of evangelicalism well enough that we can use the term "American evangelical" as a Weberian "ideal type."

27 The number of sixty million or more American evangelicals comes from the Pew Research Center (2014) U.S. religious landscape study.

28 Steensland and Goff (2014).

29 Emerson and Smith (2000); Smidt (2013); and C. Smith (1998, 2000).

30 See, e.g., the collected essays included in Brint and Schroedel (2009a, 2009b) and Steensland and Goff (2014). See also the important monographs on evangelical social engagement: Elisha (2011); Emerson and Smith (2000); Hunter (1983, 1987, 2010); D. M. Lindsay (2007); Markofski (2015); Smidt (2013); C. Smith (1998, 2000); and Young (2006).

31 Sewell (1996:842).

32 Elisha (2011); Emerson and Smith (2000); Hunter (2010); Smidt (2013); and C. Smith (1998).

33 See, e.g., Hunter (2010); D. M. Lindsay (2007); Noll (1994); Stephens and Giberson (2011); and Worthen (2014).

34 See, e.g., E. Bernstein's (2007, 2010) work on evangelical activism in the area of sex trafficking.

35 For some exceptions, see E. Bernstein (2007, 2010); and Elisha (2011).

36 See the essays in Steensland and Goff (2014) for some recent attempts to better understand how the evangelical subculture links with public and social engagement.

37 C. Smith (1998:178).

38 C. Smith (1998:183, 186).

39 See also Emerson and Smith (2000).

40 Hunter (2010).

41 C. Smith (1998:217).

42 An outstanding online resource for understanding the history of adoption, foster
care, and other child welfare activities in the United States is *The Adoption History Project*, run by the historian Ellen Herman out of the University of Oregon
(Herman 2012). I also refer readers to Herman's (2008) important book *Kinship by
Design*.

43 Kidd (2014).

44 Carp (2002).

45 These children were frequently not "orphans" in the sense that they had lost both
of their parents. In fact, Brace himself calculated that about 47 percent of the
"orphans" had one or both parents living. Brace explained that this 47 percent
of children who were placed out on orphan trains were simply the children of
extremely poor people who were growing up neglected on the streets of New York
(M. Holt 1992).

46 M. Davis (2011). Commenting on the impetus for the orphan trains, Davis writes,
"This Christian evangelical humanitarianism movement was the harbinger of
future adoption efforts based on rescuing innocent children from 'adverse' situations as is currently played out in Christian agencies focusing on international
adoptions" (2011:32).

47 Adams (1995); and M. Davis (2011).

48 B. Holt (1956).

49 This account is based on my interview of Paul and Robin Pennington in Austin,
Texas, on June 27, 2013.

50 Several leaders referred to Paul Pennington as the "father of the orphan care
movement" during interviews.

51 Christian Alliance for Orphans (2016–2017).

52 Member congregations can be found at "The National Church Alliance Network"
of the Christian Alliance for Orphans (n.d.).; the 517 member congregations were
present on the website as of March 17, 2016.

53 The year 2014 was the last year with official numbers on Orphan Sunday provided
by CAFO. The numbers can be found in the "2013 Investor Report and Orphan
Care Movement Update" (Christian Alliance for Orphans 2014).

54 As of March 18, 2016, the names and locations of the Orphan Sunday regional and
international coordinators can be found at the Orphan Sunday website (Christian
Alliance for Orphans, n.d.-b).

55 See, e.g., Barna Group (2013:36); Bergeron (2012:252); Kovacs (2009:26–27);
Morton (2014:15); and Rosati and Rosati (2011:174).

56 As quoted in Joyce (2013b:41).

57 Christian Alliance for Orphans (n.d.-a).

58 Christian Alliance for Orphans (n.d.-h).

59 Christian Alliance for Orphans (n.d.-g).

60 Christian Alliance for Orphans (n.d.-e).

CHAPTER 1. WHAT EVANGELICAL ORPHAN BOOM?

1   Joyce (2013b:41) quotes a movement leader, Jason Kovacs, as saying this in a public meeting, but she either misunderstands or misrepresents the intent of the message. As I show in the following chapter, Kovacs sees adoption as the natural result of a Christian's proper understanding of their place in the family of God and God's passion to see vulnerable children in loving families.

2   Moore (2009).

3   Cruver (2011).

4   Merida and Morton (2011).

5   See, e.g., Bennett (2011); Cruver (2011); Darke and McFarland (2014); T. Davis (2008); Merida and Morton (2011): Moore (2009, 2015); and Morton (2014).

6   See Daly (2015).

7   For example, Kelly Rosati, vice president of community outreach for Focus on the Family, told the *National Review* in a March 2015 interview that "there are more than 300,000 churches in the United States. Just let that math sink in. If just one family in every three churches adopted a child, we could literally eliminate the list of kids awaiting adoption in the U.S. That sounds like an achievable goal to me" (NRInterview 2015). See also statements in Medefind (2010b); and Wiebe (2010). See also similar statements made by Marc Andreas of Bethany Christian Services (Andreas 2010). And on the home page of the ABBA Fund (n.d.-c), as of March 2015, they write, "Did you know that if just one family in every three churches in the United States adopted a waiting child every child in the US would be adopted!" Elsewhere, at their "Adoption Facts" page, under "Church Adoptions," they reiterate, "If 1 family in every 3 churches in the US adopted a waiting child, every waiting child in the US would have a forever family" (ABBA Fund, n.d.-a).

8   For news outlets, see Charles (2012); Crary (2013); Draper (2010); Eckholm (2013); Johnson (2014); M. Jones (2013); Lang (2014); Riley (2008, 2010); Schwarzschild (2013); Simon (2007); and P. Smith (2011). For critics, see Barcella (2013, 2014); *Indian Country Today Media Network* staff (2013); Joyce (2009b, 2011, 2013a, 2013b, 2013c, 2013d, 2013e); Kerry and Niels (2009); Riben (2007, 2010, 2012); Smolin (2012b); and Springer-Mock (2013). For movement leaders, see Barna Group (2013); Brinton and Bennett (2015); and Christian Alliance for Orphans (2014). For sympathetic defenders, see Bryars (2013); Foust (2010); French (2013); Hill (2013); Merritt (2013); Roach (2009); and Stetzer (2013).

9   Joyce (2013b).

10 See, e.g., Barcella (2013, 2014); Joyce (2013a); Smolin (2012b).

11 Barna Group (2013); Brinton and Bennett (2015); Christian Alliance for Orphans (2014); Foust (2010); Morton (2014); Roach (2009).

12 Brinton and Bennett (2015:13); emphasis mine.

13 Brinton and Bennett (2015:38); emphasis mine.

14 *The Child Catchers* (Joyce 2013b) is filled with anecdotes about churches or Christian families acting to adopt children from overseas. Books written by orphan

care leaders are also filled with short anecdotes about Christians catching vision for adoption and fostering. See, e.g., Carr (2013); Merida and Morton (2011); and Morton (2014). Indeed, a whole genre of Christian literature has emerged within the last decade or so in which evangelical Christians describe their ministry to orphans overseas. The tacit implication one may draw from reading these accounts is that this sort of activity is happening with a good deal of consistency. See, e.g., Benkert and Chand (2012); Bentley (2006); Chapman (2010); Daly (2007); K. Davis (2012); Díaz-Ortiz and Gachagua (2014); Gifford (2011); Guckenberger (2008, 2011, 2012, 2013, 2014); Martin (2007); and Mitchell (2007). For a specific example of anecdotes that get repeated, see accounts of what I call the "Colorado Miracle" in Barna Group (2013:51–52); Draper (2010); and Riley (2010).

15 These leaders include the president of the Christian Alliance for Orphans, Jedd Medefind; president and CEO of Focus on the Family, Jim Daly; and prominent megachurch pastors and authors David Platt and Francis Chan.

16 Barna Group (2013:14).

17 Bernal et al. (2007); Bonham (1977); Tyebjee (2013).

18 Crary (2013); Joyce (2013b).

19 For "culture of adoption," see e.g., Haskins (2012); Kovacs (2009); Moore (2009); Platt (2010); and the Southern Baptist Convention (2009). For "culture of orphan care," see, e.g., Kovacs (2011); Merida and Morton (2011); and Platt (2015).

20 M. Davis (2011); and Herman (2008). Though forms of fostering could be found in the late 1800s, foster care did not take on its current form and formal relationship to the government until 1974, with the Child Abuse Prevention and Treatment Act (Wildeman and Waldfogel 2014).

21 Fisher (2003); and Wildeman and Waldfogel (2014).

22 See my discussion of important national data sources for adoption and fostering in Appendix A.

23 Fisher (2003).

24 The tabulation can be found at National Center for Heatlth Statistics (2015a).

25 Child Welfare Information Gateway (2016).

26 Children's Bureau (1998–2015).

27 A recent publication from the Child Welfare Information Gateway (2016) provides an excellent compilation of data sources from state courts and various federal agencies to construct a picture of national adoption trends. Unfortunately, more up-to-date numbers for "other" types of adoptions are currently unavailable.

28 Dave Thomas Foundation for Adoption (2013:8); and Quiroz (2007:8–9).

29 See data from Curtain, Abma, and Kost (2015).

30 Joyce (2013c).

31 For example, see Medefind (2010a).

32 For AFCARS, see Children's Bureau (1998–2015).

33 Briggs (2012:chap. 7).

34 The number of American evangelical adults varies by how one measures evangelicalism (see Hackett and Lindsay 2008). C. Smith (1998) estimates that there are
over twenty million evangelical adults, but Pew Research Center (2014) estimates
that there are over sixty million evangelical adults. Some operationalizations of
"evangelical" would put the number at around one hundred million (Hackett and
Lindsay 2008).

35 Carr (2013:chap. 7); and Merida and Morton (2011:chap. 7).

36 Child Welfare Information Gateway (2016).

37 Zylstra (2016).

38 Dave Thomas Foundation for Adoption (2013:8); and Quiroz (2007:8–9).

39 Bergeron (2012); and Elliot (2012).

40 Gilmore (2013).

41 Brown, Sigvaldason, and Bednar (2007); Geiger, Hayes, and Lietz (2013); and
Gillis-Arnold et al. (1998).

42 Rosati and Rosati (2011).

43 Draper (2010). Also see Andreas (2010).

44 Charles (2012).

45 Barna Group (2013:51–52).

46 The numbers of children waiting to be adopted from foster care by state can be
found at Children's Bureau (2015b). The Kids Count Data Center, maintained by
the Annie E. Casey Foundation (n.d.), also provides interactive tables from which
one can view national statistics on children in foster care.

47 See Children's Bureau (2015a).

48 Bernal (2007); Bonham (1977); Fisher (2003); Malm and Welti (2010); and Park
and Hill (2014).

49 Bachrach, London, and Maza (1991); Bausch (2006); Bernal et al. (2007); Bonham
(1977); M. Davis (2011); Hollingsworth (2000); J. Jones (2009); Lamb (2008); Park
and Hill (2014); and Van Laningham, Scheuble, and Johnson (2012).

50 Hollingsworth (2000); Malm and Welti (2010); Tyebjee (2003); and Van Laningham, Scheuble, and Johnson (2012).

51 Bachrach, London, and Maza (1991); M. Davis (2011); Park and Hill (2014); and
Tyebjee (2003).

52 Van Laningham, Scheuble, and Johnson (2012).

53 Belanger, Copeland, and Cheung (2008); Bernal et al. (2007); Goodman and Kim
(1999); Hollingsworth (2000); and Lamb (2008).

54 Bernal et al. (2007); Bonham (1977); and Tyebjee (2003).

55 Bernal et al. (2007); Fisher (2003); Malm and Welti (2010); and Tyebjee (2003).

56 Bausch (2006); Greil et al. (2010); Hayford and Morgan (2008); Park and Hill
(2014); and Jennings (2010).

57 Greil et al. (2010); Jennings (2010); Shreffler, Johnson, and Scheuble (2010); and
Van Laningham, Scheuble, and Johnson (2012).

58 Gillis-Arnold et al. (1998); and Orme et al. (2006).

59 Brown, Sigvaldason, and Bednar (2007); Geiger, Hayes, and Lietz (2013); and Gillis-Arnold et al. (1998).

60 De Maeyer et al. (2014); and Gillis-Arnold et al. (1998).

61 Brown, Sigvaldason, and Bednar (2007); De Maeyer et al. (2014); Geiger, Hayes, and Lietz (2013); Gillis-Arnold et al. (1998); Helm, Peltier, and Scovatti (2006); and Rodger, Cummings, and Leschied (2006).

62 Barna Group (2013).

63 Barna Group (2013:14).

64 Barna Group (2013:24).

65 Barna Group (2013:15).

66 See definitions at Barna Group (2016b).

67 Barna Group (2016a). As Wuthnow shows, George Barna has a history of adjusting his religious categories to be more or less restrictive, often in rather arbitrary and unconventional ways by social scientific standards. For critiques of Barna and other modern polling firms, like Pew and Gallup, see Wuthnow (2015).

68 See Appendix A for full details about sampling and survey methodology.

69 Jones (2009).

70 See the results from the 2007 National Foster Care Adoption Attitudes Survey (Dave Thomas Foundation for Adoption 2007).

71 D. M. Lindsay (2007); and C. Smith (1998, 2000).

72 This slogan (a quote from Isaiah 1:17) is often found on CAFO literature and websites. For example, see Christian Alliance for Orphans (n.d.-f).

73 Barcella (2013, 2014); and Joyce (2013a, 2013b, 2013c).

74 Barna Group (2013:14); and Brinton and Bennett (2015:38).

75 T. Davis (2008).

76 See the Evangelical Council for Financial Accountability website for annual giving reports (n.d.).

77 Carr (2013); Darke and McFarland (2014); and Elliot (2012).

CHAPTER 2. CULTURE BUILDING FOR CHANGE

1 Hunter (1983, 1987); Woodberry and Smith (1998); and Wuthnow (1988).

2 C. Smith (1998:10); emphasis his. The evangelical commitment to theological distinctiveness should not be taken to mean that evangelicals refuse to accommodate American cultural preferences. Rather, evangelicalism—being largely an "Americanized Christianity" (Kyle 2006) and, thus, heavily influenced by religious market forces—is extremely flexible in its "packaging" for the purposes of engaging with society (D. M. Lindsay 2007; Shibley 1996; and C. Smith 1998).

3 D. M. Lindsay (2007); and Noll (1994).

4 D. M. Lindsay (2007:4).

5 Hunter (2010:4). Although Hunter states early on that this mindset is not limited to evangelicals alone, the vast majority of the examples he cites of this mindset are that of famous evangelicals like Charles Colson, James Dobson, Bill Bright, Jim Wallis, and others.

6 Hunter (2010:6); emphasis his.

7 Elisha (2011); Hunter (2010); Kyle (2006); D. M. Lindsay (2007); Shibley (1996); and C. Smith (1998, 2000).

8 C. Smith (1998:187).

9 Hunter (2010); and C. Smith (2000).

10 Schmalzbauer (2014); C. Smith (2000); and Wuthnow (1988).

11 Hunter (2010).

12 See also Elisha (2011); Emerson and Smith (2000); Kyle (2006); Reynolds and Offutt (2014); Smidt (2013); and C. Smith (1998).

13 Elisha (2011).

14 Benkert and Chand (2012); Bentley (2006); Chapman (2010); Daly (2007); K. Davis (2012); Díaz-Ortiz and Gachagua (2014); Gifford (2011); Guckenberger (2008, 2011, 2012, 2013, 2014); Martin (2007); and Mitchell (2007).

15 Christianson (2007a, 2007b); Gillespie (2006); Gumm (2011); Purvis, Cross, and Sunshine (2007); Schooler and Atwood (2008); and Tebos, Woodwyk, and Eldridge (2011).

16 Barna Group (2013); Bennett (2011); Bergeron (2012); Bohlender and Bohlender (2013); Borgman (2014); Caldwell (2011); Carr (2013); Cruver (2011); Darke and McFarland (2014); T. Davis (2008); Ellicott (2010); Elliot (2012); Gardner (2003); Maggard and Maggard (2013); Merida and Morton (2011); Moore (2009, 2012); Morton (2014); Platt (2010, 2011, 2013, 2015); Rosati and Rosati (2011); J. Weber and P. Pennington (2006); and Wong (2005). The four books by the evangelical mega-church pastor David Platt (2010, 2011, 2013, 2015) enjoin evangelicals to embrace a radically sacrificial lifestyle. Each book includes passages that talk about Christian adoption as examples of this lifestyle, and thus, while these books are not written with the singular goal to mobilize Christians toward adoption and orphan care, they nevertheless advertise adoption and orphan care as manifestations of radically obedient Christian living. Platt himself is an adoptive father and frequently speaks on behalf of orphan care and CAFO.

17 Barna Group (2013); Cruver (2011); and Moore (2009).

18 Snow and Benford (1988).

19 Joyce (2013b:41).

20 These titles are from the 2011, 2013, and 2014 Christian Alliance for Orphans Summit programs (these program lists are in my possession).

21 Purvis (n.d.)

22 Southern Baptist Convention (2009).

23 Piper (2011:97).

24 Platt (2011:31–32).

25 Kovacs (2009, 2011).

26 Ashland Avenue Baptist Church (n.d.).

27 Moore (2009).

28 Moore (2009:19).

29 Moore (2009:73).

30 Moore (2009:168).

31 "Abba" is an Aramaic word for "father" that is used in reference to God himself three times in the New Testament (Mark 14:36; Romans 8:15; and Galatians 4:6). Christians understand "Abba" as it is used in the New Testament to convey a particularly intimate relationship with God as a father. The reference is used strategically by Cruver (2011), Moore (2010), and evangelical orphan care organizations like the ABBA Fund to convey God's love for "fatherless" children.

32 Moore (2010).

33 Kovacs (2009:26).

34 Kovacs (2011:87).

35 Merida and Morton (2011:80).

36 In my interview with Tony Merida, he expressed that his thinking on the subject of the "culture of orphan care" had been influenced by Russell Moore both through their personal relationship and through Moore's book *Adopted for Life* (2009).

37 T. Davis (2008:49).

38 Merida and Morton (2011:105).

39 Merida and Morton (2011:130).

40 Bergeron (2012:23).

41 Bergeron (2012:75).

42 Bergeron (2012: 192–193).

43 Bergeron (2012:63–65).

44 Elliot (2012:25).

45 Medefind (2013a:35).

46 Piper (2002:33–34).

47 Merida and Morton (2011:116).

48 Bennett (2011:41); emphasis his.

49 Bennett (2011:48).

50 Bennett (2011:52).

51 Moore (2009:173).

52 Kovacs (2009:26).

53 Kovacs (2011:88).

54 Kovacs (2011:83–84).

55 Merida and Morton (2011:81); emphasis theirs.

56 Morton (2014:41).

57 Morton (2014:44).

58 Morton (2014:47).

59 Carr (2013:149).

60 Carr (2013:133).

61 Carr (2013:134).

62 Carr (2013:141–142).

63 Kovacs (2011:88).

64 Carr (2013:165).

65 Moore (2009:168).

66 Moore (2009:186).

67 Merida and Morton (2011:83).

68 Merida and Morton (2011:92).

69 Merida and Morton (2011:81).

70 *STUCK* is a documentary made by Craig Juntunen, adoptive father of three Haitian children and founder of Both Ends Burning, an advocacy organization that seeks to create awareness about legal barriers to adoption and to pressure the U.S. government to break down those barriers. Although neither Juntunen nor Both Ends Burning as an organization is religious, the *STUCK* documentary was heavily promoted and watched by those in the orphan care movement. The CAFO website even promoted the *STUCK* documentary for several months in 2013. The documentary was shown at the 2013 CAFO Summit, and CAFO president Jedd Medefind personally endorsed the film on video. I also saw a number of leaders in CAFO attend the Both Ends Burning "(Un)Stuck" march on Washington, DC, on May 17, 2013.

71 Haskins (2012:57).

72 Haskins (2012:59).

73 Haskins (2012:61).

74 Haskins (2012:63).

75 D. M. Lindsay (2007).

76 C. Smith (1998).

77 Bennett (2011).

78 C. Smith (1998:189).

79 Hunter (2010:27).

CHAPTER 3. ORPHANS NEED FAMILIES! JUST NOT *THOSE* FAMILIES

1 Christian Alliance for Orphans (n.d.-i).

2 Cruver (2011:15); emphasis his.

3 P. Yancey (2003:63).

4 Lynerd (2014); and Noll (2003). Certainly, the Puritans are not the only theological and ideological forbears of American evangelical thought. There are numerous other important cultural strands woven within American evangelicalism. Most prominently, perhaps, are free-will individualism and populism (and its corollary, anti-intellectualism), inherited from various thinkers such as Locke, Wesley, and the philosophers of the Revolutionary War period and cultivated through the Second Great Awakening and premillennial dispensationalism of the 1800s (see Hatch 1989; and Noll 1994, 2003).

5 Piper (2002:33–34).

6 This is not to say that evangelical Christians never find themselves in partnership with non-evangelicals around certain social issues. The sociologist Elizabeth Bernstein (2007, 2010) has done extensive research on evangelical Christians joining forces with abolitionist feminists against international sex trafficking.

Yet, as Bernstein acknowledges, these evangelicals are often of a younger, more progressive strain of evangelicalism, and their "partnership" with liberal feminists often seems to be more of an agreement about practical goals, and unity against a common foe (traffickers), rather than an example of constant cooperation.

7 For a review, see Lamont and Molnar (2002).

8 Bourdieu (1984).

9 These observations about group boundaries increasing in specificity as groups grow in size and complexity are as old as sociology itself (Durkheim 1893/2014; Simmel 1955; and M. Weber 1978).

10 Douglass (1966, 1973).

11 Lamont (1992, 1999, 2000); and Lamont and Fournier (1992).

12 Douglass (1966, 1973).

13 Becker (1999); and Chaves (1996, 1997).

14 Lamont and Molnar (2002); and Williams (2004).

15 M. Bernstein (1997); Gamson (1992); Hunt and Benford (2004); Taylor and Whittier (1992); and Williams (2004).

16 Coser (1956); Hunt and Benford (2004); Simmel (1955); and Snow and Soule (2010).

17 M. Bernstein (1997).

18 All of Kay Warren's quotes are found in Kwon (2010).

19 Snow and Soule (2010).

20 Lifeline Children's Services (n.d.).

21 ABBA Fund (2015).

22 ABBA Fund (n.d.-b).

23 America World Adoption (n.d.).

24 Oftentimes, this goal however, is constrained by whether or not the agency is receiving money from the government, which is the case when placing foster children into families. In these cases, Lifeline and Bethany are constrained by government non-discrimination guidelines. In private adoptions, however, orphan care organizations can hold to the standard of placing children in Christian families exclusively.

25 In fact, only one leader I interviewed was willing to allow for same-sex couples adopting children both for the practical reason that *any* family would be better than an orphanage and for the possibility that the couple would convert and repent of their homosexuality. Even in this, the leader still stated that a same-sex couple would not be ideal.

26 Most movement leaders I spoke with about the prospect of same-sex couples adopting or fostering children were careful to point out that they did not mean any animosity or hostility toward same-sex couples as people. On the contrary, they affirmed a desire to love them as Christians. And yet, they felt that, being convinced that God prescribes the man-woman marriage as the only morally acceptable family form, they could not support same-sex adoption.

27 Christian Alliance for Orphans (2016).

28 C. Smith (1998).

29 Brinton and Bennett (2015:13).

CHAPTER 4. SO, WHY DID YOU ADOPT?

1 In 2011, the U.S. Children's Bureau published a report on the cost of adoption and available resources to help defray adoption costs. Public agency (foster care) adoptions ranged from $0 to $2,500; licensed private agency adoptions ranged from $5,000 to $40,000; independent adoptions ranged from $8,000 to $40,000; facilitated/unlicensed adoptions ranged form $5,000 to $40,000; and intercountry adoptions ranged from $15,000 to $30,000 (Child Welfare Information Gateway 2011). The costs indicated for intercountry adoption can actually be much higher than $30,000, depending on the home country.

2 For the sake of anonymity, I have intentionally changed wording and details to prevent readers from finding this fundraising page online. Nothing of the essence has been altered.

3 Bauch (2006); Hollingsworth (2000); Jennings (2010); Malm and Welti (2010); and Zhang and Lee (2011).

4 Malm and Welti (2010); and Zhang and Lee (2011). Malm and Welti draw on data from the National Survey of Adoptive Parents (National Center for Health Statistics 2007) to examine the motivations of parents pursuing private domestic, international, or foster care adoption. They find that, among those who pursued private domestic adoption (like the Bakers), the top three reasons given were that (1) they wanted an infant, (2) they wanted a healthy child, and (3) they had some other reason, such as "lower cost/risk." These motivations are consistent with those described by the Bakers.

5 The 2013 National Foster Care Adoption Attitudes Survey (Dave Thomas Foundation for Adoption 2013) reported that, among respondents who had considered adoption, the vast majority would prefer a child who is younger; not part of a sibling group; and does not have any physical or mental disabilities, chemical dependencies, or behavioral issues. The respondents believe that foster children have experienced abuse and neglect from their birth parents, and a majority of whites stated that they would prefer a white child. These concerns and preferences are entirely consistent with those communicated by the Bakers.

6 Mills (1940).

7 Mills (1940:908).

8 Mills (1940:913).

9 Munson (2008:162).

10 Merida and Morton (2011); and Moore (2009).

11 Not all of these leaders promote evangelical vocabularies of motive. I only list these leaders to show that many of the most visible leaders in the orphan care movement were initially drawn to adoption, in large part, because of their own fertility/fecundity issues.

12 Because of the implications of that fact—that many of these leaders were unable to have children biologically prior to their own adoptions and, so, their adoptions, at least in part, might have been motivated by a self-interested desire for children—several were not forthcoming about their struggles with infertility. Indeed, for some I had to ask directly (and repeatedly) or find out through blogs or their own writings.

13 Hill (2012).

14 Pierre (2012).

15 DiMaggio (1997); Gladwell (2005); Greene (2013); Haidt (2012); Kahneman (2011); and Vaisey (2009).

16 Vaisey (2009:1683).

17 Haidt (2012).

18 Lichterman (1992:426).

19 Lichterman (1992:426–427).

20 Vaisey (2009).

21 Bourdieu (1984); Giddens (1984); and Vaisey (2009).

22 Hout, Greeley, and Wilde (2001).

23 Joyce (2013a).

24 Benford and Snow (2000); and Snow and Benford (1988).

25 Munson (2008).

26 Cruver (2010).

27 Platt (2015).

28 Platt (2011:139).

29 Brinton and Bennett (2015:7, 24).

30 Malm and Welti (2010); and Zhang and Lee (2011).

31 DiMaggio (1997); Mills (1940); and Vaisey (2009).

32 McAdam (1986); and Munson (2008).

CHAPTER 5. COSTS NOT COUNTED

1 Hunter (2010); D. M. Lindsay (2007); Noll (1994); Stephens and Giberson (2011); and Worthen (2014).

2 Hunter (2010); D. M. Lindsay (2007); and Noll (1994).

3 C. Smith (1996).

4 Emerson and Smith (2000); Hunter (2010); and C. Smith (1998).

5 Evangelical leaders recognize this tendency within American evangelicalism. Several books within the past few years, for example, have been written to help churches and grassroots evangelicals think more carefully about what their social engagement accomplishes and how to help vulnerable populations without ultimately doing more harm than good (e.g., Corbett and Fikkert 2012; Darke and McFarland 2014; and Lupton 2011).

6 E. Bernstein (2007, 2010).

7 Because the Twietmeyers have already received a great deal of media attention and because they have made themselves visible by leading nonprofits and

agreeing to be interviewed by magazines and news shows, I decided to keep their actual names in my account.

8 This is a pseudonym.

9 Joyce (2013b).

10 Moore's original article title and subtitle have been modified since first publication; see Moore (2010).

11 Cruver (2011:86).

12 Carr (2013:189).

13 Purvis, Cross, and Sunshine (2007).

14 Believing in the "central role of the local church" represents one of the "core principles" of CAFO (Christian Alliance for Orphans, n.d.-c).

15 See Corbett and Fikkert (2012); and Lupton (2011).

CHAPTER 6. WHAT WILL A MATURE EVANGELICAL MOVEMENT LOOK LIKE?

1 See Finke and Stark (2005); Johnstone (2007); Niebuhr (1929); Roberts and Yamane (2012); Troeltsch (1931); and M. Weber (1973).

2 Johnstone (2007); and Roberts and Yamane (2012).

3 Chaves (2011); and Putnam and Campbell (2010).

4 Finke and Stark (2005).

5 Variations of this typology have been around for years, and thus I am unsure to whom I should attribute it. Over time I have revised the definitions of these terms myself, and I am not drawing on another author's categories here.

6 See Medefind (2010a).

7 Joyce (2013b).

8 As I pointed out in the introduction, most of the articles between 2007 and 2014 criticizing the evangelical orphan care movement have been by or based on the work of Kathryn Joyce. See Barcella (2013, 2014); *Indian Country Today Media Network* staff (2013); Joyce (2009b, 2011, 2013a, 2013b, 2013c, 2013d, 2013e); Schwarzschild (2013); and Springer-Mock (2013).

9 Jedd Medefind himself penned an online response to *The Child Catchers* published in the New York Times and on the CAFO website (Medefind 2013b, 2013c, 2013d). And David Smolin guest edited the Spring 2012 issue of the *Journal of Christian Legal Thought* (Smolin 2010a), which included his formal critique of the orphan care movement as well as responses from movement leaders like Dan Cruver and Jedd Medefind.

10 See, e.g., Medefind (2013b, 2013c).

11 Elliot (2012:206).

12 For excellent studies on the Promise Keepers movement in the United States, see Bartkowski (2004); and Williams (2001).

13 I have given a version of this scenario to dozens of evangelical friends and acquaintances over the last year. While they are certainly not a representative sample of evangelicals, their responses are instructive. As expected, a high

percentage choose A or C, meaning they would rather (A) stay focused on Christ, but be ineffective, practically speaking, or (C) shut their doors completely. Their explanations are consistent with pietistic idealism—the *ultimate* goal is to see people eternally saved, and providing *only* for physical needs stops short of that. But a significant percentage also choose B, indicating they would become secular as an organization while becoming more effective practically. Almost no one ever explains this choice by saying that serving peoples' physical needs is important in and of itself regardless of whether people are spiritually saved. Rather, they virtually always say they could minister to someone's spiritual needs individually or secretly, rather than as an organization, or they say that the service itself may somehow point the vulnerable to Christ, if not directly. Even here, evangelicals who choose B are still thinking through pietistic idealism.

14 Elliot (2012:206).

15 C. Smith (1998).

CONCLUSION

1 C. Smith (1998).

2 Durkheim (1912/1995); and Haidt (2012).

3 C. Smith (1998:186).

4 C. Smith (1998).

5 Emerson and Smith (2000).

6 Brinton and Bennett (2015); Carr (2013); and Darke and McFarland (2014).

7 For tithing, see Chaves and Miller (1999); and C. Smith and M. Emerson (2008). For sharing the faith, see Stetzer (2012).

8 Chaves (2004).

9 Elliot (2012:206).

10 For poverty, see Reynolds and Offutt (2014). For sex trafficking, see E. Bernstein (2007, 2010). For racial conflict, see Christerson, Edwards, and Emerson (2005); Marti and Emerson (2014); Lichterman, Carter, and Lamont (2009); and Shelton and Emerson (2012). For environmental degradation, see Kearns (2014). For evangelical engagement of all of these issues, see Markofski (2015); and Samson (2014).

11 Emerson and Smith (2000).

12 Carr (2013:134). See also Moore (2009:156–159).

13 Emerson and Smith (2000:130–131).

14 Christerson, Edwards and Emerson (2005); Edwards (2008); and Lichterman, Carter, and Lamont (2009).

15 Marti and Emerson (2014:183).

16 Marti and Emerson (2014:184).

17 Marti and Emerson (2014:184).

18 E. Bernstein (2007, 2010); and Platt (2015).

19 Brinton and Bennett (2015); and Darke and McFarland (2014).

20 Emerson and Smith (2000:130–131).

21 E. Bernstein (2007, 2010).

22 E. Bernstein (2007, 2010).

23 For example, see Kouri (2010).

24 Joyce (2013b).

25 M. Weber (1904/1949); emphasis his.

26 Emerson and Smith (2000); and D. M. Lindsay (2007).

27 H. Lindsay (2009).

28 Smolin (2012b).

29 Keller (2010).

30 G. Yancey (2003).

31 Edin and Kafalas (2005); and Wilson (2009).

32 Sweeney and Raley (2014).

APPENDIX A

1 These included (alphabetically by author) *Somebody's Children* by Laura Briggs (2012); *The Child Catchers* by Kathryn Joyce (2013b; also see her other articles associated with this topic); and "Of Orphans and Adoption" by David Smolin (2012b).

2 For example, see Jerolmack and Khan (2014).

3 Fisher (2003).

4 For a discussion of data sources, see M. Davis (2011).

5 For information about the National Survey of Family Growth, see National Center for Health Statistics (2015b). For information about the National Survey of Adoptive Parents, see National Center for Heatlth Statistics (2007). For information about the National Foster Care Adoption Attitudes Surveys, see Dave Thomas Foundation for Adoption (n.d.). The two FRAMES surveys consisted of one telephone survey (fielded from June 25, 2013 to June 29, 2013) and one online survey (fielded from July 29, 2013 to August 1, 2013). While the specific methodology for the FRAMES surveys is not available online, Barna has published survey methodology for similar studies that can be found at Barna Group (n.d.).

REFERENCES

ABBA Fund. n.d.-a. "Adoption Facts." www.abbafund.org.

ABBA Fund. n.d.-b. FAQ's. www.abbafund.org.

ABBA Fund. n.d.-c. Home page. www.abbafund.org.

ABBA Fund. 2015. *Combined Application for Setting Up a Family Adoption Fund as Part of the ABBA Fund's Christian Family Adoption Grant Fund and Applying for an Interest-Free Covenant Loan*. www.abbafund.org.

Adams, David Wallace. 1995. *Education for Extinction: American Indians and the Boarding School Experience, 1875–1928*. Lawrence: University Press of Kansas.

Andreas, Marc. 2010. "Church and State Working Together for Orphans." *Capital Commentary*, April 9. Center for Public Justice. www.cpjustice.org.

America World Adoption. n.d. *Mission + Vision*. www.awaa.org.

Annie E. Casey Foundation. n.d. *Kids Count Data Center*. http://datacenter.kidscount.org.

Ashland Avenue Baptist Church. n.d. "Adoption." www.ashlandlex.org.

Bachrach, Christine A., Kathryn A. London, and Penelope L. Maza. 1991. "On the Path to Adoption: Adoption Seeking in the United States, 1988." *Journal of Marriage and Family* 53(3):705–718.

Barcella, Laura. 2013. "How the Christian Right Perverts Adoption: The Evangelical Adoption Boom Is Driven by Creepy Links between the Christian Right and a Billion-Dollar Industry." *Salon*, May 4. www.salon.com.

Barcella, Laura. 2014. "Adoptees Like Me 'Flip the Script' on the Pro-adoption Narrative." *New York Times*, November 13. www.nyt.com.

Barna Group. n.d. "Survey Methodology." *Barna: Cities*. http://cities.barna.org.

Barna Group. 2013. *Becoming Home: Adoption, Foster Care, and Mentoring—Living Out God's Heart for Orphans*. Grand Rapids, MI: Zondervan.

Barna Group. 2016a. "America's Faith Segments Are Divided on Presidential Race." *Research Releases in Culture and Media*, February 25. www.barna.com.

Barna Group. 2016b. *Glossary of Barna's Theographics and Demographics*. www.barna.com.

Bartkowski, John P. 2004. *The Promise Keepers: Servants, Soldiers, and Godly Men*. New Brunswick, NJ: Rutgers University Press.

Bausch, Robert S. 2006. "Predicting Willingness to Adopt: A Consideration of Demographic and Attitudinal Factors." *Sociological Perspectives* 49(1):47–65.

Bean, Lydia, and Brandon Martinez. 2014. "Evangelical Ambivalence toward Gays and Lesbians." *Sociology of Religion* 75(3):395–417.

Becker, Penny Edgell. 1999. *Congregations in Conflict: Cultural Models of Local Religious Life*. New York: Cambridge University Press.

Belanger, Kathleen, Sam Copeland, and Monit Cheung. 2008. "The Role of Faith in Adoption: Achieving Positive Adoption Outcomes for African American Children." *Child Welfare* 87(2):99–123.

Benford, Robert D. 1997. "An Insider's Critique of the Social Movement Framing Perspective." *Sociological Inquiry* 67:409–430.

Benford, Robert D., and David A. Snow. 2000. "Framing Processes and Social Movements." *Annual Review of Sociology* 26:611–639.

Benkert, Levi, and Candy Chand. 2012. *No Greater Love: One Man's Radical Journey through the Heart of Ethiopia*. Carol Stream, IL: Tyndale House.

Bennett, Daniel J. 2011. *A Passion for the Fatherless: Developing a God-Centered Ministry to Orphans*. Grand Rapids, MI: Kregal.

Bentley, Lisa Misraje. 2006. *Saving Levi: Left to Die . . . Destined to Live*. Colorado Springs, CO: Focus on the Family.

Bergeron, Lawrence E. 2012. *Journey to the Fatherless: Preparing for the Journey of Adoption, Orphan Care, Foster Care, and Humanitarian Relief for Vulnerable Children*. Bloomington, IN: WestBow.

Bernal, Raquel, Luojia Hu, Chiaki Moriguchi, and Eva Nagypal. 2007. "Child Adoption in the United States: Historical Trends and the Determinants of Adoption Demand and Supply, 1951–2002." Working paper, preliminary and incomplete. http://faculty.wcas.northwestern.edu/~cm0938/adoptAEA.pdf.

Bernstein, Elizabeth. 2007. "The Sexual Politics of the 'New Abolitionism.'" *Differences: A Journal of Feminist Cultural Studies* 18(5):128–151.

Bernstein, Elizabeth. 2010. "Militarized Humanitarianism Meets Carceral Feminism: The Politics of Sex, Rights, and Freedom in Contemporary Antitrafficking Campaigns." *Signs: Journal of Women in Culture and Society* 36(1):45–71.

Bernstein, Mary. 1997. "Celebration and Suppression: The Strategic Uses of Identity by the Lesbian and Gay Movement." *American Journal of Sociology* 103:531–565.

Bohlender, Randy, and Kelsey Bohlender. 2013. *The Spirit of Adoption: Winning the Battle for the Children*. Shippensburg, PA: Destiny Image.

Bonham, Gordon S. 1977. "Who Adopts: The Relationship of Adoption and Social-Demographic Characteristics of Women." *Journal of Marriage and Family* 39:295–306.

Borgman, Brian. 2014. *After They Are Yours: The Grace and Grit of Adoption*. Adelphi, PA: Cruciform Press.

Bourdieu, Pierre. 1984. *Distinction: A Social Critique of the Judgment of Taste*. Cambridge, MA: Harvard University Press.

Briggs, Laura. 2012. *Somebody's Children: The Politics of Transracial and Transnational Adoption*. Durham, NC: Duke University Press.

Brint, Steven, and Jean Reith Schroedel, eds. 2009a. *Evangelicals and Democracy in America*, vol. 1: *Religion and Society*. New York: Russell Rage Foundation.

Brint, Steven, and Jean Reith Schroedel, eds. 2009b. *Evangelicals and Democracy in America*, vol. 2: *Religion and Politics*. New York: Russell Rage Foundation.

Brinton, Sara, and Amanda Bennett. 2015. *In Defense of the Fatherless: Redeeming International Adoption and Orphan Care*. Ross-shire, Scotland: Christian Focus.

Brown, Jason D., Nadine Sigvaldason, and Lisa M. Bednar. 2007. "Motives for Fostering Children with Alcohol-Related Disabilities." *Journal of Child and Family Studies* 16:197–208.

Bryars, Rachel B. 2013. "Amidst Criticism, the Call to Care for Orphans." Washington Institute for Faith, Vocation, and Culture. www.washingtoninst.org.

Caldwell, Mardie. 2011. *Called to Adoption: A Christian's Guide to Answering the Call*. Nevada City, CA: American Carriage House.

Campolo, Tony. 2009. *Is Jesus a Republican or Democrat? And 14 Other Polarizing Issues*. Nashville, TN: Thomas Nelson.

Carp, E. Wayne. 2002. "Introduction: A Historical Overview of American Adoption." In *Adoption in America: Historical Perspectives*, edited by E. Wayne Carp, 1–26. Ann Arbor: University of Michigan Press.

Carr, Johnny. 2013. *Orphan Justice: How to Care for Orphans beyond Adopting*. Nashville, TN: B&H Publishing Group.

Chapman, Mary Beth. 2010. *Choosing to See: A Journey of Struggle and Hope*. Grand Rapids, MI: Revell.

Charles, Tyler. 2012. "Fostering Hope: How the Church Is Changing the Face of Foster Care and Adoption in the U.S." *Relevant*, no. 58 (July/August). www.relevantmagazine.com.

Chaves, Mark. 1996. "Ordaining Women: The Diffusion of an Organizational Innovation." *American Journal of Sociology* 101(4):840–873.

Chaves, Mark. 1997. *Ordaining Women: Culture and Conflict in Religious Organizations*. Cambridge, MA: Harvard University Press.

Chaves, Mark. 2004. *Congregations in America*. Cambridge, MA: Harvard University Press.

Chaves, Mark. 2011. *American Religion: Contemporary Trends*. Princeton, NJ: Princeton University Press.

Chaves, Mark, and Sharon L. Miller. 1999. *Financing American Religion*. Walnut Creek, CA: AltaMira.

Child Welfare Information Gateway. 2005. *Voluntary Relinquishment for Adoption*. Washington, DC: U.S. Department of Health and Human Services, Administration for Children and Families, Children's Bureau. www.childwelfare.gov.

Child Welfare Information Gateway. 2011. *Costs of Adopting*. Washington, DC: U.S. Department of Health and Human Services, Administration for Children and Families, Children's Bureau. www.childwelfare.gov.

Child Welfare Information Gateway. 2016. *Trends in U.S. Adoptions: 2008–2012*. Washington, DC: U.S. Department of Health and Human Services, Administration for Children and Families, Children's Bureau. www.childwelfare.gov.

Children's Bureau. 1998–2015. Adoption and Foster Care Analysis and Reporting System (AFCARS) reports. Washington, DC: U.S. Department of Health and Human Services, Administration for Children and Families. www.acf.hhs.gov.

Children's Bureau. 2015a. *Adoptions of Children with Public Child Welfare Agency Involvement by State, FY 2005–FY 2014.* Washington, DC: U.S. Department of Health and Human Services, Administration for Children and Families. www.acf.hhs.gov.

Children's Bureau. 2015b. *Children in Public Foster Care on September 30th of Each Year Who Are Waiting to Be Adopted, FY 2005–FY 2014.* Washington, DC: U.S. Department of Health and Human Services, Administration for Children and Families. www.acf.hhs.gov.

Christerson, Brad, Korie L. Edwards, and Michael O. Emerson. 2005. *Against All Odds: The Struggle for Racial Integration in Religious Organizations.* New York: NYU Press.

Christian Alliance for Orphans. n.d.-a. "About." https://cafo.org.

Christian Alliance for Orphans. n.d.-b. "Coordinators." *Orphan Sunday.* http://orphan sunday.org.

Christian Alliance for Orphans. n.d.-c. "Core Principles." https://cafo.org.

Christian Alliance for Orphans. n.d.-d. "The National Church Alliance Network." https://cafo.org.

Christian Alliance for Orphans. n.d.-e. "The Orphan's Matchbox" (blog). https://cafo.org.

Christian Alliance for Orphans. n.d.-f. *Orphan Sunday.* http://orphansunday.org.

Christian Alliance for Orphans. n.d.-g. "Orphan Sunday Resources." *Orphan Sunday.* http://orphansunday.org.

Christian Alliance for Orphans. n.d.-h. "Summit." https://cafo.org.

Christian Alliance for Orphans. n.d.-i. "What Is Orphan Sunday? *Orphan Sunday.* http://orphansunday.org.

Christian Alliance for Orphans. 2014. "2013 Investor Report and Orphan Care Movement Update." https://cafo.org.

Christian Alliance for Orphans. 2016. "FAQs." *Orphan Sunday.* http://orphansunday .org.

Christian Alliance for Orphans. 2016–2017. "Next Steps." https://cafo.org.

Christianson, Laura. 2007a. *The Adoption Decision: 15 Things You Want to Know before Adopting.* Enumclaw, WA: WinePress.

Christianson, Laura. 2007b. *The Adoption Network: Your Guide to Starting a Support System.* Enumclaw, WA: WinePress.

Corbett, Steve, and Brian Fikkert. 2012. *When Helping Hurts: How to Alleviate Poverty without Hurting the Poor . . . and Yourself.* Chicago: Moody Publishers.

Coser, Lewis. 1956. *The Functions of Social Conflict.* New York: Free Press.

Crary, David. 2013. "Christian Evangelical Adoption Movement Perseveres amid Criticism, Drop in Foreign Adoptions." *Fox News U.S.,* October 28. www.foxnews.com.

Cruver, Dan. 2010. "Adoption, adoption, and Caring for Orphans." *Together for Adoption,* November 15. www.togetherforadoption.org.

Cruver, Dan, ed. 2011. *Reclaiming Adoption: Missional Living through the Rediscovery of Abba Father*. Adelphi, PA: Cruciform Press.

Curtin, Sally C., Joyce C. Abma, and Kathryn Kost. 2015. *2010 Pregnancy Rates among U.S. Women*. Washington, DC: Centers for Disease Control and Prevention, National Center for Health Statistics. www.cdc.gov.

Daly, Jim. 2007. *Finding Home: An Imperfect Path to Faith and Family*. Colorado Springs, CO: David C. Cook.

Daly, Jim. 2015. "Let's Make This Headline Happen: 'Church Wipes Out Foster Care Adoption List.'" *DalyFocus*, September 4. Focus on the Family. www.focusonthe family.com.

Darke, Philip, and Keith McFarland. 2014. *In Pursuit of Orphan Excellence*. Grand Rapids, MI: Credo House.

Dave Thomas Foundation for Adoption. n.d. "Foster Care Adoption Attitudes Research." Columbus, OH: Dave Thomas Foundation for Adoption. https://davethomasfounda tion.org.

Dave Thomas Foundation for Adoption. 2007. *National Foster Care Adoption Attitudes Survey: November 2007 Executive Summary*. Dublin, OH: Dave Thomas Foundation for Adoption. https://davethomasfoundation.org.

Dave Thomas Foundation for Adoption. 2013. *National Foster Care Adoption Attitudes Survey: 2013 Executive Summary and Detailed Findings*. Columbus, OH: Dave Thomas Foundation for Adoption. https://davethomasfoundation.org.

Davis, Katie. 2012. *Kisses from Katie: A Story of Relentless Love and Redemption*. New York: Howard Books.

Davis, Mary Ann. 2011. *Children for Families or Families for Children: The Demography of Adoption Behavior in the U.S.* New York: Springer.

Davis, Tom. 2008. *Fields of the Fatherless: Discover the Joy of Compassionate Living*. Colorado Springs, CO: David C. Cook.

De Maeyer, Skrallan, Johan Vanderfaeillie, Femke Vanschoonlandt, Marijke Robberechts, and Frank Van Holen. 2014. "Motivation for Foster Care." *Children and Youth Services Review* 36:143–149.

Díaz-Ortiz, Claire, and Samuel Ikua Gachagua. 2014. *Hope Runs: An American Tourist, a Kenyan Boy, a Story of Redemption*. Grand Rapids, MI: Revell.

DiMaggio, Paul. 1997. "Culture and Cognition." *Annual Review of Sociology* 23:263–287.

Douglas, Mary. 1966. *Purity and Danger*. London: Routledge & Kegan Paul.

Douglas, Mary. 1973. *Natural Symbols: Explorations in Cosmology*. 2nd ed. London: Barrie & Rockliff.

Draper, Electa. 2010. "Adoption Initiative Halves Numbers of Kids Needing Families." *Denver Post*, March 4. www.denverpost.com.

Durkheim, Émile. 1893/1984. *The Division of Labor in Society*. New York: Free Press.

Durkheim, Émile. 1912/1995. *The Elementary Forms of Religious Life*. New York: Free Press.

Eckholm, Erik. 2013. "Eager to Adopt, Evangelicals Find Perils Abroad." *New York Times*, May 31. www.nytimes.com.

Edin, Kathryn, and Maria J. Kefalas. 2005. *Promises I Can Keep: Why Poor Women Put Motherhood before Marriage*. Berkeley: University of California Press.

Edwards, Korie. 2008. *The Elusive Dream: The Power of Race in Interracial Churches*. New York: Oxford University Press.

Elisha, Omri. 2011. *Moral Ambition: Mobilization and Social Outreach in Evangelical Megachurches*. Berkeley: University of California Press.

Ellicott, Cheryl. 2010. *This Means War: Equipping Christian Families for Fostercare or Adoption*. Spokane, WA: Stillwater Sweet.

Elliot, Diane Lynn. 2012. *The Global Orphan Crisis: Be the Solution—Change Your World*. Chicago: Moody Publishers.

Emerson, Michael O., and Christian Smith. 2000. *Divided by Faith: Evangelical Religion and the Problem of Race in America*. New York: Oxford University Press.

Evangelical Council for Financial Accountability (n.d.). Home page. www.ecfa.org.

Farrell, Justin. 2011. "The Young and the Restless? The Liberalization of Young Evangelicals." *Journal for the Scientific Study of Religion* 50(3):517–532.

Finke, Roger, and Rodney Stark. 2005. *The Churching of America, 1776–2005: Winners and Losers in Our Religious Economy*. New Brunswick, NJ: Rutgers University Press.

Fisher, Allan P. 2003. " 'Not Quite as Good as Having Your Own'? Toward a Sociology of Adoption." *Annual Review of Sociology* 29:335–361.

Foust, Michael. 2010. "An Adoption Movement? Agencies Say Interest on Rise." *Baptist Press*, July 20. www.bpnews.net.

French, David. 2013. "Left Launches Attack on Evangelical Adoption." Opinion. *Christian Post*, April 26. www.christianpost.com.

Gamson, William A. 1992. *Talking Politics*. New York: Cambridge University Press.

Gardner, Michelle. 2013. *Adoption as a Ministry, Adoption as a Blessing*. Enumclass, WA: WinePress.

Geiger, Jennifer Mullins, Megan H. Hayes, and Cynthia A. Lietz. 2013. "Should I Stay or Should I Go? A Mixed Methods Study Examining the Factors Influencing Foster Parents' Decisions to Continue or Discontinue Providing Foster Care." *Children and Youth Services Review* 35:1356–1365.

Giddens, Anthony. 1984. *The Constitution of Society: Outline of the Theory of Structuration*. Berkeley: University of California Press.

Gifford, Elizabeth. 2011. *The House of Hope: God's Love for the Abandoned Orphans of China*. Grand Rapids, MI: Monarch Books.

Gillespie, Natalie Nichols. 2006. *Successful Adoption: A Guide for Christian Families*. Nashville, TN: Thomas Nelson.

Gillis-Arnold, Renee, Sedahlia Jasper Crase, Dahlia F. Stockdale, and Mack C. Shelley. 1998. "Parenting Attitudes, Foster Parenting Attitudes, and Motivations of Adoptive and Nonadoptive Foster Parent Trainees." *Children and Youth Services Review* 20:715–732.

Gilmore, Jennifer. 2013. "The Dark, Sad Side of Domestic Adoption: One Family's Long Quest to Adopt a Baby." *Atlantic*, April 30. www.theatlantic.com.

Gladwell, Malcolm. 2005. *Blink: The Power of Thinking without Thinking*. New York: Little, Brown.

Goodman, Joan F., and Stacy Kim. 1999. "The American Adoption of Indian Children from Mother Theresa's Orphanages." *Adoption Quarterly* 3(2):5–27.

Greeley, Andrew, and Michael Hout. 2006. *The Truth about Conservative Christians: What They Think and What They Believe*. Chicago: University of Chicago Press.

Greene, Joshua. 2013. *Moral Tribes: Emotion, Reason, and the Gap between Us and Them*. New York: Penguin.

Greil, Arthur, Julia McQuillan, Maureen Benjamins, David R. Johnson, Katherine M. Johnson, and Chelsea R. Heinz. 2010. "Specifying the Effects of Religion on Medical Helpseeking: The Case of Infertility." *Social Science and Medicine* 71:734–742.

Guckenberger, Beth. 2008. *Reckless Faith: Let Go and Be Led*. Grand Rapids, MI: Zondervan.

Guckenberger, Beth. 2011. *Relentless Hope: Extracting the Precious from the Worthless*. Cincinnati, OH: Standard.

Guckenberger, Beth. 2012. *Tales of the Not Forgotten*. Cincinnati, OH: Standard.

Guckenberger, Beth. 2013. *Tales of the Defended Ones*. Cincinnati, OH: Standard.

Guckenberger, Beth. 2014. *Tales of the Ones Led Out*. Cincinnati, OH: Standard.

Gumm, Julie. 2011. *Adopt without Debt: Creative Ways to Cover the Cost of Adoption*. Phoenix, AZ: Black Boot.

Hackett, Conrad, and D. Michael Lindsay. 2008. "Measuring Evangelicalism: Consequences of Different Operationalization Strategies." *Journal for the Scientific Study of Religion* 47:499–514.

Haidt, Jonathan. 2012. *The Righteous Mind: Why Good People Are Divided by Politics and Religion*. New York: Pantheon.

Haskins, Jeremy. 2012. "From Church Pews to Church Plants: Adoption Culture and the World Mission." In *A Guide to Adoption and Orphan Care*, edited by Russell D. Moore, 56–63. Louisville, KY: SBTS Press.

Hatch, Nathan O. 1989. *The Democratization of American Christianity*. New Haven, CT: Yale University Press.

Hayford, Sarah R., and S. Philip Morgan. 2008. "Religiosity and Fertility in the United States: The Role of Fertility Intentions." *Social Forces* 86(3):1–26.

Helm, Amanda, James W. Peltier, and Carol Scovotti. 2006. "Understanding Antecedents to Recruiting Foster Care and Adoptive Parents: A Comparison of White and African-American Families." *Health Marketing Quarterly* 23:109–129.

Herman, Ellen. 2008. *Kinship by Design: A History of Adoption in the United States*. Chicago: University of Chicago Press.

Herman, Ellen. 2012. *The Adoption History Project*. http://pages.uoregon.edu/adoption.

Hill, Megan. 2012. "Adopting a Kid, Not a Cause." *Christianity Today*, September 21. www.christianitytoday.com.

Hill, Megan. 2013. "The Good Heart of the Adoption Movement." *Christianity Today*, May 3. www.christianitytoday.com.

Hollingsworth, Leslie D. 2000. "Who Seeks to Adopt a Child? Findings from the National Survey of Family Growth." *Adoption Quarterly* 3:1–23.

Holt, Bertha. 1956. *The Seed from the East*. Los Angeles. Oxford Press.

Holt, Marilyn Irvin. 1992. *The Orphan Trains: Placing Out in America*. Lincoln: University of Nebraska Press.

Hout, Michael, Andrew Greeley, and Melissa J. Wilde. 2001. "The Demographic Imperative in Religious Change in the United States." *American Journal of Sociology* 107(2):468–500.

Hunt, Scott A., and Robert D. Benford. 2004. "Collective Identity, Solidarity, and Commitment." In *The Blackwell Companion to Social Movements*, edited by David A. Snow, Sarah A. Soule, and Hanspeter Kriesi, 433–458. Malden, MA: Blackwell.

Hunter, James D. 1983. *American Evangelicalism: Conservative Religion and the Quandary of Modernity*. New Brunswick, NJ: Rutgers University Press.

Hunter, James Davison. 1987. *Evangelicalism: The Coming Generation*. Chicago: University of Chicago Press.

Hunter, James Davison. 2010. *To Change the World: The Irony, Tragedy, and Possibility of Christianity in the Late Modern World*. New York: Oxford University Press.

Indian Country Today Media Network staff. 2013. "'Serial Adopters': How Evangelicals Are Exploiting the Orphan Market." *Indian Country Today Media Network*, September 23. http://indiancountrytodaymedianetwork.com.

Jennings, Patricia K. 2010. "'God Had Something Else In Mind': Family, Religion, and Infertility." *Journal of Contemporary Ethnography* 39:215–237.

Jerolmack, Colin, and Shamus Khan. 2014. "Talk Is Cheap: Ethnography and the Attitudinal Fallacy." *Sociological Methods and Research* 43(2):178–209.

Johnson, Annysa. 2014. "Religious Families Find Calling to Foster Care." *Milwaukee Journal Sentinel*, March 15. www.jsonline.com.

Johnston, Hank, and Bert Klandermans, eds. 1995. *Social Movements and Culture*. Minneapolis: University of Minnesota Press.

Johnstone, Ronald J. 2007. *Religion in Society: A Sociology of Religion*. 8th ed. Upper Saddle River, NJ: Pearson.

Jones, Jo. 2009. "Who Adopts? Characteristics of Men and Women Who Have Adopted Children." National Center for Health Statistics Data Brief no. 12. Washington, DC: U.S. Department of Health and Human Services, Centers for Disease Control and Prevention, National Center for Health Statistics. www.cdc.gov.

Jones, Maggie. 2013. "God Called Them to Adopt. And Adopt. And Adopt." *New York Times*, November 14. www.nytimes.com.

Joyce, Kathryn. 2009a. *Quiverfull: Inside the Christian Patriarchy Movement*. Boston: Beacon Press.

Joyce, Kathryn. 2009b. "Shotgun Adoption." *Nation*, August 26. www.thenation.com. Reprinted as "Preying on the Desperate: The Religious Right's Adoption Racket." *Alternet*, August 28, 2009. www.alternet.org.

Joyce, Kathryn. 2011. "The Evangelical Adoption Crusade." *Nation*. www.thenation.com.

Joyce, Kathryn. 2013a. "Orphan Fever: The Evangelical Movement's Adoption Obsession." *Mother Jones*. Mother Jones, May/June. www.motherjones.com.

Joyce, Kathryn. 2013b. *The Child Catchers: Rescue, Trafficking, and the New Gospel of Adoption*. New York: Public Affairs.

Joyce, Kathryn. 2013c. "The Evangelical Orphan Boom." *New York Times*, September 22. www.nytimes.com.

Joyce, Kathryn. 2013d. "'The Child Catchers': Evangelicals and the Fake-Orphan Racket." *Daily Beast*, April 24. www.thedailybeast.com.

Joyce, Kathryn. 2013e. "The Problem with the Christian Adoption Movement." *Huffington Post*, June 2. www.huffingtonpost.

Juntunen, Craig, producer. 2013. STUCK. Documentary. Scottsdale, AZ: Both Ends Burning.

Kahneman, Daniel. 2011. *Thinking, Fast and Slow*. New York: Farrar, Straus & Giroux.

Kearns, Laurel. 2014. "Green Evangelicals." In *The New Evangelical Social Engagement*, edited by Brian Steensland and Philip Goff, 157–178. New York: Oxford University Press.

Keller, Timothy. 2010. *Generous Justice: How God's Grace Makes Us Just*. New York: Dutton.

Kerry and Niels. 2009. "The Religious Right and Adoption." *Pound Pup Legacy*, September 13. http://poundpuplegacy.org.

Kidd, Thomas S. 2014. *George Whitefield: America's Spiritual Founding Father*. New Haven, CT: Yale University Press.

Kouri, Julie. 2010. "Insurmountable Orphan Odds vs. Our God." *Together for Adoption*, July 28. www.togetherforadoption.org.

Kovacs, Jason. 2009. "Creating a Culture of Adoption in Your Church." In *Our Adoption in Christ: What It Means for Us and for Orphans*, by Together for Adoption, 26–27. n.p.: Together for Adoption. www.togetherforadoption.org.

Kovacs, Jason. 2011. "Adoption and Missional Living." In *Reclaiming Adoption: Missional Living through the Rediscovery of Abba Father*, edited by Dan Cruver, 83–94. Adelphi, MD: Cruciform Press.

Kwon, Lillian. 2010. "Kay Warren Questions Christianity of Persons Who Neglect Orphans." *Christian Post*, April 24. www.christianpost.com.

Kyle, Richard. 2006. *Evangelicalism: An Americanized Christianity*. New Brunswick, NJ: Transaction Publishers.

Lamb, Kathleen A. 2008. "Exploring Adoptive Motherhood: Adoption-Seeking among Hispanic and Non-Hispanic White Women." *Adoption Quarterly* 11(3):155–175.

Lamont, Michele. 1992. *Money, Morals, and Manners: The Culture of the French and American Upper-Middle Class*. Chicago: University of Chicago Press.

Lamont, Michele. 1999. *The Cultural Territories of Race: Black and White Boundaries*. Chicago: University of Chicago Press.

Lamont, Michele. 2000. *The Dignity of Working Men: Morality and the Boundaries of Race, Class, and Immigration*. Cambridge, MA: Harvard University Press.

Lamont, Michele, and Marcel Fournier, eds. 1992. *Cultivating Differences: Symbolic Boundaries and the Making of Inequality*. Chicago: University of Chicago Press.

Lamont, Michele, and Virag Molnar. 2002. "The Study of Boundaries in the Social Sciences." *Annual Review of Sociology* 28:168–195.

Lang, Anna. 2014. "Paul and Robin Pennington Have Helped Thousands of Orphans Find Homes." *People* magazine, January 23. www.people.com.

Lichterman, Paul. 1992. "Self-Help Reading as a Thin Culture." *Media, Culture and Society* 14(3):421–447.

Lichterman, Paul, Prudence L. Carter, and Michele Lamont. 2009. "Race-Bridging for Christ? Conservative Christians and Black-White Relations in Community Life." In *Evangelicals and Democracy in America*, vol. 1: *Religion and Society*, edited Steven Brint and Jean Reith Schroedel, 187–220. New York: Russell Sage.

Lifeline Children's Services. n.d. *Qualifications*. http://lifelinechild.org.

Lindsay, D. Michael. 2007. *Faith in the Halls of Power: How Evangelicals Joined the American Elite*. New York: Oxford University Press.

Lindsay, Hugh. 2009. *Adoption in the Roman World*. New York: Cambridge University Press.

Lupton, Robert D. 2011. *Toxic Charity: How Churches and Charities Hurt Those They Help (and How to Reverse It)*. New York: HarperCollins.

Lynerd, Benjamin T. 2014. *Republican Theology: The Civil Religion of American Evangelicals*. New York: Oxford University Press.

Maggard, Ron, and Ransom Maggard. 2013. *Why Care for Orphans*. Hope Sound, FL: Baptist Evangelism.

Malm, Karin, and Kate Welti. 2010. "Exploring Motivations to Adopt." *Adoption Quarterly* 13:185–208.

Markofski, Wes. 2015. *New Monasticism and the Transformation of American Evangelicalism*. New York: Oxford University Press.

Marti, Gerardo, and Michael O. Emerson. 2014. "The Rise of the Diversity Expert: How American Evangelicals Simultaneously Accentuate and Ignore Race." In *The New Evangelical Social Engagement*, edited by Brian Steensland and Philip Goff, 179–199. New York: Oxford University Press.

Martin, W. C. 2007. *Small Town, Big Miracle: How Love Came to the Least of These*. Colorado Springs, CO: Focus on the Family.

McAdam, Doug. 1982. *Political Process and the Development of Black Insurgency: 1930–1970*. Chicago: University of Chicago Press.

McAdam, Doug. 1986. "Recruiting to High-Risk Activism: The Case of Freedom Summer." *American Journal of Sociology* 92(1):64–90.

McCarthy, John D., and Mayer N. Zald. 1977. "Resource Mobilization and Social Movements: A Partial Theory." *American Journal of Sociology* 82:1212–1241.

Medefind, Jedd. 2010a. "Strong on Zeal, Thin in Knowledge." *Christianity Today*, February 3. www.christianitytoday.com.

Medefind, Jedd. 2010b. "Study: Difficult Future Awaits Most Foster Children." Christian Alliance for Orphans, April 9. https://cafo.org.

Medefind, Jedd. 2013a. *Becoming Home: Adoption, Foster Care, and Mentoring—Living Out God's Heart for Orphans*. Barna Group FRAMES series. Grand Rapids, MI: Zondervan.

Medefind, Jedd. 2013b. "In-Depth Analysis of THE CHILD CATCHERS." Christian Alliance for Orphans, July 2. https://cafo.org.

Medefind, Jedd. 2013c. "Analysis of THE CHILD CATCHERS—Part II." Christian Alliance for Orphans, July 9. https://cafo.org.

Medefind, Jedd. 2013d. "When Evangelicals Adopt Children Abroad." *New York Times*, September 26. www.nytimes.com.

Merida, Tony, and Rick Morton. 2011. *Orphanology: Awakening to Gospel-Centered Adoption and Orphan Care*. Birmingham, AL: New Hope Publishers.

Merritt, Jonathan. 2013. "Exploring Adoption." *Books and Culture (B&C): A Christian Review*, September/October. www.booksandculture.com.

Meyer, David S. 2014. *The Politics of Protest: Social Movements in America*. 2nd ed. New York: Oxford University Press.

Mills, C. Wright. 1940. "Situated Actions and Vocabularies of Motive." *American Sociological Review* 5(6):904–913.

Mitchell, Rob B. 2007. *Castaway Kid: One Man's Search for Hope and Home*. Colorado Springs, CO: Focus on the Family.

Moore, Russell. 2009. *Adopted for Life: The Priority of Adoption for Christian Families and Churches*. Wheaton, IL: Crossway.

Moore, Russell D. 2010. "Abba Changes Everything: Why Every Christian Is Called to Rescue Orphans." *Christianity Today*, July 2. www.christianitytoday.com.

Moore, Russell D., ed. 2012. *A Guide to Adoption and Orphan Care*. Lexington, KY: SBTS Press.

Moore, Russell D. 2015. *Adoption: What Joseph of Nazareth Can Teach Us about This Countercultural Choice*. Wheaton, IL: Crossway.

Morton, Rick. 2014. *KnowOrphans: Mobilizing the Church for Global Orphanology*. Birmingham, AL: New Hope.

Munson, Ziad W. 2008. *The Making of Pro-life Activists: How Social Movement Mobilization Works*. Chicago: University of Chicago Press.

National Center for Health Statistics. 2007. National Survey of Adoptive Parents. Washington, DC: Centers for Disease Control and Prevention. www.cdc.gov.

National Center for Health Statistics. 2015a. "Adoption and Nonbiological Parenting." *Key Statistics from the National Survey of Family Growth—A Listing*. National Survey of Family Growth. Washington, DC: Centers for Disease Control and Prevention. www.cdc.gov.

National Center for Health Statistics. 2015b. National Survey of Family Growth. www.cdc.gov.

Niebuhr, H. Richard. 1929. *The Social Sources of Denominationalism*. New York: Meridian.

Noll, Mark A. 1994. *The Scandal of the Evangelical Mind*. Grand Rapids, MI: Eerdmans.

Noll, Mark. 2003. *The Rise of Evangelicalism: The Age of Edwards, Whitefield, and the Wesleys*. Downers Grove, IL: InterVarsity Press.

NRInterview. 2015. "Adopting Beauty and Dignity." *National Review*, March 5. www.nationalreview.com.

Orme, John G., Cheryl Buehler, Michael McSurdy, Kathryn W. Rhodes, Mary Ellen Cox, and David A. Patterson. 2006. "Parental and Familial Characteristics of Family Foster Care Applicants." *Children and Youth Services Review* 26:307–329.

Park, Nicholas K., and Patricia Wonch Hill. 2014. "Is Adoption an Option? The Role of Importance of Motherhood and Fertility Help-Seeking in Considering Adoption." *Journal of Family Issues* 35(5):601–626.

Pew Research Center. 2014. *Religious Landscape Study*. Washington, DC: Pew Research Center. www.pewforum.org.

Pierre, Dennae. 2012. "Adoption: Not a Justice Cause but a Spiritual Reality." *Christianity Today*, October 4. www.christianitytoday.com.

Piper, John. 2002. *Brothers, We Are Not Professionals: A Plea to Pastors for Radical Ministry*. Nashville, TN: Broadman & Holman.

Piper, John. 2011. "Adoption: The Heart of the Gospel." In *Reclaiming Adoption: Missional Living through the Rediscovery of Abba Father*, edited by Dan Cruver, 95–107. Adelphi, MD: Cruciform Press.

Platt, David. 2010. *Radical: Taking Back Your Faith from the American Dream*. Colorado Springs, CO: Multnomah Books.

Platt, David. 2011. *Radical Together: Unleashing the People of God for the Purpose of God*. Colorado Springs, CO: Multnomah Books.

Platt, David. 2013. *Follow Me: A Call to Die. A Call to Live*. Colorado Springs, CO: Multnomah Books.

Platt, David. 2015. *Counter Culture: A Compassionate Call to Counter Culture in a World of Poverty, Same-Sex Marriage, Racism, Sex Slavery, Immigration, Abortion, Persecution, Orphans and Pornography*. Carol Stream, IL: Tyndale House.

Purvis, Karyn. n.d. "Creating a Healthy Adoption Culture in Your Church" (video). Empowered To Connect. http://empoweredtoconnect.org.

Purvis, Karyn B., David R. Cross, and Wendy Lyons Sunshine. 2007. *The Connected Child: Bring Hope and Healing to Your Adoptive Family*. New York: McGraw-Hill.

Putnam, Robert D., and David E. Campbell. 2010. *American Grace: How Religion Divide and Unites Us*. New York: Simon & Schuster.

Quiroz, Pamela Anne. 2007. *Adoption in a Color-Blind Society*. Lanham, MD: Rowman & Littlefield.

Reynolds, Amy, and Stephen Offutt. 2014. "Global Poverty and Evangelical Action." In *The New Evangelical Social Engagement*, edited by Brian Steensland and Philip Goff, 242–264. New York: Oxford University Press.

Riben, Mirah. 2007. "Adoption and the Role of the Religious Right." *Counter Currents*, November 4. www.countercurrents.org.

Riben, Mirah. 2010. "Prophecy, Proselytizing and Profit: Adopting Christian Soldiers." *Dissident Voice*, January 1. http://dissidentvoice.org.

Riben, Mirah. 2012. "Is the War on Abortion Heating Up? *NewsBlaze*, March 11. http://newsblaze.com.

Riley, Naomi Schaefer. 2008. "Defend the Orphan: An Age-Old Christian Lesson Gets a New Lease on Life." *Wall Street Journal*, August 29. www.wsj.com.

Riley, Naomi Schaefer. 2010. "Adoption Season for Evangelicals: A Biblical Mandate to Help Children, Especially Those in Foster Care." *Wall Street Journal*, September 24. www.wsj.com.

Roach, David. 2009. "Adoption Ministries Thriving at SBC Churches." Southwestern Life, August. www.sbclife.net.

Roberts, Keith A., and David Yamane. 2012. *Religion in Sociological Perspective*. 5th ed. Thousand Oaks, CA: Sage.

Rodger, Susan, Anne Cummings, and Alan W. Leschied. 2006. "Who Is Caring for Our Most Vulnerable Children? The Motivation to Foster in Child Welfare." *Child Abuse and Neglect* 30:1129–1142.

Rosati, Kelly, and John Rosati. 2011. *Wait No More: One Family's Amazing Adoption Journey*. Carol Stream, IL: Tyndale House.

Samson, Will. 2014. "The New Monasticism." In *The New Evangelical Social Engagement*, edited by Brian Steensland and Philip Goff, 94–108. New York: Oxford University Press.

Schmalzbauer, John. 2014. "Whose Social Justice? Which Evangelicalism? Social Engagement in a Campus Ministry." In *The New Evangelical Social Engagement*, edited by Brian Steensland and Philip Goff, 50–72. New York: Oxford University Press.

Schooler, Jayne E., and Thomas C. Atwood. 2008. *The Whole Life Adoption Book: Realistic Advice for Building a Healthy Adoptive Family*. Colorado Springs, CO: NavPress.

Schwarzschild, Todd. 2013. "Red Flags Wave over Uganda's Adoption Boom." *CNN*, March 2. www.cnn.com.

Sewell, William H., Jr. 1992. "A Theory of Structure: Duality, Agency, and Transformation." *American Journal of Sociology* 98:1–29.

Sewell, William H., Jr. 1996. "Historical Events as Transformations of Structures: Inventing Revolution at the Bastille." *Theory and Society* 25:841–881.

Shelton, Jason., and Michael O. Emerson. 2012. *Blacks and Whites in Christian America: How Racial Discrimination Shapes Religious Convictions*. New York: NYU Press.

Shibley, Mark A. 1996. *Resurgent Evangelicalism in the United States: Mapping Cultural Change since 1970*. Columbia: University of South Carolina Press.

Shreffler, Karina M., David R. Johnson, and Laurie K. Scheuble. 2010. "Ethical Problems with Infertility Treatments: Attitudes and Explanations." *Social Science Journal* 47:731–746.

Simmel, Georg. 1955. *Conflict and the Web of Group Affiliations*. New York: Free Press.

Simon, Stephanie. 2007. "Campaign Calls for Christians to Adopt Needy Kids." *Los Angeles Times*, May 13. http://articles.latimes.com.

Smelser, Neil J. 1963. *Theory of Collective Behavior*. New York: Free Press.

Smidt, Corwin E. 2013. *American Evangelicals Today*. Lanham, MD: Rowman & Littlefield.

Smith, Christian, ed. 1996. *Disruptive Religion: The Force of Faith in Social Movement Activism*. New York: Routledge.

Smith, Christian. 1998. *American Evangelicalism: Embattled and Thriving.* Chicago: University of Chicago Press.

Smith, Christian. 2000. *Christian America? What Evangelicals Really Want.* Berkeley: University of California Press.

Smith, Christian, and Michael O. Emerson. 2008. *Passing the Plate: Why American Christians Don't Give Away More Money.* New York: Oxford University Press.

Smith, Peter. 2011. "Adoption Growing among Evangelical Christians." *Louisville Courier-Journal,* January 18.

Smolin, David M., guest ed. 2012a. Special issue on adoption. *Journal of Christian Legal Thought* 2, no. 1.

Smolin, David M. 2012b. "Of Orphans and Adoption, Parents and the Poor, Exploitation and Rescue: A Scriptural Critique of the Evangelical Christian Adoption and Orphan Care Movement." *Regent Journal of International Law* 8:267–324.

Snow, David A., and Robert D. Benford. 1988. "Ideology, Frame Resonance, and Movement Participation." *International Social Movement Research* 1:197–218.

Snow, David A., Burke E. Rochford, Steven Wordon, and Robert Benford. 1986. "Frame Alignment Processes, Micromobilization, and Movement Participation." *American Sociological Review* 51:464–481.

Snow, David A., and Sarah A. Soule. 2010. *A Primer on Social Movements.* New York: W. W. Norton.

Southern Baptist Convention. 2009. "On Adoption and Orphan Care: Resolution No. 2." www.sbc.net.

Springer-Mock, Melanie. 2013. "Why Christians Like Me Should Listen to Critiques of Evangelical Adoption." *Nation,* May 17. www.thenation.com.

Steensland, Brian, and Philip Goff, eds. 2014. *The New Evangelical Social Engagement.* New York: Oxford University Press.

Steensland, Brian, Jerry Z. Park, Mark D. Regnerus, Lynn D. Robinson, W. Bradford Wilcox, and Robert D. Woodberry. 2000. "The Measure of American Religion: Toward Improving the State of the Art." *Social Forces* 79(1):291–318.

Stephens, Randall J., and Karl W. Giberson. 2011. *The Anointed: Evangelical Truth in a Secular Age.* Cambridge, MA: Belknap Press of Harvard University Press.

Stetzer, Ed. 2012. "New Research: Churchgoers Believe in Sharing Faith, but Most Never Do." *Christianity Today,* August 13. www.christianitytoday.com.

Stetzer, Ed. 2013. "Evangelicals and Adoption: An Evil Obsession? *Christianity Today,* April 19. www.christianitytoday.com.

Sweeney, Megan M., and R. Kelly Raley. 2014. "Race, Ethnicity, and the Changing Context of Childbearing in the United States." *Annual Review of Sociology* 40:539–558.

Tarrow, Sidney. 1983. "Struggling to Reform: Social Movements and Policy Change during Cycles of Protest." Western Societies Paper no. 15. Ithaca, NY: Cornell University Press.

Taylor Verta, and Nancy E. Whittier. 1992. "Collective Identity in Social Movement Communities: Lesbian Feminist Mobilization." In *Frontiers in Social Movement*

Theory, edited by Aldon Morris and C. Mueller, 104–129. New Haven, CT: Yale University Press.

Tebos, Susan, Carissa Woodwyk, and Sherrie Eldridge. 2011. *Before You Were Mine: Discovering Your Adopted Child's Lifestory*. Grand Rapids, MI: Zondervan.

Tilly, Charles. 1978. *From Mobilization to Revolution*. Reading, MA: Addison-Wesley.

Tilly, Charles. 2004. *Social Movements, 1768–2004*. Boulder, CO: Paradigm.

Together for Adoption. *Our Adoption in Christ: What It Means for Us and for Orphans*. n.p.: Together for Adoption. www.togetherforadoption.org.

Troeltsch, Ernst. 1931. *The Social Teaching of the Christian Churches*, vol. 1. New York: Macmillan.

Tyebjee, Tyzoon. 2003. "Attitude, Interest, and Motivation for Adoption and Foster Care." *Child Welfare* 82(6):685–705.

Vaisey, Stephen. 2009. "Motivation and Justification: A Dual-Process Model of Culture in Action." *American Journal of Sociology* 114(6):1675–1715.

Van Laningham, Jody L., Laurie K. Scheuble, and David R. Johnson. 2012. "Social Factors Predicting Women's Consideration of Adoption." *Michigan Family Review* 16(1):1–21.

Wallis, Jim. 2006. *God's Politics: Why the Right Gets in Wrong and the Left Doesn't Get It*. San Francisco: HarperSan Francisco.

Weber, Jason, and Paul Pennington. 2006. *Launching an Orphans Ministry in Your Church*. Little Rock, AR: Family Life.

Weber, Max. 1904/1949. *The Methodology of the Social Sciences*. Edited by E. Shils and H. Finch. New York: Free Press.

Weber, Max. 1973. "On Church, Sect, and Mysticism." *Sociological Analysis* 34:140–149.

Weber, Max. 1978. *Economy and Society*. Berkeley: University of California Press.

Wiebe, Elizabeth. 2010. "Wait No More." Christian Alliance for Orphans, September 9. https://cafo.org.

Wildeman, Christopher, and Jane Waldfogel. 2014. "Somebody's Children or Nobody's Children? How the Sociological Perspective Could Enliven Research on Foster Care." *Annual Review of Sociology* 40:599–618.

Willer, Robb. 2009. "Groups Reward Individual Sacrifice: The Status Solution to the Collective Action Problem." *American Sociological Review* 74(1):23–43.

Williams, Rhys, ed. 2001. *Promise Keepers and the New Masculinity: Private Lives and Public Morality*. Lanham, MD: Lexington Books.

Williams, Rhys. 2004. "The Cultural Contexts of Collective Action: Constraints, Opportunities, and the Symbolic Life of Social Movements." In *The Blackwell Companion to Social Movements*, edited by David A. Snow, Sarah A. Soule, and Hanspeter Kriesi, 91–115. Malden, MA: Blackwell.

Wilson, William Julius. 2009. *More than Just Race: Being Black and Poor in the Inner City*. New York: W. W. Norton.

Wong, Kristin Swick. 2005. *Carried Safely Home: The Spiritual Legacy of an Adoptive Family*. Grand Haven, MI: FaithWalk.

Woodberry, Robert D., and Christian Smith. 1998. "Fundamentalism et al.: Conservative Protestants in America." *Annual Review of Sociology* 24:25–56.

Worthen, Molly. 2014. *Apostles of Reason: The Crisis of Authority in American Evangelicalism*. New York: Oxford University Press.

Wuthnow, Robert. 1988. *The Restructuring of American Religion: Society and Faith since World War II*. Princeton, NJ: Princeton University Press.

Wuthnow, Robert. 2015. *Inventing American Religion: Polls, Surveys, and the Tenuous Quest for a Nation's Faith*. New York: Oxford University Press.

Yancey, George. 2003. *One Body, One Spirit: Principles of Successful Multiracial Churches*. Downers Grove, IL: InterVarsity.

Yancey, Philip. 2003. *Rumors of Another World: What on Earth Are We Missing?* Grand Rapids, MI: Zondervan.

Young, Michael P. 2006. *Bearing Witness against Sin: The Evangelical Birth of the American Social Movement*. Chicago: University of Chicago Press.

Zhang, Yuanting, and Gary R. Lee. 2011. "Intercountry versus Transracial Adoption: Analysis of Adoptive Parents' Motivations and Preferences in Adoption." *Journal of Family Issues* 32:75–98.

Zylstra, Sarah Eekhoff. 2016. "Why International Adoptions by Americans Have Hit a 35-Year Low." *Christianity Today*, April 7. www.christianitytoday.com.

INDEX

4M model of ministry evolution (movement, ministry, machine, monument), 187–188, 193. *See also* sect-church continuum or process

Abba, 264n31
ABBA Fund, 77, 108–109, 116, 124, 150, 210, 236–237, 259n7, 264n31
abortion, 2, 88–89, 104, 131–132, 135, 154, 206, 228. *See also* pro-life activism and values
accommodation: churches unwilling, 31, 162–171, 182–183; and multiracial congregations, 228; with secular state, 31, 186–188, 192–193, 200
Adopted for Life, 72, 74, 141, 155–156, 238, 264n36. *See also* Moore, Russell
adoption: and abortion, 2, 88–89, 131–132, 135, 154, 206, 228; and birthmothers, 2, 35, 37, 137, 224, 247; and consumerism, 50; data on, 37–51, 53–54, 59–61, 246–248; declining numerically, 37–42; and designer babies, 50; as family growth strategy, 54–55, 133–138; and fundraising, 130–131; ideal family for, 97, 109–125, 226; intercountry, 15, 21, 36, 39–42, 48, 50, 64, 130, 135–136, 138, 144, 146, 162, 171, 190–191, 213, 217, 248, 267n1, 267n4; as limited in its ability to solve orphan crisis, 226–229; motivations for, 2, 33, 54–55, 137–138, 267n4, 267n5; in New Testament, 221–222; by non-relatives, 42–49; as plan B, 151–153; private agency, 21, 37, 39–40, 42, 48–50, 130–138, 192, 202, 212, 246, 266n24,

267n1, 267n4; and pronatalism, 55–56, 148, 153–154; religion and, 36, 54–55; as rescue, 1, 56, 75, 91–92, 98–99, 142–143, 161, 177–178, 183, 188–189, 200, 217–219, 256n7; in Roman world, 222; and salvation analogy, 177–178, 221–224; and singles, 30, 44, 107–109, 116, 121–127, 226; theology of, 73–93, 105–106, 176–178, 196–197, 221–224; transracial, ix–xi, 50, 88, 136, 138; trends in, 29, 37–51, 53–54. *See also* foster care
Adoption and Foster Care Analysis and Reporting System (AFCARS) data, 42–49, 52–54, 247
The Adoption History Project, 258n42
adoption theology, 73–93, 105–106, 176–178, 196–197, 221–224
Africa, 24, 41–42, 119, 136, 162, 164, 172, 179, 183
America World Adoption (AMA), 17, 112–113, 150, 210, 238, 245
anti-structuralism, 10, 29, 31, 160–161, 176, 204, 207–208, 213–217, 227–229. *See also* cultural schemas; evangelicals; individualism
Ashland Avenue Baptist Church, 74

Barna Group: *Becoming Home*, 52, 56–59, 71; claims about Christians adopting or fostering, 35–36, 56–57; FRAMES data, 54, 58–61, 248, 271n5; "practicing Christian" measure, 57–58; problematic research methodology, 57–59, 262n67; reanalysis of FRAMES data, 59–62

ABOUT THE AUTHOR

Samuel L. Perry is Assistant Professor of Sociology and Religious Studies at the University of Oklahoma. He received his Ph.D. in sociology from the University of Chicago. He also holds a Th.M. from Dallas Theological Seminary. His research explores the changing dynamics of religion and family life in the United States. He is currently working on a forthcoming book about the ways pornography affects American families and religion.